In Case of Katrina

In Case of Katrina

Reinventing the Church in Post-Katrina New Orleans

Ellen Blue

CASCADE *Books* • Eugene, Oregon

IN CASE OF KATRINA
Reinventing the Church in Post-Katrina New Orleans

Copyright © 2016 Ellen Blue. All rights reserved. Except for brief quotations in critical publications or reviews, no part of this book may be reproduced in any manner without prior written permission from the publisher. Write: Permissions, Wipf and Stock Publishers, 199 W. 8th Ave., Suite 3, Eugene, OR 97401.

Cascade Books
An Imprint of Wipf and Stock Publishers
199 W. 8th Ave., Suite 3
Eugene, OR 97401

www.wipfandstock.com

PAPERBACK ISBN: 978-1-62564-140-3
HARDCOVER ISBN: 978-1-4982-8500-1
EBOOK ISBN: 978-1-5326-0182-8

Cataloguing-in-Publication data:

Names: Blue, Ellen.

Title: In Case of Katrina : Reinventing the church in post-Katrina New Orleans / Ellen Blue.

Description: Eugene, OR: Cascade Books, 2016 | Includes bibliographical references.

Identifiers: ISBN 978-1-62564-140-3 (paperback) | ISBN 978-1-4982-8500-1 (hardcover) | ISBN 978-1-5326-0182-8 (ebook)

Subjects: LCSH: Hurricane Katrina, 2005—Religious aspects. | Hurricanes—Religious aspects—Louisiana—New Orleans. | Church work with disaster victims.

Classification: LCC HV553 B5 2016 (print) | LCC HV553 (ebook)

Manufactured in the U.S.A.   08/03/16

To Jim, Jeff, and Valery,
who first lived through Katrina
and then lived through the writing of this book
and whom I love even more than I love New Orleans

Contents

Acknowledgments | ix
Abbreviations | xii

1 Introduction | 1
2 United Methodism in New Orleans: Historical Context | 16
3 The Storm | 27
4 The Process: Or, How the Church Decided to Decide | 41
5 First Grace UMC: Where the City Worships | 71
6 "Specialized Focus" Ministries | 97
7 Four Congregations Partner in Ministry | 112
8 "Holler Back If You Can Hear Me" | 133
9 What's God Got to Do with It? | 153
10 It's Time | 173

Appendix: Explanation of Some United Methodist Terms | 207
Bibliography | 215

Acknowledgments

Thanks are due to the many people who helped me learn about the church in New Orleans and the aftermath of Katrina and how the two have intersected. I am especially grateful for a Lilly Faculty Fellowship, a $30,000 grant that allowed me to spend an entire sabbatical year, 2008–9, in New Orleans. Participating in the Association of Theological Schools (ATS) conference for grant recipients in 2009 was immensely helpful in moving my project along.

I am grateful to Phillips Theological Seminary for approving a year-long sabbatical so I could live in New Orleans for fourteen months of research. Sandy Shapoval, Clair Powers, and other members of the Phillips library staff are wonderfully competent individuals who find joy in helping with research projects. Our former dean, Dr. Don Pittman, was willing to schedule an innovative course, "The Church's Response to Katrina," immediately after the storm, and I have since taught it several times, including a version for doctoral students taught with our dean, Dr. Nancy Claire Pittman. Students in those courses include Diane Burl, Jim Cinocca, Marsha Evans, Marvin Ewertt, Steven Fieldcamp, Barbara Fyffe, Angela Gage, Judy Hall, Ron Hayes, Larry Jordan, Tiffany Kirkland, Samuel Lee, Randy Lewis, Todd Mallory, Kathy Morris, Jennifer Pasco, Chad Perceful, Evon Siegel, Kent Smith, Nathan Smith, Matthew Thompson, Lori Walke, Mark Whitley, Susan Whitley, and Lexie Williams. Janet Barrow and Steven Williams completed a practicum in Urban Ministry in the city in the summer of 2014. Dean Nancy Pittman and I co-taught a doctoral course in New Orleans in January 2015; the topic was women's leadership after Katrina and students included Devon McAnally, Lorri Kentner, Dayne Kinkade, Lara Blackwood Pickrel, Ellen Strickland and Connie Wacht. Seeing New Orleans and its churches through all of these students' eyes was very helpful.

I am grateful to the Newcomb College Center for Research on Women (NCCROW) at Tulane, where I was a Visiting Scholar in 2008–9. This provided me with library privileges and an opportunity to publish a small segment of my findings about women involved in the recovery. Some portions of that document have made their way into this book.

Friendship and conversation with other scholars in New Orleans was invaluable. Dr. Martha Ward and Dr. Catherine Wessinger deserve special mention in that regard.

The cooperation of UMC bishop William Hutchinson; provost Don Cottrill; the Mission Zone executive, Martha Orphe; and district superintendents Freddie Henderson, Ralph Ford, Ramonalynn Bethley and Hadley Edwards was absolutely essential both in the seminary courses and in the success of this project. I am deeply grateful for the time they spent and their willingness to have their work scrutinized.

I am especially grateful to Kathy Moore, executive assistant to the bishop in Louisiana, who has eased my way through this project many times and in many ways. More importantly, I cannot imagine that the work of the bishop (William Hutchinson from 2000 to 2012 and now Cynthia Fierro Harvey) would have been accomplished nearly so effectively had it not been for her skill and dedication.

I extend thanks to all the pastors whose churches my students or I visited. Lay people, including June Sanchez of Hartzell UMC, discussed their experiences with my classes. Bob Mann, a UMC layman who was then Communications Director for Governor Kathleen Babineaux Blanco met with my class on more than one occasion and spoke with honesty and integrity about what happened from his point of view. The United Methodist clergy and laity of Louisiana, especially those of our congregations in New Orleans, deserve admiration, and they certainly have mine.

Because we visited with individuals in every denomination represented among the students in any given class, I also thank the Presbyterian, Episcopalian, Unitarian Universalist, African Methodist Episcopal, and United Church of Christ clergy and laypeople who met with us. Roman Catholic layman Bill Quigley, Sister Jane Remson, OCarm, and Sister Mary Daniel, OP, spent time with us and helped students understand larger storm-related issues within the community.

I have talked about the work of the UMC in post-Katrina New Orleans in formal settings, such as the "United Methodism at Forty" conference held at Emory University and the "Cultures of Rebuilding Conference" sponsored by the Louisiana State Museum and UNO, and in less formal settings such as visits with mission teams from Oklahoma and Michigan and Maryland and in adult Sunday school classes in Tulsa. Each invitation to present helped me think through the material I had gathered.

Acknowledgments

I appreciate the work of cartographer Jakob Rosenzweig, who created the maps, and videographer Eric Gremillion, who furnished me with raw footage of Grace UMC's decommissioning and a photograph taken from it for use in this volume. Deaconess Pat Hoerth presented liturgical elements used here at a conference at Phillips Theological Seminary.

My research assistant in 2009–10, Yuki Schwartz, completed extensive work in organizing my massive piles of research materials collected since the day after landfall, and Eric Meyer continued her work in 2012–14, as did Travis Ewton in 2014–16. I appreciate their attention to detail, especially on the final formatting. Editor David Lott helped tremendously with organizing the manuscript at a critical stage of the process, and I appreciate his work. Cascade Books' patience as the book writing stretched out just like storm recovery has been an unexpected and much appreciated gift.

My daughter, Valery Williams, helped me research previous disasters; my son, Jeff Blue, was in the city as a first responder during Katrina and spoke with my class each time I taught it; and they, their spouses, and my grandchildren, Jourdan, Devin, and Elise, have helped make my time in the city a delight. My husband, Jim Wilson, accompanied me on almost all of my post-Katrina journeys to New Orleans, both short and long, and Jim's love for the city is a gift to me, too.

Abbreviations

DS—District Superintendent
FEMA—Federal Emergency Management Agency
GBCS—General Board of Church and Society
GBGM—General Board of Global Ministries
LANO—Louisiana Association of Nonprofit Organizations
MEC—Methodist Episcopal Church
MECS—Methodist Episcopal Church, South
RMN—Reconciling Ministries Network
UCC—United Church of Christ
UMC—United Methodist Church
UMCOR—United Methodist Committee on Relief
UMW—United Methodist Women

1

Introduction

*Save me, O God; for the waters
are come in unto my soul.*
—Psalm 69:1 (KJV)

Hurricane Katrina made landfall on August 29, 2005. What happened next has been well documented. Floodwalls that were not built to specifications broke and 80 percent of the city flooded, a good bit of it taking more than ten feet of water. That water, full of every foul thing from toxic chemicals to sewage to unretrieved dead humans and animals, stayed in the city and in its buildings for weeks before the United States Army Corps of Engineers pumped it out.

The toll of lives lost and lives devastated was immense. Many of these losses were experienced and borne alone. Others occurred in situations with no privacy at all and were displayed by images shown around the world.

Sociologist Kathleen Tierney called Katrina "one of a handful of true catastrophes to strike the United States." Katrina "brought into sharp relief both the astounding ineptitude of governmental systems and the systemic violence of a society characterized by equally astounding patterns of inequality and injustice." A disaster scholar called Katrina "'the mother of all Rorschachs,' a dark crystal whose every facet yields important insights for a wide array of academic disciplines."[1]

One of those disciplines was the study of religion. And so, less than six months after the floodwalls broke, I took my first group of theological students from Phillips Seminary to New Orleans for a class called "The Church's Response to Katrina." The course had almost nothing to do with disaster response, insofar as that involves food, clothing, and shelter for flood survivors. Our task, rather, was to explore how the church was beginning

---

1. Laska, "Mother of Rorschachs," cited in Tierney, "Critical Disjunctures," 251–52.

to rethink its mission in a city that had suddenly been radically altered. How was it making decisions about who the church was to be and what it was to do in a circumstance where many of its limiting circumstances, like longstanding commitments to badly located structures with dwindling congregations, had been altered?

Deciding which churches and agencies could reopen and deciding how ministers in the devastated area should be selected and paid were among the unprecedented problems Katrina brought—issues that I knew would be pertinent to my students as they led congregations in a changing cultural and religious landscape. But practical matters of congregational life were not our only concern. We studied theologies that underlie works of mercy and those that underlie work toward justice, two related and yet quite separate kinds of ministries. We discussed the theme of exile. We pondered the question of theodicy: if an all-good God created the world, where does evil come from? We considered the real-life results of various beliefs about how God is active in the world.

Always, we paid attention to the rich and varied aspects of Christianity and culture in one of the most religiously interesting cities in this country, if not the world. Even before Katrina, New Orleans had an immense store of material for the student of religion, and since the flood, the city has been an unprecedented laboratory for those who want to know how religions do and do not change.

That class and all the repetitions of it have been a key part of my larger project—exploring the struggle of the United Methodist Church's Louisiana conference (composed of all UMC churches in the state) to rethink its mission in portions of south Louisiana devastated by Hurricanes Katrina and Rita in August and September of 2005. It focuses almost exclusively on churches in greater New Orleans, for reasons described below. The key question I address in this extended case study is how the church has been redefining itself in an area where its structures and infrastructure were almost completely destroyed.

Cell by Cell

"In 2005, America had watched New Orleans drown on national television. It was, some said, like watching a good friend suffer a massive stroke." Filmmaker June Cross made this comment at the end of *The Old Man and the Storm*, her documentary about one family's struggle to return to the Lower Ninth Ward which aired as the January 6, 2009, episode of PBS's *Frontline*. Cross's imagery about the city as stroke victim captured my attention.

The comment prompted me to think about how a patient does, or does not, recover from a serious brain injury. Having developed a neurological disease after a car wreck in 1999, I have done a bit more reading in this area than the average person. Though it was once believed that a damaged brain cannot be repaired, researchers now know that healing can occur in the brain and that it can do so through several internal mechanisms. One of these is the body's ability to compensate for a blockage in circulation by creating or enlarging other channels through which the blood can flow.

This process of creating collateral circulation is by no means instantaneous; rather, it is gradually accomplished on what could be thought of as a cell-by-cell basis. This work occurs within the brain without our conscious direction; we cannot draw designs and make deliberate decisions to route our blood through this channel and not that one. Even though we know some of the things that can foster recovery and can decide to do those things, often healing "just happens" or else it doesn't.

The recovery of a devastated city is far more reliant on human decision making, although, in the case of New Orleans, that has not been as deliberate as some hoped. Healing the trauma and paralysis has been full of error caused by human frailties, human ignorance, and ethical failures. Ignorance about how to fix things was exacerbated by a widespread lack of understanding about how and why the city was doing what it did before the storm. The city has been no more guaranteed of success than is an individual stroke patient. Indeed, the odds in some ways seemed lower.

There have been striking parallels to the "cell-by-cell" redevelopment I imagine collateral circulation in the brain must require. The recovery in New Orleans must happen person-by-person and house-by-house. The recovery of the Christian community has sometimes been church-by-church. For United Methodism, though, a larger directing structure has also played a role. That process is at the heart of this book.

Seeking New Direction

In the wake of Katrina, the wreckage not only of iconic buildings but also of key infrastructural givens such as street signs made the city a nightmare to navigate, even for longtime citizens. The landscape had altered so dramatically that people who knew the city well had difficulty finding their way around when they returned. This lack of street signs and landmarks for navigating around the city became a metaphor for needing new directions, or just new direction. But people also needed something that had not changed, and many expected that to be their church.

For most of my adult life, I've heard the mainline church critiqued as being too much like a country club. There are churches I've attended, churches I've visited, and churches I've served as pastor that have been unwilling to reach out to their cities or their neighborhoods or even to new people who come through their doors on Sunday morning. Surely most pastors have encountered at least one congregation who maintained that they would just love to reach out in mission but couldn't because maintaining their building took all the money and energy available.

Truthfully, many of the buildings constructed in the mid-twentieth century when a larger percentage of the population got up and went to Sunday school each week are far too large for their dwindling group of stalwarts in the twenty-first century. As Tom Frank notes, "The older denominations have an enormous overhead to carry from their previous institutional successes."[2] Nostalgia, sentiment, or even a feeling of ownership prevents many congregations from being willing to downsize or relocate. One of my parishioners once proclaimed in my hearing, "This church will move over my dead body." I think that is indeed how it will happen, though by now it may have to move over her daughter's, as well.

For congregations whose buildings were all but destroyed by the flooding after Katrina, that problem seemed to have solved itself. Along with the building, their reason or excuse for not serving their community was destroyed. No longer hampered by aging buildings that needed more and more money to keep the *status quo*, they were invited to make a clear and conscious choice about how to position themselves vis-à-vis the rest of the neighborhood and city.

Framed this way, the invitation calls forth an "obvious" answer: of course, congregations should not isolate themselves but should reach out in service to obey Jesus' commands and live out the calls of the gospel. However, this ignores another reality that church leaders in New Orleans had to acknowledge: the term "sanctuary" means more than just an auditorium-like room designed for a large group of people to hear a sermon and participate in Christian rituals. In medieval times, the term referred to a practice of considering those who had taken refuge within the walls of a church to be safe from removal by authorities. After Katrina, people wanted churches to be a sanctuary for those displaced and disoriented by catastrophe. How to balance the two pressing needs—taking an opportunity to change and meeting a felt need for no change—is at the heart of what my students and the church itself have had to wrestle with since the storm.

---

2. Frank, *Polity, Practice, and the Mission*, 30.

Scattered and Strewn

Jazz provides another apt metaphor for how the church came to make its own decisions. Katy Reckdahl, a superb writer who was working for the *Times-Picayune* when Katrina struck and who now freelances for the *New Orleans Advocate*, noted, "It's not a coincidence jazz started here. This city ad libs everything it does." Reckdahl was part of a panel discussing the role of music at the "Cultures of Rebuilding" conference in November 2008. Fred Kasten, a public radio announcer and host, used the word "improvisational" to describe the entire recovery. And Larry Blumenfeld, editor of *Jazziz* magazine, said that some national organizations came to help but were unable to be effective "because they didn't take into account how weird things are here." Reckdahl added, "And how poor the people are."

Jed Horne, author of one of the smartest books on the Katrina event, used another apt analogy. He wrote about a woman who returned to New Orleans to see her home one last time before it was bulldozed. While she was in the city, she reflected on her church and the meaningful spiritual life she'd participated in there. She thought that the church alone would be worth coming back for, but "then it struck her. There was no Battleground Baptist. Yes, the maroon-brick building still stood there, but Katrina had shredded and scattered its congregation, like a Mardi Gras Indian tearing apart last year's costume before setting to work on a new one."[3]

Churches in New Orleans and their members were rather like strings of beads that were torn apart and scattered by the wind. Yet, for United Methodists, because of the connectional structure of the church, the string that held the beads together was still intact. The pastors appointed by the Louisiana conference relate primarily to the conference rather than to the local congregations where they served. The bishop of the United Methodist Church (UMC) in Louisiana, William Hutchinson, announced very soon after the storm that the conference would try to arrange placements for all the displaced clergy, but that their salaries and benefits would be paid until the end of December no matter what. He made this pledge having no plan for where the money would come from, but believing that it was the right thing to do. The conference year runs from July 1 to June 30, and before long, the conference announced that salaries and benefits would be covered until the next July.

Some of the larger churches in Louisiana and nearby states were able to take on an extra staff person temporarily and pay their salaries. Ellen Alston, pastor at Covenant United Methodist Church in St. Bernard Parish

---

3. Horne, *Breach of Faith*, 386.

in 2005, wound up in the northwest corner of the state as an associate at Grace Community Church in Shreveport. When my first Katrina class traveled from Tulsa to New Orleans, we spent a night there on the way, and the students interviewed her. Six months after the storm, Alston still felt deep grief over the loss of her home and her church and the scattering of her congregation. She pointed to the New Testament parable about a shepherd who left ninety-nine sheep in the wilderness to search for one that had strayed, and said, "Living through this is like being a shepherd who knows where one sheep is and has ninety-nine that are missing."[4]

Alston was one of ninety United Methodist pastors who were displaced by Katrina and by Hurricane Rita which struck southwest Louisiana just three weeks later. Seventy churches in south Louisiana could not reopen at first and required financial assistance to support their clergy. Methodism's connectional structure meant that congregations which lost their self-sufficiency when members were unable to return were not simply abandoned. Nevertheless, the church did not try to restore itself to its exact pre-storm situation. Decisions about which buildings should and should not be rebuilt in their former locations were difficult. What pastors should be appointed to the devastated area? How would they be paid? Which service agencies should be re-opened or put into place? In a city whose post-storm demographics were almost completely unclear, there was no obvious answer to the question of how the church should decide how to decide these issues. Creative solutions were attempted, some of which are documented and evaluated here in order to help the church both in future disasters and in its everyday practices.

Setting Boundaries for This Study

When I was in seminary, I had trouble remembering the word *apophatic*. I usually thought about apophatic theology using other names—negative theology or the *via negativa*. It is based on the idea that the Deity is so unknowable and indescribable that the only way to talk about God is to begin by talking about what God is not. God is *not*, for instance, limited by time and space.

I have learned through experience that the best way to describe this project and this book is also to begin by talking about what they are *not*. Many people have thought that if I'm writing about the post-Katrina church, I must be writing about how the church does disaster response. "No," I say,

---

4. Ellen Alston, interview with the author and students, March 13, 2006, Shreveport, LA.

"the fact that people need food, water, and clothing and to have their homes rebuilt is predictable. The idea that the church should help with all that is not in dispute. I don't need to write about that."

Then you must be studying how the church could have done that work better or how it should do it the next time, they would suggest. "No," I say, "that's not my focus. The church really did a very good job with disaster response, and if it could have been improved, that is someone else's book to write."

Students who took my "Church's Response to Katrina" immersion classes in New Orleans faced similar questions. "If you're not going to help anybody while you're there, why are you going?" their parishioners wondered. Later they'd ask, "You went all the way down there and didn't spend even one day working?" By "working," they'd mean something like "driving nails." Mucking and gutting (the process of clearing a flooded house out down to its studs) is not easy, anywhere, at any time, and in the subtropical climate zone, it is especially exhausting. And the students, who knew very well that they had worked extremely hard every waking minute on the trip would have to respond, "No, we didn't do any of that." Still, I would contend that the work the students did was even harder.

Along with not being about disaster response, there are a number of other things that this project is not. Each time I taught a Katrina class, for instance, we did visit leaders from every denomination represented among that group of students. The students and I learned a lot, and some of it is documented in this volume. Nevertheless, this book does not address the situation of hundreds of either nondenominational or congregationally autonomous churches in the city. If enough of these congregations' members came back with enough money, they rebuilt and reopened the church; if enough of them didn't come back, it remained closed. These kinds of churches are omitted from this project not because they are not important; they are omitted because their decision-making process was comparatively simple. The pastor and people could decide whether their congregation could reopen without dealing with a hierarchy or a larger church that might have its own opinions and hold some authority or decision-making power.

New Orleans congregations affiliated with several of the mainline denominations were in a different position. Episcopalian, Roman Catholic, United Methodist, and Presbyterian (USA) churches, for instance, had a nationwide or worldwide network with which they were in some form of covenant, where the ownership of the property rested with an entity other than the local church, and where others in their network might be expected to bear at least some financial responsibility for those affected by

Katrina. Yet the situations that these mainline denominations faced differed significantly.

Indeed, the situation in the Roman Catholic Church became extreme, as described in Chapter 4. In one videotaped *Times Picayune* interview with the archbishop of the diocese of New Orleans, a reporter's follow-up question is as telling as anything the archbishop said with regard to how the Catholics' decisions about church closures affected New Orleanians. When the archbishop closed a comment by saying, "I am at peace with myself," the reporter responded in a tone that approached disbelief, "Really? Why?"[5]

While Roman Catholicism is the dominant Christian denomination in New Orleans, United Methodism is well represented there; the district reported 25,553 members in June 2005.[6]

Other mainline denominations have far fewer churches in New Orleans, and the UMC's racial/ethnic diversity is unduplicated, as most of the other groups' congregations were Anglo. About half the affected UMC congregations were African American and half were Anglo; a Latino and a Korean UMC congregation in New Orleans were also affected, as was a Native congregation, Clanton Chapel, in Dulac, Louisiana.

This unique combination of diversity and connectional structure makes United Methodism especially fruitful for study. In congregationally autonomous denominations, the decision about whether and how to rebuild rests solely with the congregation itself. The UMC's trust clause, a part of its governance since the time of Methodism's founder, John Wesley (1703–1791), means that the larger church holds title to each congregation's physical structures. Furthermore, our system of clergy itinerancy means that although pastors are paid by the individual congregations they serve, they are not hired by the congregations, but appointed to service in a location, one year at a time, by the bishop. Thus, the larger body was intimately involved in decision making.

Setting boundaries not just in terms of religious representation, but also geographically, was imperative if I hoped to create a manageable project. When Hurricane Rita hit southwest Louisiana and re-flooded part of southeast Louisiana just three weeks after Katrina, a church official in New Orleans began calling the phenomenon "Kat-rita." Rita was in fact a more powerful storm than Katrina—at that time, the fourth strongest storm ever in the Atlantic Basin—but it came ashore in a far less populated area that was largely rural rather than urban. Further, despite the amount of destruction in southwest Louisiana, it was a different kind of destruction than in

---

5. Pope, "Exclusive Interview with Archbishop."
6. Rhoads, ed., *Journal of the Thirty-Fifth Session*, S66.

New Orleans, because water came in and went back out, rather than being trapped.[7] Including the area impacted by Rita in this study was impossible. Including all the area impacted by Katrina was impractical. Eventually, I decided that not all of the New Orleans District should be involved, as the situation in Greater New Orleans was unique. Thus, the churches in Greater New Orleans were those I considered.

Methodology and Organization

My Social Location

I am a woman who is academically trained as a historian, a theologian, and a pastor. I am an ordained minister in the Louisiana conference of the United Methodist Church.[8] Since 2002, I have taught at a mainline Protestant seminary in Oklahoma where most of our students are in training for ordination. I have tenure, have been promoted to the rank of full professor, and hold a named chair. I earned a PhD from Tulane University, an MDiv from Southern Methodist University, and an MA and a BS from the University of Louisiana, Monroe.

My pastoral experience includes seven years in greater New Orleans pastorates, including a mixed-race congregation in New Orleans East; an Anglo middle-class congregation in Metairie; and an Anglo middle- to upper-middle-class congregation in Harahan. I pastored an African American congregation in downtown Monroe, Louisiana, for a year during my internship.

I benefit from white privilege. I have been aware of that privilege since I was four or five years old, though I certainly did not have that language then. However, I undoubtedly do not grasp all the aspects of my white privilege even now in my early sixties.

Born and raised in a small town in central Louisiana, I fell in love with New Orleans as a child and consider it to be my home, both spiritual and otherwise. I still have strong family connections to New Orleans, as my children and grandchildren live there. My son's pre-Katrina home had to be bulldozed after the storm, and he owns an empty lot where it used to stand.

---

7. According to Tidwell, Rita "still atomized coastal communities like Holly Beach and Cameron, Louisiana, and destroyed or damaged 70 percent of the housing stock as far inland as Lake Charles. The salinity of in-rushing ocean water, meanwhile, contaminated vast rice fields and cattle fields all along southwest Louisiana, not unlike the ancient fields of Carthage sown with salt by invading Roman armies." (*Ravaging Tide*, 94)

8. I am an ordained elder in full connection in the Louisiana Annual Conference. I am appointed to an extension ministry as a seminary professor.

Being a first responder, he stayed in the city during Katrina's landfall. He was a police officer at Tulane Hospital and Medical School located in downtown New Orleans. He was there during the storm's landfall on Monday, and was not airlifted out until Friday. By then he and other staff had evacuated over 1,600 patients and employees from their hospital, along with two hundred critically ill patients from Charity Hospital which was so near that patients could be floated across the street in plastic tubs. It was a week that none of us ever wish to repeat.

Most important of all, I have lived in New Orleans both before and after the storm, actively studying its layers upon layers of pre-Katrina and post-Katrina culture, including those reflected in the UMC. My sabbatical from Phillips Theological Seminary and the grant funding detailed in the acknowledgments allowed me to live in New Orleans full time from June 2008 through August 2009. That fourteen-month immersion gave me an exceptional opportunity for research. Additionally, I have been in the city for month-long and summer-long residencies several times since Katrina, and made dozens of shorter trips.

My Methods

Texts on methodology for qualitative research often address the question of voice for the presentation of the results. For instance, Chiseri-Strater and Sunstein discuss the importance of reminding the reader occasionally about an author's "fixed position" so the reader will remain conscious "of the ways you come to know *the way you know*."[9] Even more on point is Rossman and Rallis's consideration of voice. Acknowledging the difficulty of finding the right voice for presenting qualitative findings, they suggest that a blend of third and first persons allows a writer to acknowledge her subjectivity and reveal who she is in a way that frees her to tell the story of others.[10]

In order to construct what amounts to an extended case study, I have drawn on my experience and identity as a historian, a qualitative researcher, and a feminist theologian. For me, the occasional use of the first person is a deliberate statement of those various personal identities. It is something I have been reflecting on for years, and something that I practice purposefully in various formats.

It must already be clear that my status as a researcher on this project has been complicated. The most accurate way to describe my methodology is to say that I have been a participant observer, though that term is complex

---

9. Chiseri-Strater and Sunstein, *FieldWorking*, 57–59. Italics theirs.
10. Rossman and Rallis, *Learning in the Field*, 337–39.

in itself. Scientists recognize the "observer effect," acknowledging that the very act of measurement changes the results. In truth, I have made no effort to refrain from having an impact on the results, though I am sure that such an impact was very small. But I did have some impact, occasionally deliberate, such as my giving money directly to particular churches or programs that I wanted to see succeed or helping to promote fundraisers through my Facebook page. Much more of my impact was not consciously directed, occurring as an inevitable byproduct of my interviews with scores of people involved in the recovery.

Every time I (or in some instances, my students and I) had conversations with individuals involved in the recovery, they were given a chance to reflect on their work in a way they would not otherwise have been doing at that time (or perhaps ever). In crisis mode, it is all people can do to handle urgent pressures and minute-to-minute decisions that will determine whether their loved ones, homes, and workplaces will survive. During recovery, they make countless decisions that may determine whether institutions to which they have given their lives will thrive or even survive. When there are so many dire needs that last for so long, simply maintaining an even keel from week to week and month to month takes every scrap of energy available.

Being asked, often for the first time, about the deeper meaning behind their decisions and their actions gave people a chance to look at their work from a different angle. It offered a moment for the kind of explicit theological reflection that might otherwise not have been at the top of their to-do list. It made space for them to think about not just one congregation or one ministry, but rather the church as a whole. I would guess it was rare for persons who spent an hour reflecting with me to approach their next task in precisely the same frame of mind they were in before we started.

Occasionally I was able to supply some language that allowed people to think differently about what they were doing. I filled in some historical context for the situations in which various church leaders found themselves. The term "'The New Normal" was so common and so apt, especially in the early months after Katrina, that it must have been easy to forget what the "Old Normal" was and how it had developed. Knowing how things were in 2005 and 1965 and 1915 and 1895 provides an understanding of how previous splits and mergers in the church occurred, where cooperation has been successful before, and how resentments and distrust have developed. Both the Christian hope and our lived experiences show that the past does not have to dictate the future, but this does not mean that we shouldn't learn what the past has to teach us and attempt to apply that learning to current decision making.

My work has been qualitative and similar to ethnographic field work in nature.[11] Along with traditional academic research in books and journals, I attended and observed worship at thirty-two United Methodist churches in the area, including African American, Anglo, Korean, Latino, Native American, and mixed-race congregations; I attended worship at a number of those congregations multiple times over the course of several years. Moreover, where there are Methodists, there are meetings. I went to annual conferences and to district-wide preconference meetings. I attended preachers' meetings and clergy retreats. I went to clergy parties to celebrate Christmas and to celebrate Mardi Gras, parties to say welcome to new clergy in the New Orleans district, and parties to say farewell to those who were leaving.

I conducted dozens of interviews with reporters, musicians, professors, executives in several Christian denominations, church pastors, leaders of the United Methodist Women (UMW), and laypeople, including young people living in intentional community at First Grace UMC. I gleaned information from more informal visits. I talked with adult Sunday school classes and local United Methodist Women (UMW) and volunteer groups from other states. I visited various UMC agencies, including several established after the storm, and talked to the people who began them.

I heard many lectures given by scholars and panel presentations by community organizers. I went to political forums, attended panel discussions, and film screenings at local universities. I read local newspapers of all types and read bulletin boards at coffeehouses. I presented papers on the post-Katrina church at a number of scholarly conferences and learned from feedback there. I attended performances where artists interpreted the Katrina experience through their own media. These included film screenings of locally produced documentaries, a dance performance called *Shelter* by the Urban Bush Women, and a play called *Swimming Upstream* written by Eve Ensler and a group of New Orleans women.[12] Art installations I visited around the city told the story visually.

---

11. Naples, *Feminism and Method*, 49–66. In a chapter called, "The Insider/Outside Debate: A Feminist Revisiting," Naples questions the assumption that genuine "outsider" status can possibly be maintained through a sustained investigation of this sort. Overall, my methodology bears similarities to that described by Nicholas Ng-A-Fook in *An Indigenous Curriculum of Place*, 64–65.

12. Bebelle et al., *Swimming Upstream*.

Description of the Volume

In this Introduction, I have explained my own methodology, background, and personal connections to New Orleans. In Chapter 2, I provide an abbreviated narrative of some of the history that brought the UMC to the place it found itself in 2005. Chapter 3, "The Storm," gives a brief overview of the flood itself and some of the events it precipitated. It begins a discussion of the effects of the Katrina Diaspora and the exile.

The next four chapters detail the work of the United Methodist Church following Katrina. Chapter 4, "The Process," is a key chapter, as it lays out the ways the United Methodist Church began addressing the situation. The following five chapters report some of the results of using that process. Chapter 5 describes one of the more successful and most interesting creations that the storm helped bring about, First Grace UMC, a merger of an African American congregation and an Anglo congregation that has formed a unique relationship with the recovering city. Chapter 6 deals with the course of ministry with Latino/as in Greater New Orleans. Chapters 7 and 8 deal with a wide variety of post-Katrina congregations and ministries.

My closing chapters explore the theological underpinnings of the church's work. It was tempting to place the material in Chapter 9 at the beginning of the book, but by the time the project was nearly complete, it became clear to me that the theological understandings of the church are so intimately tied to its future that the most appropriate placement was next to Chapter 10, where my hopes for what the church will accomplish in the days ahead are written.

Conclusion

The opening of Psalm 69 was a recurring theme in the months after the storm: "Save me, O God; for the waters are come in unto my soul" (v. 1, KJV). From the Bible open to that psalm at the registration desk of the Dominican Conference Center to the poster of a kitten that used a more modern translation that located the waters not in the writer's soul but rather up to his neck, the verse seemed to appear all over the city. The next verses read, "I sink in deep mire, where there is no standing: I am come into deep waters, where the floods overflow me. I am weary of my crying: my throat is dried: mine eyes fail while I wait for my God" (vv. 2–3).

Certainly that psalm captures the feelings of those of us who love New Orleans and all who inhabit it. As I was finishing this book, I rewatched Spike Lee's documentary film on Katrina, *When the Levees Broke*. Horrified and sickened all over again, I found myself in a fetal position on the couch. At that point, I began to observe myself from a physical standpoint and realized that my face felt out of shape because of my sadness. In fact, "sadness" is too tame a word; I was grief stricken, heartbroken.[13]

Just a few days after the storm, I drove a pickup truck, the bed full of furniture and household goods for my son and his family, from Oklahoma to Abita Springs, a town on the north shore of Lake Pontchartrain. We passed through vast areas that had lost all their power sources. Describing that drive to others, I would say, "It's the mile-after-mile-ness of it," knowing even that could not convey the experience. I knew full well what a pastor meant when he told my class, "People felt abandoned and afraid. Those two things together create a rich kind of anger."[14]

One of the things that made me and others especially angry was the suggestion by many that New Orleans was not worth saving, and should be abandoned, since there was no practical way to protect it from future catastrophes. Too many times people standing in a church building in Oklahoma would ask me, quite seriously, "Why should we even think about rebuilding that city?"

Answering that requires reminding the questioner that the Mississippi River drains all or part of thirty-one of the fifty states. The strategic and economic importance of the port of New Orleans, located where the Mississippi drains into the Gulf of Mexico, can be established with that one fact alone. Coastal areas in the twenty-three states that border the Atlantic, the Pacific, or the Gulf of Mexico—46 percent of all the states—are just as vulnerable as New Orleans was and is. Indeed, although it was not comparable with Katrina in any category of damage, Sandy's landfall in New Jersey in October 2013 should serve as a reminder that the Gulf Coast is not the only danger zone within the United States.

Psalm 69 also helped to raise the question of the Deity's involvement, which made for some bad, maddening theology. While the bodies of people who died still floated in the floodwaters, prominent televangelists who seem always to get press coverage for their pronouncements about a vengeful God were insisting that the situation was the fault of New Orleanians who tolerated or perpetrated all that sexual sinfulness. New Orleanians angrily pointed out that the French Quarter where Bourbon Street is located and the gay-friendly Marigny neighborhood were the places that did *not* flood, and that if the televangelists and those in agreement with them were correct,

---

13. Lee and Pollard, *When the Levees Broke*.

14. Rob Weber, interview by the author and students, March 13, 2006, Shreveport, LA.

then God must have very bad aim. These facts, however, appeared to make no impact on the televangelists' side of the discussion.

Some talk about the storm's having laid open a wound, revealing what is needed for healing. For those with eyes to see, Katrina exposed a level of racism that many had previously denied. The circumstances of those who had no car and nowhere to go are still denied by a few, but others have faced the truth of what life can be like for individuals who live in poverty. Even the landfall on the twenty-ninth day of the month—that period when money has run out for the month and it is not yet payday—made the difference between staying and going for lots of New Orleanians.

Anger, hopelessness, blame, judgment—understanding all these and how they affected the church's response requires looking more deeply into the realities on the ground in New Orleans following Katrina, as well as grasping some of the history and practices of the Methodist church from its very origins. In the next two chapters, then, we will consider these in broad detail before zeroing in on the real lives of congregations that were key to helping the city emerge from despair and meet its challenges head-on.

2

United Methodism in New Orleans: Historical Context

In the introduction, I spoke briefly of the connectional structure of the United Methodist Church, and of how its clergy relate first to their conferences before they do to their individual congregations. This UMC terminology is explained in the Appendix. These dimensions of United Methodism are perhaps unique within American Christianity—mainline Protestantism, in particular—and helps explain why the church was able to respond as it did to Katrina. And to understand how it is that Methodism developed these traits, we must look briefly at its historical roots, both in England and in its arrival in America.

English Roots

Contemporary believers—as well as observers of religion—may well have lost sight of the fact that Methodism has its roots in the Church of England, whose early history is marked by several centuries of bloodshed and a war for supremacy in England. Indeed, King Henry VIII's action to establish an English church apart from the Roman Catholic Church in the 1530s was still causing bloody strife in 1746 at the Battle of Culloden, when the Jacobites made one final effort to invade England and install a Catholic monarchy. Over one thousand people died that day alone. John Wesley, considered the founder of Methodism, and a priest in the Church of England, was forty-six years old at the time.

While it is not necessary to recount all complex events that ensued during those two centuries—with Protestants and Catholics vying not just for the English crown, but also subjecting one another to various forms of oppression—we should not underestimate the extreme religious traumas that shaped the world into which Wesley was born. In 1660, following a brief period after the English Civil War when the country was governed under a Protectorate led by Oliver Cromwell, Church of England polity and doctrine were restored along with the monarchy. All clergy were then required to conform to the reinstated Thirty-Nine Articles of Religion, the church's historical doctrinal statements first established in 1563. Those who could not were called "Noncomformists" or "Dissenters" and turned out of the priesthood. John Wesley's paternal grandfather was among them. He "was ejected from his living and, as was typical of many nonconformists, spent the remaining years of his life in a variety of pulpits and prisons."[1]

The Restoration did not bring religious peace. Many hundreds of public executions for the crime of practicing the wrong religion (which was Protestantism under Mary Stuart, called "Bloody Mary," and Catholicism under Elizabeth I) had been carried out since the Act of Supremacy in 1534, and even Parliament's approving an Act of Toleration in 1689 did not end the strife and bloodshed. This Act meant that groups "who could not adhere to the traditional Church of England's faith were 'tolerated' in the sense that they were allowed to exist legally under certain prescribed conditions."[2] The Roman Catholic and Unitarian churches had no legal right to exist, but other groups could practice so long as their preachers were licensed and meetings occurred only in registered locations. Individuals not willing to adhere to Church of England beliefs faced significant restrictions. In order to attend a university, vote in elections, hold public office, or hold a commission in the armed forces, a person had to subscribe to the Thirty-Nine Articles of Religion.

Thus, religious conflict was not an abstract idea for John Wesley, but a reality that cost thousands of British lives during his own lifetime. Violence was part of his personal life experience, too. His journal records his being attacked by angry mobs on several occasions. I think the frightening legacy and powerful threat of religious violence kept him from making a formal break with the church. Methodist historian Richard Heitzenrater concludes, "It is no wonder on these grounds alone that Wesley would vehemently oppose those in his movement who favored separation."[3]

But just what was his movement? It began when John Wesley was a student at Oxford and several young men gathered to encourage one another to live holy lives. He was ordained, and though he remained a priest of the Church of England for the rest of his life, Wesley was persuaded to

---

1. Heitzenrater, *Wesley and the People Called Methodists*, 15.
2. Ibid., 15.
3. Ibid., 17.

move outside the church—literally, outside—and he frequently preached outdoors to miners and other working people.

Wesley believed that salvation was available to every human, and that each of us can choose whether to answer God's call. He insisted that a good Methodist, and indeed a good Christian, was defined not by anything a person might believe, but rather by what a person does. He thought that although we can do so only as we are empowered by God's grace, humans are responsible for making life on Earth conform more nearly to what God would have it be. He was, in other words, attentive to an aspect of theology that would become closely identified with Methodists during the Social Gospel movement, the doctrine of the Kingdom of God. Deeply concerned with those who were marginalized, Wesley insisted that all Methodists should spend time getting to know those who were in need. He established free health clinics, opened schools for poor children, and practiced microlending. He taught that no one should accumulate more wealth or possessions than he or she needed to provide necessities for themselves and their families.

Such teaching was not always welcome among the relatively affluent Church of England congregations, and most of their congregations where he preached made it clear that he was not welcome to return. Despite (or because of) the challenge he presented to the prevailing church, his movement grew rapidly and spread across the British Isles. Nevertheless, he continued to insist that Methodists should receive Eucharist at Church of England churches and that the Methodists were not and should not be a separate church.

Methodism in the United States

The result of all this is that Methodism was formally established in North America, in what would become the United States of America, rather than in England. Its governance and character paralleled that of the new republic. This has immense significance in terms of how the church regards leadership. While United Methodism is certainly not completely democratic or nonhierarchical, Methodism began in a far more democratic fashion than Wesley would have liked, and in the 220 intervening years has become still more democratic.

Because the Church of England was an established church, when the colonies declared their independence, its priests were recalled back to England. Since Wesley had insisted that Methodism remain affiliated with the Church of England and had written a pamphlet condemning the colonial rebellion, Methodist preachers judged it wise to leave the country, too. Only Francis Asbury remained, and he maintained a very low profile during the war.

Wesley was concerned about the thousands of Methodists on this continent who did not have opportunity to partake of the sacraments (baptism and Holy Communion). He acted on a theological conviction he had held for some time; based on his reading of the New Testament in the Greek, he believed a priest had as much authority to ordain ministers as bishops did. He ordained two individuals to come to America where they were to ordain others, including Asbury. Wesley intended for Asbury and Thomas Coke to be "superintendents" of the Methodist church in the new country.

Asbury was the one individual who had the most influence on the new American denomination. Asbury soon began using the title "bishop" instead of "superintendent," which annoyed Wesley to no end. Asbury's choosing of his title signaled a step away from Wesley's authority, yet it was not a personal power grab. In fact, Asbury indicated that he would accept the office "only if elected by an American Conference."[4]

This move sealed a relatively democratic future for Methodism. While Queen Elizabeth II is still head of the Church of England, there is no monarch in the United States and no one person who can govern the church. Changes in governance occur only at General Conference, a quadrennial gathering of elected delegates. Bishops, the persons who hold the highest ecclesiastical offices, are barred from voting on anything that occurs at those General Conferences.

Further, from a system where initially only clergy in full connection (who were all white males) voted on issues of governance, the church has moved over the years to a system where laity elect as many delegates to General Conference as clergy do, where African Americans can be ordained in full connection, where women are ordained in full connection, and where women and people of color are represented among our Council of Bishops. We have by no means achieved full equality of all people within the UMC or brought complete justice into our church. My assessment as a historian, though, is that we have continually, albeit far too slowly, moved in the right direction when it comes to sharing leadership more widely. That undoubtedly made a difference in post-Katrina New Orleans.

---

4. Ibid., 291.

Methodism in New Orleans

Although it is tempting to say that the post-storm church in New Orleans has not returned to its normal situation, that statement would probably exaggerate its pre-storm normality. True, the situation had been relatively unchanged for several decades prior to 2005. Furthermore, most people who showed up for worship on Sunday probably did not realize the extent to which the building where they gathered occupied its particular location due to conflict among people who all considered themselves Methodists. This section will paint just a few broad strokes about New Orleans Methodism, including a very simple (and therefore very incomplete) description of the origins of some its racial/ethnic diversity.

The Methodist Episcopal Church (MEC) was formally established in Baltimore in 1784. John Wesley was a strong and vocal opponent of slavery, and the stance of the MEC was originally a firm opposition to slavery. It was not long before the personal convictions of men like Bishop Francis Asbury, who agreed with Wesley, gave way to what they saw as an overwhelming need to keep the church in the North and the South together. Racism crept (or sometimes stormed) into the MEC, and early schisms had to do with how persons of color were treated. It would be folly to try to chronicle all the splits and mergers in Methodism in this chapter or even this book. However, there are a few that are germane to the UMC's situation in New Orleans.

The first of these occurred in 1787 with Richard Allen's departure from an MEC congregation in Philadelphia over racial discrimination. This resulted in the eventual creation of the African Methodist Episcopal Church (AME). A few years later, the African Methodist Episcopal Zion Church (AMEZ) organized in New York City, also sparked by local discrimination. Both the AME and the AMEZ still exist as denominations completely unattached to the UMC; they have congregations in New Orleans, but these are not discussed in this book.

In 1844, the MEC experienced a massive breakup over the ethics of enslaving humans. The schism had been coming for some time as the movement toward abolition of slavery grew stronger in country and church. The catalyst was when MEC Bishop James Andrews was expelled from the episcopacy because his wife had inherited an enslaved person whom the bishop refused to free, maintaining that it was against the law in Georgia to free a slave. As a result, most white Methodists in the South split away and formed the Methodist Episcopal Church, South (MECS) in 1845. The MECS *Book of Discipline* was essentially the same as that of the MEC, but the prohibition against slavery was simply omitted.

Nevertheless, even in states where most congregations chose to affiliate with the MECS, there were still some white congregations who remained with the MEC. Other MEC congregations were planted by missionaries from the North after the Civil War. Thus, New Orleans was home to white membership MECS congregations, to white membership MEC congregations, and to black membership MEC congregations.

In 1870, after the Civil War but long before the 1939 reunion, another African American denomination, the Colored Methodist Episcopal Church, came out of the MECS. It changed its name to the Christian Methodist Episcopal Church (CME) in the mid-twentieth century. Enslaved persons had previously attended MECS worship with their owners (though in separate seating), but many desired to have their own denomination after they achieved freedom. Further, many white MECS members preferred to segregate their churches than to attend with freed black people. To achieve segregation, the MECS intentionally fostered the creation of a separate denomination. The CME still exists, unaffiliated with the UMC; it has congregations in New Orleans, but these, too, are not discussed in this book.[5]

The two classic histories of the UMC in Louisiana are those of Robert Henry Harper (published in 1949) and that of Walter Vernon (published in 1987).[6] Some recent monographs include information on Methodist history that plays a pivotal role in the post-Katrina story. They explore various aspects of how issues of race, class, and gender have shaped the history of the city, and when it comes to New Orleans, these issues are very, very complicated.

In *The Great Southern Babylon*, Alecia Long discusses the infamous Storyville. Created in 1897, Storyville was a district zoned for legal houses of prostitution. It was located just lakeside (roughly north) of the French Quarter. Storyville was full of brothels that ranged from mansions to flophouses, along with establishments for drinking, dancing, and live music. As the city made the decision to create the district, it disregarded the fact that there were institutions within its boundaries which did not want prostitution legalized and which would no longer find the district a suitable location once such legalization occurred. These included several African American membership churches.

Long's book documents the struggle of the MEC congregation called Union Chapel, including court cases brought by black organizations to try

---

5. Today, the Pan-Methodist movement brings together AME, AMEZ, CME and UMC representatives to engage in conversations about the reuniting of these denominations. It is possible that these will eventually lead to fruition, but at this time the AME, AMEZ and CME congregations in New Orleans are in no way tied to the UMC.

6. Harper, *Louisiana Methodism*; Vernon, *Becoming One People*.

to prevent the church's being included in Storyville. "Court testimony and related contemporary documents reveal that before and during 1897, the Union Chapel was a thriving, well-attended church that had its sights set on the education and edification of its own. According to one source, the Union Chapel's commodious facility was one of the largest and finest African American church buildings, surpassing most other 'churches of color in the State in size and beauty.'" Reports indicated that there were three hundred active members "and a total attendance of about six hundred that assembled regularly on Sundays, Tuesdays and Fridays." The Sunday school program provided 170 children with regular "religious instruction and teaching."[7] Then, one Sunday morning, a police officer stopped families trying to bring their children to Sunday school and told them that children were no longer allowed in the district.[8]

The lawsuit to keep the district from being formed around Union Chapel eventually wound up being appealed all the way to the United States Supreme Court. Long recounts the history of the lawsuit and considers the impact of racism and the prior *Plessy v. Ferguson* decision in 1896 (also based on an incident in New Orleans) on these events. She concluded, "In creating Storyville, the city sought to separate respectable New Orleanians from prostitutes. In the process, city leaders implied a rough equality between its population of 'lewd and abandoned women' both white and black, and the African Americans who lived, went to school, and worshiped in the neighborhood. The Story Ordinances placed people of color on a plane with prostitutes and other sexual sinners, both conceptually and in terms of physical proximity."[9]

Eventually, around 1915, the pastor and leaders of Union Chapel decided to worship together with the members of the Pleasant Plains Church whose building had been "demolished" by a storm. At first they gathered in a school building but later rented a stable for meetings. "They began . . . to console each other with the thought, 'Since there was no place for us in the Inn, we went to the stable.'" With the assistance of their bishop, who put up his Procter & Gamble stock as collateral for a loan, the congregations purchased a building and called the new merged body Grace MEC.[10] They eventually settled into a large structure at 2001 Iberville Street.

Grace is one of the two congregations that merged into First Grace UMC after Katrina. It is important to recognize that the predecessors of

---

7. Long, *Great Southern Babylon*, 136.
8. Vernon, *Becoming One People*, 173.
9. Long, *Great Southern Babylon*, 138.
10. Vernon, *Becoming One People*, 173–74.

Grace Church had already been forced to move despite significant resistance on the part of the Union Chapel members. The Pleasant Plains move was occasioned by their building's destruction, which was no doubt a trauma for its members. When Grace merged with First UMC after Katrina and left their building for First UMC's, there was already a bone-deep history of pain resulting from the people's being forced to move their church from one location to another. The story of how Grace merged with First UMC is recounted in Chapter 5, but each of the events mentioned in this chapter played a part in creating the circumstances, the ethos, the personality, and the soul not just of Grace UMC and First UMC, but of every UMC congregation in New Orleans.

The Storyville district was closed down when the United States became involved in World War I in 1917, on the insistence of the United States Navy. The local narrative says that as troops were about to leave the port of New Orleans, many men were prone to treat themselves to a last night of revelry; by the time they reached Europe, they were displaying symptoms of sexually transmitted disease and therefore had to be sent home again. However, there were also significant reform efforts underway in the city at the time. Rhetoric of the day usually dealt with ensuring the morality of the fighting force; no doubt some did object solely on the grounds of prostitution being immoral. However, different reformers had different motives, and some were concerned about the exploitation of women, while others were incensed about the interracial sex that happened in the district. In the end, local officials who wanted to preserve the district and those who profited financially from Storyville were trumped not by local objections but by the military and the war effort. It hardly seems necessary to say that prostitution in New Orleans did not end with the dismantling of the Storyville district. Sex for hire of all descriptions, including human trafficking, continues there today as it does in cities across the United States and around the world.

In another monograph, *Religion and the Rise of Jim Crow in New Orleans*, James Bennett examines the roles of the Roman Catholic Church and the Methodist Episcopal Church (MEC). He addresses both the complicity of the MEC in the construction of legal segregation and the resistance that the MEC offered to it. He notes that the existence of the CME, AME, and AMEZ alongside the MEC "created a unique pattern in the American religious landscape." No other Protestant group except Presbyterians had enough black church members for the option of a separate denomination to be viable. Neither Episcopalians nor Congregationalists "claimed substantial numbers of black churches or clergy." Although the MEC faced "the unique challenge of contending with rival Methodist organizations as well as with competing Baptist and, especially in New Orleans and Atlanta,

Congregationalist churches," he writes, "no tradition approached the success of the M. E. Church in retaining black and white members in the same denomination. Well into the twentieth century, the M. E. Church was the only substantially biracial Protestant denomination."[11]

Neither the close of the Civil War nor the ending of Reconstruction was a strong enough catalyst to precipitate reunion between the MEC and the MECS. It was not until 1939, more than seven decades after Lee's surrender, when they reunited to form The Methodist Church.[12] There were fewer than a handful of major denominations that did not split apart over issues of race and slavery in the years preceding the Civil War. Compared to some, the 1939 reunion for Methodists seems quick. Presbyterians did not repair their antebellum rupture until the 1980s. Southern Baptists are still a separate church.

It is a serious mistake to assume that all MEC members were "liberal" and all MECS members were "conservatives," or that formerly MEC congregations are automatically progressive today and that former MECS congregations are automatically conservative. There was significant racial prejudice and discrimination in the MEC and, as my book on St. Mark's Community Center in New Orleans demonstrates, many MECS women in the late 1800s and early 1900s worked courageously toward racial tolerance and equality. *St. Mark's and the Social Gospel* examines the work of MECS deaconesses at a French Quarter settlement house. They ran a first-come, first-served health clinic where both black and white New Orleanians were served with no separate waiting or treatment rooms. Most of the white Southern deaconesses trained at Scarritt College in Nashville, where many of them joined the local chapter of the National Association for the Advancement of Colored People (NAACP). Their legacy is explored in a bit more depth in the section on St. Mark's UMC in Chapter 8.[13]

The MEC also opened a community center in New Orleans in the early 1920s. It was affiliated with People's MEC, located on Simon Bolivar in Central City. Women from MEC churches around the city, many of which had African American congregations, formed the Ruth Carter Auxiliary to

---

11. Bennett, *Religion and the Rise*, 15.

12. The Methodist Protestant denomination was also included in this merger into The Methodist Church, along with the MEC and MECS. The Methodist Protestants had split from the MEC and created their church in 1830. Their issues included the right of laity to vote on church governance questions and opposition to electing bishops to the office for life. During the 1939 proceedings, the Methodist Protestants from Mississippi walked out, and there are still a few congregations which use the Methodist Protestant denominational label in Mississippi and a handful of other Southern states.

13. Blue, *St. Mark's and the Social Gospel*.

support the work at People's."[14] Although Bennett did note that "women in home missions would continue as one of the last and often unremarked-upon examples of racial interaction, laying the groundwork for the interracial women's organizations that preceded the Civil Rights movement," he did not mention the work at People's or explore any other women's work in his book.[15] The auxiliary and People's were still involved in ministry when Katrina struck, and the current status of the ministry is discussed in Chapter 7.

The reunion of the MEC and the MECS in 1939 was not an unmitigated success. It was achieved through a shameful compromise that segregated the newly created body, The Methodist Church, along racial lines. In order to make sure that white clergy would not have to serve under African American bishops, the church decided that bishops would be elected at the jurisdictional level and serve within the jurisdiction where they were elected. Five jurisdictions for white membership congregations and conferences were created in the United States on a geographical basis, as well as a sixth jurisdiction composed of all African American congregations and conferences that overlapped the other jurisdictions geographically. The sixth was called the Central Jurisdiction, and Bishop James Thomas has written an introduction to its history.[16]

While there are sometimes good reasons for minority groups to maintain their own separate structures, the African American Methodists involved in the 1939 merger made it abundantly clear that they did not choose to be segregated in the Central Jurisdiction. That jurisdiction's existence meant that an Anglo congregation and an African American congregation located just blocks apart belonged to two different annual conferences. The white congregation belonged to the conference designated "Louisiana A," and the black congregation to "Louisiana B." Things were designed so there would be no interaction between laity or clergy of A and B at the local, district, conference, or jurisdictional levels.

The women's organizations in both South and North were proponents of the merger and had worked together more successfully in the years prior to 1939 than the churches at large. Later on, their new organization created

---

14. Several women have spoken to me about a tacit understanding regarding St. Mark's Community Center (located in the French Quarter) and People's Community Center. Both originated in the early twentieth century, St. Mark's as a project of the MECS and People's as a mission project of the MEC. The understanding which persisted even after the 1939 merger (probably because of the existence of the segregated Central Jurisdiction) was that women's groups in black membership congregations would support People's, while women's groups in white membership congregations would support St. Mark's.

15. Bennett, *Religion and the Rise*, 56.

16. Thomas, *Methodism's Racial Dilemma*.

by the merger, the Women's Society of Christian Service (WSCS), advocated for the abolishment of the Central Jurisdiction. However, complete segregation was the church's default position, and members had to make a special and deliberate effort to cooperate on anything across racial lines.

The racially segregated Central Jurisdiction was finally abolished in 1968 when The Methodist Church merged with the Evangelical United Brethren (EUB) denomination to create The United Methodist Church (UMC).[17] After 1968, it still took a couple of years to combine the structures of Louisiana A and Louisiana B, so that the anniversary of today's integrated conference is calculated from 1971. However, even when that administrative merger was accomplished, there was still no move to integrate individual congregations around the state.

Although delegates began to meet and sit together at Annual Conference gatherings, and black and white laypeople and clergy began to serve together on boards and committees at the district level, the people who related to the UMC primarily through their local congregations saw little change in worship and in all the other matters which make up the local experience of Methodism. While some United Methodists, especially members of the United Methodist Women (UMW) organization, worked with persons of different races on a frequent basis and in a collegial way, it is impossible to deny that segregation, separation, and resentment still exist within the church. Post-Katrina decisions have both challenged and affirmed that reality.

---

17. There were no congregations in the city of New Orleans that originated in the Evangelical United Brethren (EUB) branch of the United Methodist Church.

3

The Storm

*And the mold, whether toxic or
merely revolting, was everywhere.*
—Jed Horne[1]

The Floodwalls Could
Not Hold—Things Fall Apart

When Katrina made landfall on Monday, August 29, 2005, New Orleans was by no means the only place affected. Flooding was widespread, but the flood within the city itself was different. In most locations, there was a "typical" flood—lots of water flowed in, but it also flowed back out after the storm. The damage was the kind that south Louisianans are accustomed to hearing about or even dealing with personally.

In New Orleans, floodwall breaks allowed water from Lake Pontchartrain into the city, and because the land was lower than the level of the lake, the only way to get the water back out was to pump it out. The process took three weeks. Eighty percent of the city had been inundated with water so high that people drowned in their attics.[2] Dangerous chemicals, toxins, and sewage swirled in the mix. The subtropical heat fostered the growth of various kinds of toxic mold in quantities that most people had never imagined.

UNO historian Arnold Hirsch made an important distinction about what happened then. "Katrina never claimed all of the ingredients that made up the 'perfect storm,'" he wrote, "but the course of a couple of centuries

---

1. Horne, *Breach of Faith*, 211.

2. One of the best pieces, if not *the* best piece of writing to emerge from the city after Katrina was a collection of essays by then *Times-Picayune* columnist Chris Rose. It is entitled *1 Dead in Attic*, a phrase that appeared on a house Rose drove by each day. National Guard soldiers who searched for bodies spray painted the results on the front of every house.

had enabled New Orleans to gather enough of them to produce a 'perfect disaster.'"[3] This characterization seems completely accurate; although Katrina was not a perfect storm, what happened was a perfect disaster.

The heading of this section, "The Floodwalls Could Not Hold," reflects how the understanding of that 2005 disaster has changed in the intervening years. Early on, the conversation was about what Katrina had done to the city. Then, people began to emphasize that the city had indeed "dodged the bullet" with the storm as was first thought, and that the disaster occurred because the levees had broken. This interpretation was significantly helped along by Spike Lee's award-winning documentary, *When the Levees Broke: A Requiem in Four Acts*. The DVD package features a personal message signed by Spike Lee that read, "Most people think that it was Katrina that brought about the devastation to New Orleans. But it was a breaching of the levees that put 80 percent of the city under water. It was not the hurricane."[4]

Time passed, and the explanation, "the levees broke," proved inadequate, too. The flooding was not primarily due to levees bursting or being overtopped. Instead, breaks in the floodwalls caused most of the flooding. Investigation later revealed that the walls broke because they had not been built to specifications. The United States Army Corps of Engineers had failed to oversee contractors who sank the floodwalls many, many feet less into the ground than their contracts specified.

On the part of contractors and/or the Corps, there was incompetence or dishonesty, greed or graft, laziness, or a deliberate decision not to sink the walls deep enough, and either a failure to supervise properly or else a deliberate decision on the part of supervisors to overlook the discrepancies. These actions and failures to act led directly to the deaths of over 1600 people, significantly hastened the deaths of thousands more, and visited trauma and abject misery on hundreds of thousands of New Orleanians. To blame "that bitch Katrina" is one thing. Saying "the levees didn't hold," a phrase laden with possibility that there was a sincere though mistaken belief that earthen levees were high enough and strong enough, is another. To say "contractors deliberately chose to make more money by not sinking floodwalls to the specified depths" and "for reasons yet to be determined, the Corps of Engineers did not see that the work was done correctly" moves us into another level of assigning responsibility for the tragedy. In this context, the word "sin" seems to apply.

One high-ranking Corps of Engineers official who previously headed the office in New Orleans actually apologized for not having done all that

---

3. Hirsch, "(Almost) a Walk Closer with Thee," 618.
4. Lee and Pollard, *When the Levees Broke*.

could have been done to prevent flooding.⁵ However, the courts have determined that the Corps is immune from lawsuits and therefore cannot legally be held responsible. Thus, "justice for all" cannot be accomplished here.

Why Did So Many People Stay?

It is best to acknowledge at the outset that there are some individuals whose personality is such that they would never leave their homes and belongings unattended without being driven out at gunpoint. There are some individuals who have such poor judgment that staying in New Orleans and experiencing the storm while drinking heavily at a hurricane party sounded like so much fun they were unable to resist it. There is no way to attach actual numbers to these groups, but it is certain that they made up only a tiny percentage of the people who remained in the city during landfall.⁶

Some people from outside Louisiana seem unwilling to admit that the vast majority of people who remained in the city would have left if they could. Katrina's timing was as bad as it could be. In my opinion, if landfall had occurred one week later, far fewer people would have failed to evacuate in the face of a storm that covered much of the Gulf of Mexico. By the time Katrina hit, on the twenty-ninth day of a thirty-one-day month, a very large number of residents had run out of money and would not receive any more until September. Those who have never evacuated for a storm probably do not realize how much it costs.

Thousands did not own cars; the reasonably good public transportation system in New Orleans made car ownership less of a priority than it is in other locations. Some people could rent a car and leave, but there was a limit to the cars available. Most of those who live in poverty do not have the wherewithal to rent one. Those who did own a car had to purchase gasoline in order to leave the city and more gasoline to come back. Being stalled in traffic and moving by feet and inches on the interstate for up to twenty hours uses a great deal of fuel.

Unless they had family or friends who lived far enough away for safety but also close enough to reach in a day's (slow) travel, evacuees would have to pay for a motel room for at least a couple of nights (if they were lucky enough to find one). Both people who evacuate and people who live inland from New Orleans are familiar with the sight of cars lined up all around

---

5. Pope, "Lt. Gen. Elvin 'Vald' Heiberg III."

6. Even some tourists were caught by surprise and trapped in the city. The Louis Armstrong International Airport usually closes the day before an expected landfall, long before visitors expect that it might close.

highway rest stops with whole families, adults and children, sleeping inside. Restaurants and convenience stores along evacuation routes run out of food and bottled water; their rest rooms run out of paper products. Leaving is a grueling and expensive prospect.[7]

Government Failed at All Levels

Government failed at all levels—because government performance can be summed up in that one phrase, very little space in this book is devoted to a discussion of it. Many authors have begun and others will continue to analyze precisely how particular displays of ineptness affected peoples' lives. Some authors believe and will continue to believe that the federal government did not respond quicker because a large percentage of the people who were stranded in the city were black and if they voted, probably voted for Democrats.

The images of the many thousands of people left in the city during floods were infuriating. The abandoned men, women, and children, mostly African American, mostly poor, were a living witness to the inability—and perhaps to the unwillingness—of government to protect the American people, or at least that segment of them.

FEMA, the Federal Emergency Management Agency, formed during the Carter administration, has traditionally failed to meet expectations. People in New Orleans have very sarcastic and graphic suggestions about what the F, E, M, and A stand for; fortunately the best four-word description of the agency's performance is also one of the few fit to print in this setting: "Failure to Effectively Manage Anything."

Many suspected that more than ineptness was involved, and indeed it was hard to believe FEMA head Michael Brown's assertions that he had only just found out that people were at the Convention Center when CNN had been broadcasting the information for days. Kanye West famously went to the heart of the suspicion when he spoke at "A Concert for Hurricane Relief," a benefit for the Red Cross televised live on NBC on September 2, while many people were still stranded in the city. Veering from his script, West noted that military personnel who could otherwise have been sent to help were unavailable because of the war that had them fighting elsewhere,

---

7. Adrenaline fuels the process of picking things up off the floor, piling small items of furniture on top of larger ones, boarding up windows, and bringing inside everything from the yard that could be turned into a missile by the wind. Three days later, there is no adrenaline to fuel the reversing of all these processes. It is difficult to face the job of putting everything back where it belongs.

and finally blurted out, "George Bush doesn't care about black people." Spike Lee's *When the Levees Broke* skewered officials, with the most cutting remark coming from a resident of the Lower Ninth Ward who maintained that George Bush "gave C students all over the world a bad name."[8]

Mayor C. Ray Nagin's failures, including his decision to delay an order for evacuation while he consulted with lawyers about whether the city might be sued for lost business and his refusal of Amtrak's offer to transport citizens out of harm's way, have been well publicized. By the time he did give the order, many who might have been able to get out of the city earlier could no longer do so because of traffic jamming the roads out. Delaying the order might have been linked to the widespread (and no doubt correct) belief that thousands of people would not be able to obey such an order unless the city organized transportation for them, something which it had not done and which Nagin was not even going to try to do.

Nagin has since become the only mayor in the city's history to be charged with and convicted of corruption, and he is currently serving time in a federal prison. After he was convicted on twenty of twenty-one counts, the *New York Times* wrote, "By the end of his second term, in 2010, many in the city had come to resent what they saw as a casual indifference on Mr. Nagin's part during the most demanding years any American city has known in recent decades." Bloggers and investigative reporters began uncovering his participation in illegal deals regarding city contracts and permits.[9] An entire book could be devoted to the failures of Nagin and the tactics that led to his re-election in 2006, but this is not that book.[10]

Upriver in the state capital, Baton Rouge, Governor Kathleen Blanco and her communications director, Bob Mann, were as cut off from the city during the flood as everyone else was. A dedicated UMC layman, Mann visited with my first Katrina class in March 2006 and helped students understand more about governmental response. He talked about the Posse Comitatus Act of 1878 which prevents federal troops from enforcing laws within the United States and explained the concerns that made an invitation for the Bush administration to take control of the city unacceptable for the Democratic governor. In 2006, Congress passed an exception to Posse Comitatus in the case of disasters like Katrina, but that law was later repealed.

Mann visited with my students again in January 2007. In the meantime, he had worked to name any blame he bore for the tragedy, and he began with what he called "a confessional." Near the end of the session, I

---

8. Lee and Pollard, *When the Levees Broke*.
9. Robertson, "Ex-Mayor of New Orleans."
10. Russell, "Mastermind."

found myself making a not-very-Methodist cross in the air and telling him, "You are absolved." Because he is one of the more ethical people involved in politics, his personal errors were easy to forgive, and compared with the catastrophic failure of Ray Nagin and FEMA, the state looked better.

State government's biggest failure was the Road Home program. The private company which was engaged by the state to administer it was not just unsuccessful—it was spectacularly unsuccessful. Even many of the lucky people who received some funds had a frustrating and dehumanizing experience in obtaining them. The Office of Community Development in Governor Bobby Jindal's administration took over administration of the program in 2010. Serious problems with the program have never been solved, and many families have submitted their documentation over and over. It has been such a fiasco that "sinful" is appropriate language here, too.

The Media—the Good, the Bad and the Ugly

CNN anchor Anderson Cooper covered the Gulf Coast situation and experienced the results of governmental breakdowns firsthand. He initially went to the Mississippi coast, where he found conditions he never expected to see in the United States. Then he made his way to New Orleans while the city still had no power, no working infrastructure, no safety net. He recalled how he grew into the deep relationship with the city that prompted him to keep recovery or the lack of it in the news periodically as the years passed.

After a while, he wrote, "I'm not shocked anymore by the bodies, the blunders. You can't stay stunned forever. The anger doesn't go away, but it settles somewhere behind your heart; it deepens into resolve. I feel connected to what's around me, no longer just observing. I feel I am living it, breathing it." Even in other disaster situations, there had been a hotel to go back to at night that let him feel "isolated from the destruction." In New Orleans, he said, "We are surrounded, all day, all night. There's no escape. I wouldn't want to get away even if I could. I don't check my voicemail for messages. I don't call home. I never want to leave."

New Orleanians are very familiar with the category of "never lefts," people who come to the city for a visit and simply never leave. Most of them are enchanted by the city on her good days. Cooper found that even at her worst, New Orleans still captures the heart. In the time that he wrote about, there was no power, and without power, no lights. "We're sleeping in trailers parked on Canal Street, not far from the old Maison Blanche department store where my father worked. At night sometimes, when the broadcast is done, we sit outside the trailers in small groups, staring at the silhouettes of empty buildings. We don't need to say a thing. There is a bond that's forming among us. We are in new territory, on the cliff's edge. This place has no name, and all of us know it. The city is exposed: flesh and blood, muscle, and bone. New Orleans is a fresh wound, sliced open by the shrapnel of a storm."[11]

Media coverage overall seemed to demonstrate that social order was breaking down. Rumors flowed freely, and as horrible and dangerous as things were, the stories that were reported as truth were even worse. Most outrageous were the untrue reports of events in the Superdome which Mayor Ray Nagin and the NOPD Chief Eddie Compass presented as fact on Oprah Winfrey's show. Rumors affected the course of events in a negative way, not just in the middle- and long-term, by convincing many Americans that New Orleans is inhabited by the depraved and the vicious, but also in the short-term, as helicopter rescues were halted from time to time after it was falsely reported that people were shooting at helicopters.

Five days in, reports sounded like this: "Violence has also increased on the streets of New Orleans. Armed citizens have reportedly taken over some of the relief sites. Shots have been fired at police officers and rescue helicopters. There have been reports of rapes, murders, and carjackings. Residents continue to break into stores in search of everything from food and water to guns to luxury items. The White House announced it would have zero tolerance for looters—even for those taking essential items needed to stay alive. Louisiana Governor's Kathleen Blanco warned that troops had orders to shoot to kill. She said 'These troops are fresh back from Iraq, well trained, experienced, battle tested and under my orders to restore order in the streets.' She went on to say 'They have M-16s and they are locked and loaded. These troops know how to shoot and kill and they are more than willing to do so if necessary and I expect they will.'"[12]

Some media critics began to develop side-by-side comparisons of photos that they said depicted media bias against African-American residents. Media outlets would caption pictures of white people leaving stores that had been broken into with the information that the people had "found" resources needed by their families. African-Americans in similar circumstances were pictured over a caption that called them "looters." This comparison has been much discussed, affirmed, and denied by different writers. It hit close enough to home to infuriate one of my former colleagues when another faculty member posted it on his office door.

11. Cooper, *Dispatches from the Edge*, 168–69.
12. Goodman, "Governor Gives Troops."

"Why do we have to see that?" she demanded. Why, indeed? Reality is not easy to face, and Katrina exposed realities that many Americans would prefer not to have seen.

The Gretna Bridge Incident

There were some people who were too sick to think of evacuating, and some who were completely disabled. Many of them died. Most of those who were hospitalized survived the floods. The exception was the patients at Memorial Hospital, where over forty people died. A physician and two nurses were accused of mercy killings; they were later tried for second-degree murder but acquitted.[13]

Most law enforcement personnel and first responders acted faithfully and helped others during the storm and the floods; some were simply unable to cope and a few ran away or committed suicide; others acted in horrific ways. A theological consideration of what happened might include observations about Rheinhold Niebuhr's assertion that humans act more immorally in groups than as individuals and a critique of Martin Luther's doctrine of the two kingdoms.

In a time and place where unnumbered atrocities of all kinds were committed, my own choice for "worst of the worst" was referred to later in the courts as the "Crescent City Connection blockage" and in the vernacular as "the Gretna Bridge incident." With 80 percent of the city underwater and the shelters of last resort turning people away, a number of individuals started walking across the Mississippi River bridge to get to dry land on the West Bank. Some of them actually lived on that side of the river but had been caught in the city for one reason or another. As they approached, law enforcement personnel from the city of Gretna and from Jefferson Parish (county) closed the bridge and denied them entry. They threatened the walkers with guns, even firing a warning shot, and forcibly turned them back into the flooded city.

Not surprisingly, a number of lawsuits were filed, including a class action suit. Those still active in December 2010 were dismissed by US District Judge Mary Ann Vial Lemmon. She issued a ruling that "called the blockade a 'reasonable restriction' and cited 'compelling safety and welfare' considerations, including heavy vehicular traffic on the bridge and the lack of food, water and shelter on the West Bank for evacuees." Gretna Police Chief Arthur Lawson, Jr. said the ruling backed his contention that the controversial blockade was "the correct and rational course of action. We had no food or

---

13. Fink, *Five Days at Memorial*.

water on the West Bank. . . . If I were I faced with the same situation today, I would make the same decision."[14]

Artist Steve Prince created a series of works called *Katrina Suite*, including a linoleum cut called "Katrina's Veil: Stand at the Gretna Bridge." Analyzing it, Beth McCoy wrote, "The walkers, no longer seen as citizens and survivors but hostile invaders, turned away, their faces to crumbled levees and a drowning city, their backs to dry land and a broken bridge. The *Katrina Suite*'s second piece confronts the bridge to Gretna and asserts that it has long been broken."[15]

It had been long broken, indeed. It was not just the long-term effects of slavery that persisted, nor the pain and dysfunction of Jim Crow segregation that impacted the law enforcement personnel in Gretna that day. As Howard Witt of the *Chicago Tribune* put it, "On one point, at least, nearly everyone seems to agree: Atop the bridge to Gretna, under the strain of an unprecedented crisis, the thin veneer of American civilization peeled back for a moment to reveal the atavistic, tribally protective impulses coursing beneath." For me, watching from Tulsa and knowing my son was in the city, it seemed that the whole fabric of civilization had broken down. Ronnie Harris, who had been mayor of Gretna for twenty-three years, said in response to the lawsuits' dismissal, "No one in America today can realize the collapse of civil authority that happened in the area after Katrina. . . . It was a return to basic human nature, a clannish feeling. You clung to people you know, people you trust and what's familiar and comfortable to you."

Witt summarized the legal question on which the judge had ruled as "the legality of the way Gretna officials acted on that clannish feeling." Looking back, Gretna Mayor Harris insisted, "Nobody got hurt, nobody died, but the world is left with the impression that we are a racist community, and that is incorrect and totally unfair."[16]

Responding to that assertion, Jarvis DeBerry wrote that it was "Accurate in the technical sense but not altogether true. Nobody was injured when the police officer fired his weapon, it's true, but the hurt? The hurt caused by the blockade was and remains incalculable. Consider the message the police conveyed with their actions: Your distress, your fear, your peril, they all mean nothing to us. Go back to where you came from. You'll find no refuge here. How could it not hurt when you find yourself in a life-threatening crisis and the police you encounter are indifferent to your survival? Is this not America? Exactly which American value is it that inspires law

---

14. Rioux, "Crescent City Connection."
15. McCoy, "Second Line," 68.
16. Witt, "Katrina Aftermath."

enforcement to brandish weapons at those seeking safety and then forcing them back into danger?"[17]

It is hard to imagine that persons on both sides of the barrier on the bridge were not harmed spiritually in this incident. The term "soul repair" is used to talk about the work in which returning military personnel may need to engage after suffering what is termed moral injury, but Brite Divinity School's Soul Repair Center leaders note that the work needs to be extended to others who are forced to make "difficult decisions."[18] Ten years out, much soul work remains to be done.

A Memorial to the Dead

A memorial was finally built to the estimated 1,600 to 1,800 Katrina victims who died straightaway (as over against the uncounted others who died early due to stress-related illnesses). Located close to the place where Canal Street becomes Canal Boulevard, the memorial sits on ground that was previously used as the graveyard for persons who died at Charity Hospital and had no other burial site. The area as a whole is a destination for tourists who ride the streetcar to see the above-ground tombs for which the city is famous. The memorial itself, though, is not well known among tourists or New Orleanians.

There were some eighty-five people who died whose remains were left at the coroner's office for three years, and they are interred at the memorial. They include fifty-four who had been identified. "Some families are so overwhelmed by the storm, or were so troubled before it, that they have declined to pick up the bodies of relatives." Some family members were lost in the storm, and some in diaspora could not be located by the coroner.

The office of Coroner Frank Minyard was responsible for the memorial. "Minyard's office shouldered the memorial project after organizing some 900 Katrina-related autopsies, and helping investigate 3,000 missing person's reports."[19] Jeffrey Rouse, a psychiatrist who worked with the coroner's office after the storm and who was more recently elected parish coroner, envisioned the design which incorporates a labyrinth into the circular shape used by weather scientists to depict a hurricane. Labyrinths have been used as a meditative tool for many centuries; those who walk them are invited to reflect on their journeys with the Holy as they walk.

---

17. DeBerry, "Hurt from Hurricane Katrina."
18. Brite Divinity School, "Soul Repair Center."
19. Gonzales, "Sign of Katrina Fatigue?"

Lindsay Tuggle maintained that the memorial "houses the casualties not only of a disaster but also of a diaspora." An inscription on a marble tablet reads "Most of the deceased were identified and buried by loved ones in private ceremonies throughout the nation. Here lie the remaining. The unclaimed and unidentified victims of the storm from the New Orleans area. Some have been forgotten. Some remain unknown." Tuggle considered the fact that "many families of the Katrina diaspora lacked the means to return to, and bury, their dead" as additional evidence "of the failure of recovery efforts."

A forensic anthropologist loaned to the New Orleans coroner by FEMA told a reporter that the memorial was built in part because "some families have chosen not to claim the bodies; some we cannot find families for." Tuggle wrote, "The seemingly permanent uprooting of many Katrina survivors has made the reclamation of remains practically impossible." Further, she said, "The implication that families scattered by the chaotic (and belated) evacuation 'choose' not to claim their dead perpetuates the flawed logic that pervaded many aspects of Katrina recovery, which presumes that residents chose to stay and that they now choose not to return."[20]

The Exile (The Katrina Diaspora)

Those whom Tuggle described—those who have not returned, not because they do not choose to, but because they do not have the needed means to do so—make up the Katrina Diaspora. The Katrina Diaspora is one of the most painful and least understood aspects of the tragedy. Tens of thousands of New Orleanians are still in exile in 2015. Countless people were herded onto buses or planes after the storm, and many families were separated against their will and sent to different cities. Many people were not told where they were going until they arrived, much less where their family members were being sent; trying to locate one another later was a time consuming and emotionally damaging process.

Some areas welcomed evacuees with great hospitality and sympathy. Local volunteers donated money, food, and clothing, and helped the people contact FEMA, obtain housing, and find jobs. In other areas, evacuees did not receive much of a welcome at all and were greeted and processed like criminals.

Some evacuees did not come back immediately because there were no schools open in New Orleans and very little medical care. The failure of the Road Home program to function effectively and the failure of FEMA and

20. Tuggle, "Encrypting Katrina."

insurance companies to do the right thing have complicated return, even for many residents who were not previously poor.

After the water was pumped out and the remaining residents were evacuated, voluntarily or otherwise, access to the city was denied to almost everyone. Residents could not get in to their own neighborhoods or houses. Different segments of the city were opened at different times. Some of the more affluent areas were opened first, and the Lower Ninth Ward was opened last. "Well into October, word reached [residents] that even the Lower Ninth had finally been removed from quarantine. But residents would be permitted only a quick visit called a 'look and leave,' the mayor decreed. Such visits would be under police escort, partly to prevent looting, if anything remained to be looted, partly because many structures were so badly damaged they were in danger of collapse and must not be entered."[21]

Many of the houses in Lower Nine had been knocked completely off their foundations and swept away. The Lower Ninth Ward had an unusually large percentage of homeowners, but many had inherited their property and their paperwork was lost in the flood. Because the courthouse was in a part of the city that flooded, it has been hard for many owners to demonstrate their ownership or their property lines. In the subtropical climate, vegetation of all kinds grows incredibly well, and weeds, vines, and brush have taken over uninhabited blocks. Large tracts of the area display no evidence except for the deteriorating streets that anyone ever lived there. Where are the people who lived there in 2005?

Since many New Orleanians were very poor, there were some former residents living around the country whose material circumstances were actually improved by the forced move. There are undoubtedly some that are happier in their new homes. The fact that it is now financially problematic for a family to give up their jobs and come back to New Orleans where they would have to find new jobs and start again does not mean that they do not consider themselves displaced.

It also fails to excuse Barbara Bush, the former First Lady and the mother of then President George W. Bush. She visited evacuees staying in Houston's Astrodome on September 5, just one week after landfall, and enthused that things were "really working out" for people there. She told a television reporter, "Almost everyone I've talked to says, 'We're going to move to Houston.' What I'm hearing, which is sort of scary, is they all want to stay in Texas. Everyone is so overwhelmed by the hospitality. And so many of the people in the arena here, you know, were underprivileged anyway, so this, this is working very well for them." One of the first publications on Katrina

---

21. Horne, *Breach of Faith*, 212.

and religion, *The Sky Is Crying: Race, Class and Natural Disaster*, included essays by twenty-one scholars, and five of them used this quote from Barbara Bush that New Orleanians and many other African-Americans took as a verbal slap in the face.[22] They are not the only ones who remember.

According to Cheryl Sanders, the primary theme for black theologians "is the Exodus, but exile is more morally interesting."[23] Her book, *Saints in Exile*, explores how the worship practices and social ethics of segments of the African-American Christian community have been affected by the experiences of diaspora and exile. "In a variety of ways, twentieth-century African-Americans have responded to the experience of exile and alienation in America by expressing their longing for some place or space—geographical, cultural, spiritual—where they can feel at home." The struggle continues in the twenty-first century for New Orleanians of all races and ethnicities who have still not been able to recover the lives they knew or even to return to their city or neighborhood, however altered it might be.[24]

Since music is one of the primary expressions of New Orleans culture, my Katrina courses have a theme song. "By the Rivers of Babylon" is performed by the Neville Brothers, one of the city's famous families of musicians. They recorded a Rastafarian version, not at all inappropriate for a city with such a strong Caribbean influence. The lyrics are inspired by Psalm 137, written about a time when the Hebrews have been taken into captivity and find themselves in Exile. As they sit by the waters, their captors want them to sing, but, the psalmist demands, "How can we sing the Lord's song in a strange land?" The Nevilles' version includes a descant line sung by Aaron Neville asserting that the people were taken from Zion by the wicked. It is an understandable conclusion.[25]

Disaster anthropologist Kate Browne created the film *Still Waiting* about a large African-American family from St. Bernard Parish and their struggle to return home. In 2013, she wrote that an often overlooked aspect of assisting displaced people is determining the extent to which a family possesses the "hidden key to recovery from disaster." That hidden key is understanding "how to navigate the universe of bureaucratic culture." Such navigational skills "come bundled with education and middle-class experience" and people who lack them are often unable "to trudge through the complicated and alien forms and paperwork necessary to effectively manage their cases with insurance companies, FEMA, and grant-giving agencies."

---

22. Kirk-Duggan, *Sky Is Crying*.
23. Sanders, "Conducting Effective Research."
24. Sanders, *Saints in Exile*, 143.
25. Ps 137:1–4, KJV.

They also tend to lack the ability to communicate well with "bureaucratic staffers in person or on the phone." She called for the intentional deployment of "culture brokers"—people with a foot in two cultures—to assist those impacted by disasters.[26]

For all the accusations about citizens who knew how to "game the system," it is a fact that far more urban poor people fall into the category that Browne described, those who do not have the capacity to work their way through a maze of paperwork which may or may not make sense and which may or may not get misplaced by a person who may or may not care. Having lost all their possessions and trying to deal with it all from a remote and temporary location makes it that much worse. On the tenth anniversary of Katrina, there were still New Orleanians who wanted to come home and could not.

Exile was a huge piece of the UMC's decision-making processes. The question of how many members of any given congregation would be able to return was being asked the week of the storm. In 2015, people are still returning, and it is still an important question for congregations who are considering what sort of ministries they can afford.

On a very deep level, the experience of exile impacts everyone in the city. It also played a key role in creating the primary dilemma of the church: should it meet the needs of its members for Sanctuary—a comforting place that offers, amid the chaos, the illusion of stability (one place that will never change)—or should it use its newfound flexibility to make changes that formerly seemed impossible and to live out the justice claims of the Gospel in ways that it hadn't been doing before the storm?

---

26. Browne, "Culture Brokers."

4

The Process: Or, How the Church Decided to Decide

It is common sense to take a method and try it. If it fails, admit it frankly and try another. But above all, try something.
—Franklin Delano Roosevelt

Disaster response is not what this book is about, so I will not say very much about it. The UMC is good at disaster response. The United Methodist Committee on Relief (UMCOR) excels at getting there first with seed money. Various denominations have specialties; Southern Baptists, for instance, came in early with chainsaws to clear downed trees. The UMC specializes in case management and promises, "We will be there till the last nail is nailed." After Katrina, the conference set up its own storm center, Louisiana United Methodist Disaster Response, Inc., under the direction of Darryl Tate, and ran staging areas across south Louisiana. Several were in Greater New Orleans.

By the close of 2008, over 60,000 volunteers had donated over 2.6 million hours, closing nearly 10,000 cases. Because states must repay FEMA, and FEMA gives a credit of around $19 per documented volunteer hour, work done through the UMC would save the state over $49 million; most denominations did not keep records required for this credit.[1] These are not final numbers, as the storm center stayed open for some time. Several requests in 2014 for updates did not elicit a response, probably because the principals have moved on to other tasks. Though incomplete, the numbers are impressive. There is no doubt that the staff and volunteers performed an immense part of the physical recovery.

---

1. Handout provided by Darryl Tate during interview by the author, July 27, 2009, Baton Rouge, LA.

The only significant failure that occurred in disaster response was not the responsibility of the Louisiana conference, but of UMCOR. In the community of Baldwin, 113 miles west of New Orleans, UMCOR operates the Sager Brown depot, a warehouse and shipping facility for goods gathered for disaster victims around the world.[2] Various kits are assembled there, including hygiene kits and layettes. One kit, now called a "cleaning bucket," is still commonly known as a "flood bucket." Each five-gallon container holds laundry detergent, household cleaner, dish soap, insect repellant, a scrub brush, cleaning wipes, sponges, scouring pads, clothespins and clothesline, trash bags, dust masks, and gloves. UMCOR's website claims, "Buckets Can Make a Theological 'Statement'" as "tangible signs of prayers, love, and support."[3] Their statement right after Katrina was "lack of support." Louisiana United Methodists drove to the depot and asked for buckets, but depot personnel would not let them have any. One pastor spoke bitterly at a clergy meeting of standing by his truck in sight of huge piles of buckets and being told he could not take them to his community because there was "not a procedure in place" for direct distribution. Relations improved over time but not until at least one change in personnel at the depot occurred. Eventually, a separate facility was set up for Katrina/Rita assistance.

Along with a huge amount of physical labor, the staff and volunteers of the conference's storm center offered a crucial ministry of presence to those who needed emotional recovery. A pastor recalled, "Often we were digging through rubble to help find some piece of memory that might bring comfort. . . . One group found a homeowner's wedding dress . . . They had it completely restored . . . and presented it to the homeowner on their following trip." But most times, she said, "All we could do was sit, listen and cry with the ones whose lives were forever changed."[4] That might have felt insignificant, but it was a tremendous contribution in a community where most therapists, counselors, psychologists, and psychiatrists did not return. There is a continuing need for the opportunity to tell the stories and for the production of helpful narrative in New Orleans. Rebecca Stilling, a licensed professional counselor who came back to the city early on, believes that telling the story of the storm and the many frustrations of recovery is very helpful so long as the listener exhibits a genuine sense of caring about what happened. This is the case even if that caring listener is not a trained counselor. She can confirm this from personal experience, as her cousin whose Lakeview home was flooded received assistance from church volun-

2. UMCOR, "About Us."
3. Meister, "Cleaning Buckets."
4. MacKenzie, "The 'R' Word."

teers. Stilling was on site with family members while the volunteers worked and said the opportunity to talk with outsiders who actually cared was just as valuable as the assistance in removing furniture and gutting walls.[5] All of this work was surely Christian labor.

Yet the question of whether we ought to undertake this kind of work is easily answered. There were no controversies about whether the church should be "sticking its nose into" the problems of those who could not afford to have their homes repaired. The disaster response agency's work was hard—it was heart-rending, it was perhaps in some cases lifesaving, and it was very, very well done. But in terms of complexity, it did not compare to the puzzle faced by those tasked with putting the individual churches and the district and conference back together again. That work caused controversy and downright acrimony among churches and between clergy and the conference hierarchy.

The dilemma the church faced in this area and the way the conference decided to address it are the subjects of this chapter. Despite its power to make top-down decisions, the UMC hierarchy decided that choices about which churches would be reopened, closed, or merged should, as much as possible, come from the bottom-up—that is, that decisions should spring from congregants themselves and the pastoral teams assigned to lead them and charged with helping to determine each congregation's future.

Such collaborative leadership styles led to a markedly different post-Katrina experience than that of the Roman Catholics. There, the archdiocesan hierarchy decided to close certain parishes despite vigorous protests from the congregations. Two churches were occupied by parishioners who were eventually arrested and taken to jail. By contrast, residents of New Orleans have seen no similar events accompanying the decommissioning of half-dozen United Methodist Churches in the city and the mergers that have affected more than a dozen others.

In this chapter, I will examine at some length some of the factors that informed how change was enacted in the UMC. There are brief profiles of a few key leaders, including Bishop William Hutchinson, Provost Don Cottrill, Mission Zone director Martha Orphe, and the first three DSs who served after Katrina. I will discuss the process the conference used for decision making. Finally, I will consider the different approach that the Roman Catholic archdiocese took, as it provides an important comparison.

---

5. Rebecca Stilling, LSCW, LMFT, Diplomate in Clinical Social Work, interview by the author, May 15, 2009, New Orleans, LA.

The Puzzle

The combination of racial/ethnic diversity which is unique among local mainline Protestant groups and the denomination's connectional structure which invests many kinds of power in the statewide body rather than with local congregations made the United Methodist Church a fruitful topic for study. It was perhaps the perfect situation for considering the church's struggle to redefine itself in the post-Katrina environment, where many impediments to change had been washed away.

The Louisiana conference had to begin immediately rethinking how it would do ministry in New Orleans even though it did not possess most of the data required. As the bishop put it, "One of the biggest challenges we face is the reshaping, revisioning, and rebuilding of ministry in a devastated city that will have to be rebuilt. Estimates range from 125,000 to 250,000 people who will NOT return to New Orleans. We do not know what neighborhoods will be rebuilt. We do not know what businesses will relocate in other cities. We do not know how soon hospitals and schools can be rebuilt. There is much that we do NOT know."[6]

Before Katrina, there were over 25,500 United Methodists in the New Orleans district. After Katrina, no one had any idea how many could return and when they might be able to do so. Ninety pastors were displaced across south Louisiana. Seventy UMC congregations could not initially resume services, and most did not know when or even if they would ever be able to reopen; about half of these were African American in membership and half were Anglo. The bishop almost immediately made a commitment to pay salaries and benefits for all pastors who could not be placed in another ministry setting that could furnish a salary for them temporarily. At the time, he had no clarity at all on where the conference would get the money.

The questions of how to support displaced clergy, how to insure fair treatment among congregations that varied in race and socio-economic standing, how to begin to gather the data that would be needed to make decisions—these were obvious from the beginning. It did not take long for the stickiest issue to surface, either. Whether it is deemed a theological or philosophical or simply practical issue, the dilemma that underlay almost all other decisions could be named this way: Should the UMC use its resources to meet the needs of its members for sanctuary, or should it use the opportunity to live out the justice claims of the gospel in ways that its commitment to preserving the institution and its decaying buildings had prevented before the storm?

6. William W. Hutchinson, "Report to General Board of Church and Society," October 10, 2005, Copy on file in bishop's office.

The Process: Or, How the Church Decided to Decide 45

Ralph Ford, then superintendent of the New Orleans district, had dinner with my students on our first night in the city during the January 2007 offering of my "Church's Response to Katrina" class. He spoke about the opportunity side of the situation and his struggle to get local congregations to move away from the "all I want is sanctuary" side of the equation. Many congregations were resisting the imperative to reach out to the community around their churches. "They tell me, 'They are not our people.' I say, 'No, but they are God's people.'"

He reminded members that there were people in the city who were starving and had urgent needs that were not being met. Then, he said, if they refused to respond, he would tell them that the conference would wind up padlocking their churches. He said the bishop told him that "sometimes you have to talk that way" to get people to look outside their own walls.[7] (The bishop told me and my students later that week that laypeople were complaining about his insistence that they reach out to others. He said they would tell him, "We never dealt with those people before. Why would we deal with them now?")[8]

When we got in the van after dinner, Ford's comments left my students subdued. It was their first night in the city, and they had just seen the damage, or at least a small part of it, for the very first time as we were driving in. They were filled with compassion for the people whose whole world had crumbled, and the students' pastoral instincts made them sympathetic to the survivors who wanted their churches not to change.

I, on the other hand, was delighted with how forthcoming Ford had been, because they had been immersed in this quandary just a few hours into their stay. "This is it, exactly! This is what we're here to study," I told them. They'd just seen why there was truly unprecedented need for some sort of sanctuary, for holding onto something, anything, that hadn't been altered. Then, Ford had told them how much the church needed to grab the opportunity to be unsaddled from its pre-storm mentality of simply surviving and keeping up aging buildings. He described it as a moment when the church could begin to be in true ministry with "the least of these" instead.

Knowing how to choose good over evil is easy, though deciding which is which can be difficult. Sometimes both choices are "goods," and there is no way to have both of them. Provost Don Cottrill spoke of how difficult it was "trying to be pastoral and prophetic at the same time" and juxtaposing

---

7. Ralph Ford, interview by the author and students, January 9, 2007, New Orleans, LA.

8. William Hutchinson, interview by the author and students, March 12, 2007, New Orleans, LA.

"the past with what can be in the future."[9] Even defining the choices clearly was not an easy thing to do in the midst of post-Katrina chaos. Making wise choices required understanding that both points of view about what the church should do were valid, but that both could not be fully embraced.

The Need for Sanctuary

Returnees to the city found landmarks vanished and street signs missing. Major intersections were hard to identify. I am unable to describe the level of disorientation the situation produced. Many people desperately wanted their churches to reassure them that there was continuity in at least one thing that mattered. Sister Mary Daniel, OP, told my students that when the Dominican sisters reopened their school, they painstakingly ensured that classroom space was re-created exactly, down to the same black-and-white pattern on the floors. But it was not just children who needed the reassurance of physical continuity. Everyone searched for something familiar.

Most churches *have* a sanctuary, a space devoted to formal worship activities. To *use* a church building as sanctuary, as a medieval fugitive might have done, is rare. It does still occur; undocumented immigrant Elvira Arellaño was sheltered from deportation for twelve months in 2006–2007 at Adaberto UMC in Chicago. Yet the everyday understanding of church *as* sanctuary has to do with its worship services being somewhere members can feel safe from the fast-paced and ever-changing world outside.

Familiar liturgy provides a sense of constancy. In liturgically "high" churches, many members believe you cannot meaningfully participate in a ritual unless you know the words by heart. Everything except the hymns, the Scripture readings, and the content of the sermon is expected to be almost identical from week to week. Variances will fall within a certain set of parameters. Hymns are those with which the people are familiar, and as every pastor knows, introducing new music brings controversy. The use of certain instruments, such as pipe organs, touches humans in a deep way. In congregations with so-called "lower" liturgy, worship is more informal. There may be an expectation that the Holy Spirit will guide the service from moment to moment, but even in charismatic worship, things are likely to occur in a very familiar pattern, and behavior rarely strays far from the congregation's norm.

The space in which worship occurs is expected to remain constant. Though liturgical colors for stoles, paraments, and banners vary with the season, their size and placement are consistent. They cycle in a predictable

9. Don Cottrill, interview with the author, June 21, 2007, Kenner, LA.

pattern that repeats from year to year through Advent, Christmas, Epiphany, Lent, Easter, and Pentecost. If choir members wear robes, they look the same from week to week. If clergy wear robes, their appearance is constant, too.

Recent trends in church architecture include movable chairs that allow for multiple kinds of set-ups in sanctuaries, but pews that were bolted to the floor were the norm for Katrina-affected churches. Most denominations view the choice of where to place the pulpit, lectern and Bible, baptismal font, and communion table as theological statements, so their positions are likely to remain unchanged. Permanent placement is sometimes mandated by a need to access electricity for reading lights and microphones.

Although designers of liturgy may be aware of the effects that repeating elements will have on congregants, most people in the pews have not thought through why repetition of sights and sounds (and even tastes, in the case of communion) is appealing in that context. Still, they do know that worship will evoke familiar feelings—feelings that they associate with their faith in a Deity that they hope will care for them. When a church building has been destroyed by fire, it is not uncommon for television to show parishioners saying something like, "I realize now that my church isn't a building—it's the people—and it doesn't matter where we meet." In such circumstances, the person's home and possessions were not destroyed and their fellow congregants have not been dispersed across the country. After Katrina, a huge percentage of church people had lost everything they owned, they did not know where many other members of the church or even their families were, and some of the missing might well be dead. It made it hard to take a sanguine view of further change.

Moving Out of the Sanctuaries

Given the level of disruption New Orleanians had experienced, would it be wrong to spend all the church's resources in returning things to their pre-storm state? That might depend in part on what a given church's pre-storm state was like. Then District Superintendent Freddie Henderson once complained in my hearing that when a church puts "historic" in its name, "that just means they have weeds growing on the roof and out of the gutters." Several UMC churches in the city styled their names that way and tended to meet his definition. Many other structures, like Napoleon Avenue UMC's, had extensive pre-Katrina structural and foundation problems that members did not think they had the resources to address.

Conference leaders felt the unprecedented opportunity to turn building-centric, inward-focused congregations outward for a change could not be ignored. Although everyone seemed to want his or her own church restored to precisely the same condition, there was a general understanding that using resources to return churches to a state that was tenuous before was unwise. Thus, there was a common feeling that "those other churches" should be required to change. The critique of mainstream Christianity as country club had some validity—consider Ford's report of hearing, "They are not our people"—and convincing traumatized New Orleanians that the unprecedented chance to move into genuine mission and service to neighbors was too precious to ignore seemed an uphill battle.

Pre-Katrina, membership decline and failing financial support were common in most mainline congregations. Decades of white flight to suburbs in Jefferson Parish and towns on the north shore of Lake Pontchartrain resulted in some congregations composed primarily of people who drove back to an old neighborhood on Sunday. Those who had moved when the neighborhood became "transitional"—meaning no longer all-white—were sometimes loath to have new residents enter their religious systems. The fear that the very folks they moved to get away from might start attending worship did nothing to soften the already-present reluctance of many church members to participate in ministry in their neighborhoods.

Sending money to a denomination-wide agency that will serve people "over there" who are poor, or going on a mission trip to do home repairs for a person who lives too far away to call you when the hot water heater you installed stops working are worthwhile endeavors, but they do not have the same result as getting to know the people in your changing neighborhood and asking how the church could be part of their lives. Founder John Wesley insisted that Methodists spend time with people who were poor. He engaged in extended correspondence with a woman named Miss March who did not think she should have to associate with poor people. She offered a range of excuses, including the assertion that she would be better off spending time with people of good character. Wesley asked why she thought the rich were of better character than the poor; in fact, he suggested, the opposite might well be true. Much more recently, Pope Francis asked the Vatican Almoner to leave his office and visit poor people on the streets. He asked all Catholics to spend time, even if only fifteen to thirty minutes, with individuals who are poor.[10]

---

10. Maddox, "Visit the Poor," 77–79; Associated Press, "Pope Ramps Up"; Associated Press, "Archbishop Tasked with Outreach."

In an interview in 2007, Bishop Hutchinson said, "This was the church's finest hour. It *was* the church in all its ways. We were very Wesleyan; it wasn't always intentional—we didn't go around asking, 'What Would Wesley Do?'—but his ideas of social holiness and grace applied."[11] When Wesley talked about there being no holiness except social holiness, he did not mean exactly what I would like for him to have meant, since understandings of how society is composed and how it changes were not the same in the 1700s. However, his insistence on visiting in prisons, founding schools, seeing to medical needs, preaching boldly against slavery even in cities where it was the basis for much of the wealth, and insisting that Christians should give away their money after their families' needs are met show that he was committed to an outward-focused church.

This whole discussion amounts to a questioning of what it means to be the church and what it means to be followers of Jesus—things which are not always identical. Providing sanctuary and venturing out of the sanctuary both seemed crucial to church leaders. Trying to do both or either in a time and place where trauma became the "new normal" was a challenge like none that the UMC's leaders had ever faced. The spiritual state of the city, the church as a whole, and each United Methodist individual seemed to depend on finding the right answer to the dilemma.

Some of the UMC Leaders

Bishop William Hutchinson

When Katrina struck, Bill Hutchinson had been the sitting bishop of the United Methodist Church in Louisiana for almost exactly five years. He and his wife Kay were finally getting accustomed to the abundant—perhaps overabundant—water in Louisiana after decades of living in New Mexico.

On Saturday, August 27, 2005, he presided over a called session of the Louisiana conference in Baton Rouge to consider an offer to buy the Lafon Home, a conference-owned nursing home in sight of the St. Bernard housing development in New Orleans. The delegates approved the sale. At the end of the session, Hutchinson mentioned Katrina, the storm that was brewing in the Gulf, and then left to accompany Kay to her father's funeral in Oklahoma. He was there when the floodwalls broke, leaving the Lafon Home under water.

Hutchinson had been brought up in the church and experienced a call to ministry at a youth meeting. He "deflected" the call, hoping to become

11. William Hutchinson, interview by the author, June 21, 2007, Fayetteville, AR.

a tax attorney. During his studies at the University of Oklahoma, after being bewildered by a business statistics exam, he finally gave in to what he already believed God wanted and changed his major. He went on to study at Duke Divinity School in Durham, North Carolina.[12]

Hutchinson returned to New Mexico after seminary. His appointments included founding a new church, pastoring medium-sized and large congregations, serving as a District Superintendent, and a stint as the director of the New Mexico conference's foundation. The New Mexico conference is small numerically, and they have few delegates to the quadrennial General Conference where church policy is set. Hutchinson was elected as their lead clergy delegate in 1992, 1996, and 2000. When that spot is given to a clergyperson, it indicates that colleagues see him or her as possessing what United Methodists call the "gifts and grace" for the episcopacy. He was not elected bishop in 1992 or 1996. Still, he gained much experience at the denominational level, serving on boards, agencies, and design teams. When the time came for the 2000 election, he let it be known that he had already "made the rounds" of interviewing with delegates from other conferences who would be voting and had no intention of doing it again. A fair paraphrase might be, "I'm happy to serve, but if you want me, you know where I am." Indeed, he was elected at the jurisdictional conference in Albuquerque, and he was assigned to serve in Louisiana.

His immediate predecessor bishop in Louisiana had an authoritarian view of leadership. This was evidenced both by the way he ran the annual meetings and by the way he expected the conference to fall in line with his own vision for the church. He came to Louisiana saying that he had the answer for declining membership and church health. It was a three-point plan comprised of: (1) the use of the Disciple Bible Study program in local churches; (2) the attendance of clergy and laypeople at Cursillo retreats; and (3) increased participation in the Volunteers in Mission (VIM) program.[13] These are fine programs, and they were much more thoroughly embraced by the people of Louisiana at his urging. Many who participated were spiri-

---

12. Turner, *God's Calling*, 91.

13. The Disciple Bible Study materials are published by Abingdon, a United Methodist press. Participants in Disciple I read extensively in the Bible from Genesis to Revelation, complete a workbook, and attend thirty-four weekly meetings where they view DVDs that feature Biblical scholars. The Cursillo movement was founded by Spanish Catholics in the 1940s. The three-day retreats which are intended to deepen the spirituality of laypeople and train them for leadership are now held worldwide and organized by and for people from many denominations. Through the Volunteer in Mission (VIM) program, UMC laity and clergy go at their own expense on short term trips to do construction, help with medical clinics, conduct Bible studies and Vacation Bible Schools, and work in various aspects of disaster relief in locations all around the world.

tually enriched by them. However, his plan did not reverse the decline that the UMC, like most of mainstream Protestantism, was experiencing.

When Hutchinson arrived in Louisiana in 2000, there was some unrest among a few of the clergy because he did not come in with his own vision of what Louisiana should do but rather set out to get to know the clergy, the congregations, the ethos of the conference, and the state of Louisiana, vastly different from the dry high desert of New Mexico. At an early retreat with clergy, he slipped into a cardigan sweater in a take-off on the mild-mannered host of the children's television program *Mister Rogers' Neighborhood*. The crowd loved it, since they knew how similar his personality is to the one Mr. Rogers projected onscreen. However, Hutchinson is a man who also has a temper and one who can effectively stand his ground when he is convinced of the rightness of a course of action. He was sure that he needed to get to know the people and situations in Louisiana. As he did, he began to be held in high regard.

In 2004, Hutchinson was reappointed to a second term in Louisiana. United Methodist bishops are appointed to an episcopal area for a term of four years which equals, in Methodist-speak, one quadrennium. There is a mandatory retirement age, and at the beginning of 2008, it appeared that Hutchinson would have to retire that September. However, when General Conference met that spring, they raised the age by two years, which meant that although he was eligible to retire, he could serve for one more quadrennium if he chose.[14] At the Louisiana conference gathering in June 2008, Hutchinson announced that he had told the jurisdictional episcopal committee which determines where bishops serve that he would delay his retirement for one quadrennium only if he could return to Louisiana. The delegates greeted the announcement with a prolonged standing ovation.

When Hutchinson was elected in 2000, the *United Methodist Book of Discipline* indicated that a bishop could be reassigned to the same area for a third quadrennium only if a two-thirds vote of the committee and a two-thirds vote of all the delegates concur that there are circumstances that warrant an unusual appointment. By 2008 the *Discipline* simply stated, "A bishop may be recommended for assignment to the same residence for a third quadrennium."[15] Even if the language had not changed, it seems likely that the fact that Louisiana was only three years into a recovery that was expected to take up to twelve would have been deemed sufficient cause for his reassignment. At the jurisdictional conference in July 2008, he was reappointed for his third term. After completing twelve years as Louisiana's

14. *Book of Discipline, 2008*, para. 408.1.
15. Ibid., para. 406.1.

bishop, Hutchinson retired. He and Kay returned to New Mexico. In 2012, newly elected Bishop Cynthia Fierro Harvey was named as his replacement.

Provost Don Cottrill

Don Cottrill was the originator of some of the more creative strategies the conference used. In 2005, Cottrill was serving as provost/director of Connectional Ministries, making him Hutchinson's second-in-command. When Katrina made landfall, Cottrill had been provost for a little over two years.

Cottrill had played a major role in the conference response to Hurricane Andrew in 1992. After devastating Florida as a category 5 storm, Hurricane Andrew made landfall near Morgan City, Louisiana, as a category 3. Though the damage was not comparable to Katrina's, Cottrill learned a great deal about how church and secular agencies responded. His ability to predict some of the problems that would arise after Katrina made him an invaluable part of the team, and he played a key role in developing the Mission Zone solution, explained below.

Cottrill was born in West Virginia, and after graduation from Marshall University with a degree in music, he taught and directed choirs in public schools. He belonged to a family with deep Methodist connections; his sister and two brothers are also UMC ministers. He answered his own call to ministry by attending seminary at Vanderbilt, and immediately following his studies, he served local churches in Tennessee.

In 1971, Cottrill moved to the Louisiana conference, and he served in pastorates around the state, including Rayne Memorial UMC in New Orleans. From 1974–79, he was the denomination-wide Director of Youth Ministries. He has worked in the Louisiana conference office as Assistant Director of Youth and Young Adult Ministries; as Director of Church Extension; and as Executive Director of the Council on Ministries. Along the way, he also earned a DMin from Perkins School of Theology at SMU with a focus in new church development.

Cottrill had previously been elected as the lead delegate to General Conference by his colleagues in Louisiana, a clear sign that they respected his leadership abilities. His broad experience served the conference well in the aftermath of the storm.

District Superintendent Freddie Henderson

Freddie Henderson was District Superintendent (DS) in New Orleans when Katrina hit. This was fortuitous; the presence of a well-regarded African

American in that position helped reassure members of African American congregations that their voices would not go unheard. Henderson had experience as a pastor in New Orleans and in Baton Rouge, where his wife, Gloria, was pursuing her career. He had been preaching since he received an exhorter's license as a teenager.

A graduate of Wiley College in Marshall, Texas, and of Gammon Seminary in Atlanta, Henderson was sent by his clergy colleagues as a delegate to general and jurisdictional conferences. He was appointed to the cabinet and assigned as DS in New Orleans in 1998. He and Gloria retained ownership of their home in Baton Rouge where Gloria worked, while they resided at the district parsonage on Germain Street in Lakeview.

The Hendersons experienced some of the pain and frustration that much of his district encountered following Katrina. At that time, pastors could not receive direct help from UMCOR, but because they were not homeowners in New Orleans, they were not eligible for government assistance to replace all they lost when the parsonage flooded. "We fell between the cracks," he said.[16]

When the Mission Zone program was implemented in 2006, Henderson was appointed to a position in the Conference Office in Baton Rouge, as Conference Disaster Relief Coordinator. Gloria Henderson fell ill, and she died in 2009.[17] Freddie Henderson had a stroke and died at the age of sixty-nine; his obituary in the September 29, 2013 issue of the *Baton Rouge Advocate* noted that although he had retired, he was still serving as pastor of St. Luke UMC in Baton Rouge.

District Superintendent Ralph Ford

Henderson was succeeded as District Superintendent by Ralph Ford. An Anglo pastor, Ford held degrees in vocal performance, church music, and theology, including a DMin from Perkins School of Theology at SMU. He was seen by his colleagues as someone with strong administrative gifts. Along with local pastorates, his ministries in Louisiana included service on the board of the United Methodist Foundation of Louisiana, on the conference task force for health insurance, on the board of pensions, and on the conference Commission on Finance and Administration.[18]

---

16. Freddie C. Henderson, interview by the author, June 6, 2007, Baton Rouge, LA.
17. Henderson, "Gloria Listach Henderson."
18. Ralph Ford, email to the author, November 27, 2013.

In 2008, Ford moved from the New Orleans district to the DS position in Baton Rouge, and then was appointed as Treasurer/Secretary/Statistician for the conference. He has now retired and lives in North Carolina.

Director of the Mission Zone Program Martha Orphe

After an extensive job search, the bishop hired Martha Orphe to serve as director of the Mission Zone program. Orphe (whose name is pronounced just as though the "e" had an accent mark) grew up in St. Martinville, Louisiana, but was ordained and serving in the Western Pennsylvania Conference at the time of the storm. She held a bachelor's degree in religion and philosophy from Clark Atlanta University and an MDiv from Vanderbilt. She earned a DMin from Wesley Theological Seminary with a specialty in Multicultural Urban Youth Ministry from a Womanist Perspective.[19] Womanist theology is done from the particular social location of African American women.

Because of family issues, especially the illness of close relatives, Orphe wanted to return to Louisiana. She was serving as DS in the Pittsburgh district. At that time, there had only been three female District Superintendents in Louisiana, and all were white. Since Orphe is African American, if she had not moved to another conference, it is unlikely she would have gained any experience at the DS level.

Some progress has been made in electing women of color as bishops and having women of color appointed as district superintendents in many conferences. Where the church has been unwilling to remove the stained glass barrier is in the appointment of women in general and women of color in particular as senior pastors of large, predominantly Anglo congregations. These are the jobs where the highest salaries are paid (sometimes higher than that of the bishop) and where the local laity are most likely to object to the appointment of anyone other than a white man to their pulpit. They are prone to demonstrate their offense by means of their financial giving, or more aptly, through failure to give. When a white male finishes his term as a DS, he is usually given an appointment as senior pastor at a large, Anglo-membership church. When men of color finish a term as DS, they are usually (though not always) given a position in the conference office so that a cross-racial appointment does not have to be made at a large, affluent church.

When Orphe was hired, she transferred back into the Louisiana conference. There was speculation among the clergy ranks about where a woman

---

19. Martha Orphe, email to the author, September 6, 2008.

of color would be appointed when the Mission Zone program ended. One highly placed female pastor said to me privately that she was dismayed by the bishop's decision to hire Orphe. She put it plainly: "What are they going to do with her after this?" In fact, the conference followed its usual pattern for men of color. She was given a job in the conference office, in her case as director of Multicultural Ministries. However, she did not remain there long, because when a pastor was unexpectedly discontinued from the ordination process in 2009, the bishop asked her to begin serving First Street Peck Wesley UMC, a merger of three African American congregations. She agreed to take what would surely be a difficult appointment, because many members supported the previous pastor and because the church's location in Central City is a dangerous place. She is still serving there, though another church has been added to her circuit.

District Superintendent Ramonalynn Bethley

When the Mission Zone program ended in the summer of 2008, Ramonalynn Bethley replaced both Martha Orphe and Ralph Ford, as the functions of both leaders were re-united into the DS position. Bethley was transferred to New Orleans from her position as DS in another district. Bethley, who is white, grew up in Shreveport and earned a BA in Christian Education from Centenary College. From 1984 till 1991, she served as an associate pastor in the Christian Church (Disciples of Christ), and then became youth minister at Noel UMC. In 1992, she was appointed as associate pastor at a large suburban church, and she received her MDiv from the New Orleans Theological Seminary, a Southern Baptist-affiliated school that year. Since Southern Baptists are against the ordination of women, she experienced gender discrimination there, including finding the door to the preaching classroom locked against her.

She went on to earn a DMin from Perkins School of Theology at SMU with an emphasis in evangelism. After a five-year pastorate in north Louisiana, she was appointed as DS in the Alexandria district in 2005. Three years later, she was rotated into the position in New Orleans, where she remained till 2012. She is now senior pastor at Asbury UMC in Bossier City. With an average of 450 in worship and a membership of 1,500, Asbury is the largest UMC congregation in Louisiana to have a woman as senior pastor.

The "For Now" Plan

During the year June 2006 to June 2007, the Annual Conference operated under the "For Now" Plan which recognized that no one knew with surety how to address the unprecedented destruction that Katrina, Rita, and the floodwall breaks had brought. Conference leaders would make the best decisions they could about how to proceed, but as circumstances changed, if experience showed that some other method would be more effective, the conference would shift its course.

Five weeks after landfall, Bishop Hutchinson wrote a report to the UMC's General Board of Church and Society (GBCS), whose meeting he was missing. He stated, "Whether by wind, flooding, falling trees, or storm surge, the churches and communities have been ravaged." He said that thirty churches would have to be "totally rebuilt" and that seventy-eight had "major damage and will need major work." There were twenty parsonages that would have to be rebuilt. "Many pastors own their own homes, and of course, those are additional losses," he wrote.[20]

He said people were asking him, "Where are we as a church and what are the plans for the future?" As his readers would have known, at the time of Katrina, UMCOR policy prevented the use of its funds for repairing or replacing church property. In 2009, UMCOR decided that up to 10 percent of the money raised for disaster relief could be used for repairing church-owned buildings.[21] While that will help next time a disaster strikes, it was four years too late for the conference that had to make some immediate decisions in the fall of 2005.

Furthermore, taking care of buildings paled in importance next to supporting the pastors whose paychecks had abruptly ceased. In five weeks, the conference had spent $298,925 on salary and benefits that would have been paid by local churches. Fifty-eight clergy were on salary support. Hutchinson projected that in nine months, by May 2006, the conference would spend $1,287,014 for their salary and benefits.

There was also a plunge in revenue to absorb. Apportionments are the annual obligations that each church has toward expenses of the conference and the denomination. Congregations that are not functioning do not pay their apportionments. In mid-October, the bishop estimated the 2005 loss at $470,000; lost apportionments for 2006 were expected to be $870,000. That totaled $1,340,000 in lost funds.[22]

20. William W. Hutchinson, "Report to General Board of Church and Society," October 10, 2005, Copy on file in bishop's office.

21. Kemper, "Theology Behind Disaster Relief."

22. William W. Hutchinson, "Report to General Board of Church and Society," October 10, 2005, Copy on file in bishop's office.

The Process: Or, How the Church Decided to Decide 57

After a litany of things about what would occur during recovery which the conference needed to know but did not, he wrote, "We do know that things will never be the same again. What the city will look like from a development standpoint will determine what it will look like from a church location point. That is in the infant stages of being assessed. It will be a very long term project."[23]

By March, barely six months in, the conference had made important preliminary decisions. Provost Don Cottrill was instrumental in developing the response called the Mission Zone program. He wrote to Bishop J. Woodrow Hearn, "Along with our relief efforts we are now moving into a bold venture of recasting our ministry in New Orleans. We are not merely seeking to 'put things back the way they were,' but rather to respond to the new, changed version of New Orleans. This means that we are going to try new models of ministry."[24] Rather than acting immediately to create a list of churches to close, they decided to postpone decisions "until study and work has been provided to prove the need for congregations in appropriate areas of the city," he wrote.

Cottrill said the Mission Zones, a structure for decision-making, would take effect at the conference gathering in June 2006. Along with a few "station churches" that could sustain themselves, "we will establish a grouping of seven cooperative parishes . . . constituted from congregations in neighboring communities. These churches are not strong enough to sustain ministry on their own." While some were "back in business . . . others have not reconstituted." Some buildings "are not usable, and will be evaluated as to the possibility of rebuilding, or of being abandoned."[25]

In the actual implementation of the program on-the-ground, there were two executives. District Superintendent Ralph Ford was appointed to oversee the entire New Orleans district, and the Mission Zone director, Martha Orphe, would focus on the churches in the city. Teams of clergy were assigned to each zone. "There will be a lead pastor in each parish, and from one to three associates, depending on the size and need of the parish." In an unusual move for the UMC in the USA, they planned "an equitable compensation package for the clergy in the mission zone, depending on the classification of Order or appointment." In other words, the base pay for team members was intended to be roughly equal.

---

23. Ibid.

24. Don Cottrill to Bishop J. Woodrow Hearn, March 6, 2006, letter on file in the bishop's office.

25. Ibid.

Cottrill told Hearn, "The Mission Zone leadership will offer guidance as to the future United Methodist presence needed in New Orleans." The most significant sentence in his letter was this: "Each cooperative parish will determine the future of the individual congregations and churches in the course of their ministry." It was a commitment to enabling a bottom-up decision-making process.[26]

The Mission Zones

Figure 1 is a map that depicts the assignment of churches in Greater New Orleans to the Mission Zones. Only a part of the New Orleans District was included in the program. The district is significantly larger than Greater New Orleans. It extends onto the north shore of Lake Pontchartrain, and southwest to Grand Isle, and down-river to Buras. It includes the area that experienced long-term catastrophic flooding but also includes areas that experienced no significant damage from Katrina.

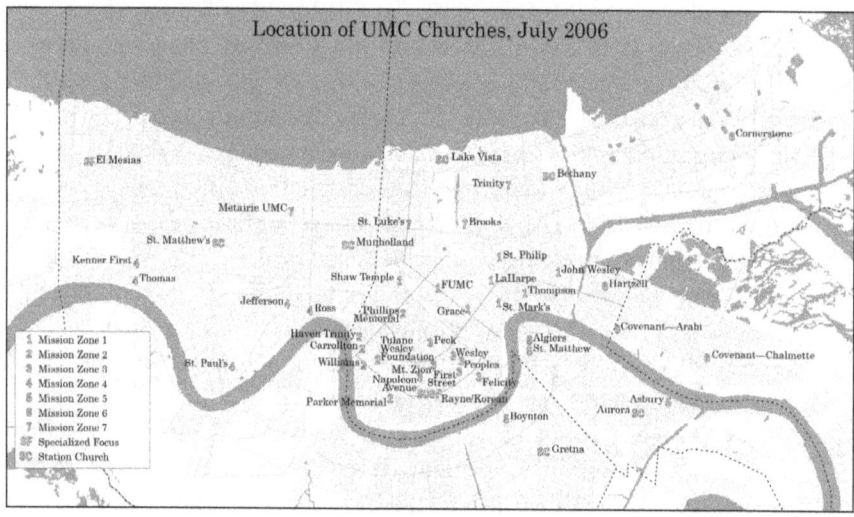

Two congregations, El Mesias UMC and the Korean UMC, were deemed "Specialized Focus Churches." Seven churches in Greater New Orleans were designated "Station Churches" which could stand alone: Gretna and Aurora on the West Bank (of the Mississippi River) which did not flood; St. Matthew's and Munholland in areas of Metairie which did not flood; and Rayne, Lake Vista, and Bethany on the East Bank in New Orleans. Neither

26. Ibid.

The Process: Or, How the Church Decided to Decide

Rayne nor Lake Vista flooded, though Rayne had extensive wind damage; of these seven, only Bethany had devastating flooding.

The thirty-eight remaining churches in Greater New Orleans were divided into seven Mission Zones.

Zone #1 was composed of eight churches: First, Grace, John Wesley, LaHarpe, St. Mark's, St. Philip, Shaw Temple, and Thompson UMCs. Shawn Anglim was team leader, and other members were Anita Dinwiddie, William Jones, and Leslie M. Taylor, Sr.

Zone #2 had six components: Carrollton, Haven Trinity, Parker Memorial, Phillips Memorial, Williams, and the Tulane Wesley Foundation. Cory Sparks was team leader, and other members were Diane Bentley, Dale Branch, and Maximillian Zehner.

Zone #3's seven churches were Felicity, First Street, Mt. Zion, Napoleon Avenue, Peck, Peoples, and Wesley. Simon Chigumira was team leader, and other members were Eunice Chigumira and Lance Eden.

Zone #4 was made up of five Jefferson Parish churches: Jefferson UMC, Kenner First, Ross, St. Paul's, and Thomas. Tracy MacKenzie was team leader, and other members were Anice Moses and Sharon Zehner.

Zone #5's four churches were located on the West Bank. They were Algiers, Asbury, Boynton, and St. Matthew. Andrew Douglas was team leader, and other members were LeKisha Reed and Ray Varnado.

Zone #6 had four churches: Cornerstone in New Orleans East; Hartzell in the Lower Ninth Ward; and two churches in adjacent St. Bernard Parish, Covenant Arabi and Covenant Chalmette. James Haynes was team leader, and other members were Jeffery Conner and Rebecca Conner.

Zone #7 included four churches: Brooks, St. Luke's, Trinity, and Metairie UMCs. Irvin Boudreaux was team leader, and other members were Jon Lord and Deborah Williams.

The goal had been to make sure that each team included both men and women and people of different races. The conference accomplished this, except that the three team members in Zone #3 were all African Americans, and Team #4 was composed only of women. They had committed to post only people who wanted to be in New Orleans, and considering the extreme living conditions in the city less than a year after landfall (including the lack of schools and adequate health care which most would consider essential for families with younger children), the mix they achieved seems impressive.

Each zone included at least one church that was up and running when the zones were implemented in July 2006. Time has revealed that most also included at least one that would never reopen, but those decisions were a long way away at that point.

The Manure Plan

The second year of the Mission Zone Program was officially titled "The Manure Plan." This was not just a nickname given by insiders to a frustrating process—rather, it is what the strategy is called in written church documents. It is actually quite apt, as the title came from a parable in Luke 13:6–9. Jesus tells of a landowner frustrated with a fig tree which is not producing figs. He tells his gardener to cut it down. The gardener counters with the suggestion that he be allowed to fertilize it for one more year; then, he says, if the tree is still not producing, he will cut it down.

The annual conference applied this parable through the decision that one year's financial support had not been enough for many of the churches to make final decisions about their futures. Salaries and other kinds of support would be furnished for one more year, while individual congregants still in exile decided whether they could return and individual congregations decided whether they could become self-supporting.

Some personnel changes occurred, as a few clergy moved around either within or out of New Orleans. Some decisions were being made about the first churches to be decommissioned. By and large, though, it was clear that for most churches, one year was not enough to get back on their feet or even to figure out whether they would ever be able to do so. At the beginning, no one anticipated how many years it would take for tens or even hundreds of thousands of New Orleanians to return home. The abject failure of government, including the Road Home program, was a primary factor. The years-long delay in FEMA's releasing flood maps which were required by lenders before people could get loans to repair their homes was inexcusable. At least one book could be devoted to the topic of why it was so difficult for people to come back quickly, but for the purposes of this discussion, it is sufficient to say that one year offered only a bare beginning of determining which neighborhoods would recover and which would not.

At the second anniversary of Katrina, two months into the Manure Plan, the bishop wrote a "Two-Year Anniversary Overview" for a United Methodist journalist. He told her, "People are still hurting. We are in the process of giving other congregations this year as a time of meeting benchmarks, which they have helped to set, and to determine if there is a future for them." Explaining that the term "Manure Plan" was based on the Lukan parable, he said, "We are putting major resources (persons and money) into the possibility of renewal and revival. We are praying for that telltale fruit that says this is a vital and viable tree. We live in the midst of renewal and hope."[27]

Indeed, hope was a theme of his communication. He continued, "Today we are seeing hope emerge as we are beginning to get a grip and a perspective on what our future might look like. It has taken much heartache, heartbreak, and heart searching to come to where we are today." He acknowledged that "our lives" and "our churches and our church ministries" were never going to be the same, but "ironically, that can be seen in a positive light now. *We are beginning to see new possibilities,* new ministries in which we can engage, and new fields of mission and evangelism that were not apparent before these two monster storms."[28]

Using Collaborative Leadership Strategies

Faced with the initial quandary, the bishop, provost, and district superintendents, in consultation with the director of church extension and transformation, the director of the United Methodist Foundation in Louisiana, and others who had input into the early assessments, could have made decisions arbitrarily. Although the annual conference must vote on the "abandonment" of any building, it seems almost certain that under the circumstances, their decisions would have prevailed. Instead, the Mission Zone strategy called for the laity and clergy teams on the ground in the city to make decisions about which churches could continue alone, which would need to merge, and which would be decommissioned.

Some of the same individuals who wanted the bishop to come to Louisiana in 2000 with a more directive approach were frustrated by what they saw as his unwillingness to push through the closure of declining congregations. Some wanted immediate action, even before the water was pumped out of the city. Some were appreciative of the process, but would not have approached it that way themselves.

Shawn Anglim, senior pastor of First Grace UMC, said,

> The way the bishop did it, it could be highly questioned and many people did. It sounded to some like a waste of money. The Catholics, basically, these churches were all in trouble before the

27. William Hutchinson, "Two-Year Anniversary Overview," email to Kathy Gilbert, UMCOM, August 28, 2007. Copy on file in bishop's office.

28. Ibid.

storm, and their bishop came in and said, "We're closing these places." I think he had every right to do it, and it's probably the way I would have done it.[29]

Anglim became grateful for the bishop's approach, because it gave his church time to succeed. However, not everyone became a convert. Tim Smith, pastor at Gretna UMC on the West Bank, was convinced that "If ever there was a time to use the hierarchy, this was it."[30]

Hadley Edwards, who as a pastor vigorously resisted the directives of the hierarchy which tried to send him to Houston after the storm and who saved Bethany UMC through that resistance, looked back later as DS and said that the church might have missed an opportunity to be more directive. "That was a great opportunity for us to really exercise the authority that the United Methodist Church has. . . . If the church had been proactive and just made a decision that this church and this church and this church are going to become one church, we are going to merge three churches and become one—but we did the best we could do under the circumstances we had, and Bishop Hutchinson led us through that."[31] The rest of his comments on this topic (which are complimentary of the bishop's hands-on leadership) are included in Chapter 8.

About five months after landfall, Hutchinson composed a long email in response to a letter of complaint from a pastor. The pastor's name is not included here, because I had access only to the bishop's response. Nevertheless, it was easy to reconstruct much of the letter's content from the bishop's answers. The pastor accused the bishop of being "secretive" about the plans for recovery, even while admitting that he had not attended a clergy meeting with the bishop held in New Orleans earlier that month to discuss that very topic. The bishop said, "I, too, wish you could have been present at meeting . . . on the 8th. At that time, I was asked about the planning process and tried my best to answer it." He then summarized what he had said at the meeting. I was surprised to see the pastor's name on this document, because his church was not damaged at all due to its being further inland.[32]

Indeed, it was my own observation—and the observation of many others with whom I've spoken—that the people who expressed the most anger at the early clergy meetings were white, male, middle-aged pastors whose churches were only minimally impacted by the storm. Although the trust

---

29. Shawn Anglim, interview by the author, June 25, 2013, New Orleans, LA.
30. Tim Smith, interview by the author, April 27, 2009, Gretna, LA.
31. Hadley Edwards, interview by the author, July 16, 2013, Metairie, LA.
32. William Hutchinson, email to [name withheld], January 22, 2006, Copy on file in bishop's office.

clause in place since Wesley's time prevents a congregation from owning their building in the sense that if they leave the United Methodist Church, they cannot take the property out of the UMC with them, repairing damage to any individual building is not the responsibility of the conference; each church is supposed to maintain insurance. Yet one pastor known for being well acquainted with UMC governance made an angry outburst at a meeting in Jefferson Parish, when we were meeting there because the city of New Orleans had not even been reopened yet. Although his church's building had comparatively minor wind damage, he demanded to know, "Why isn't my church fixed yet?" The bishop later told me that two of the stand-alone "station churches" received that designation because the pastors did not want to be part of the cooperative parishes.[33] That is certainly not true of all of them; some station churches were among the most willing to engage in cooperative ministry.

I chronicle some of the complaints to point out that the commitment to let decisions come up from the bottom was not simply a way of avoiding responsibility and criticism. Collaborative leadership is more difficult and time-consuming than autocratic leadership. Despite the inevitable frustration, it is also healthier for the organization involved.

Ronald Heifetz is a professor of leadership at Harvard University and the founding director of its Center for Public Leadership. His book, *Leadership without Easy Answers*, has become a classic in the field of adaptive leadership. Early on, he explains that "in a crisis we tend to look for the wrong kind of leadership. We call for someone with answers, decision, strength, and a map of the future, someone who knows where we ought to be going—in short, someone who can make hard problems simple." In such a situation, he insisted, "Instead of looking for saviors, we should be calling for leadership that will call us to face problems for which there are no simple, painless solutions—problems that require us to learn new ways."[34]

When I said to Hutchinson that his leadership was congruent with highly regarded theories of adaptive leadership, he said, "This has always been my philosophy of leadership. I've always led this way. It really frustrated local congregations."[35] It was a gift to have a leader who was wise enough and strong enough to admit, "I realized early on that I didn't have the answer. No one had a grasp of the whole situation. I thought that the more heads we had at the table, the better the chance we had to get it right."

---

33. William Hutchinson, interview by the author, June 21, 2007, Fayetteville, AR.
34. Heifetz, *Leadership without Easy Answers*, 2.
35. William Hutchinson, interview by the author, June 21, 2007, Fayetteville, AR.

As he put it, "You can't rely on what you've always known. It's like a war-torn country where the whole infrastructure is gone."

There was a need to trust God in the situation. By this I do not mean God as an abstract being, but rather God as manifested in the people of New Orleans. There is more on this topic in Chapter 9, a theological consideration of what occurred. There was also a need to have leaders on the ground who appreciated the methodology.

The initial configuration that put Ralph Ford as District Superintendent and Martha Orphe as Mission Zone director resulted in a number of problems. Many people involved in the zones have commented to me that they never felt they had clarity on whether they were to report to Ford or Orphe. The two of them did not appear to see eye-to-eye on important matters. However, many felt that Orphe's status as an African American gave her an understanding of the black membership churches that a white leader could not have achieved and also gave her a place to stand to offer needed critiques that might not have been tolerated from a white pastor. (When one tiny group of elderly people kept on insisting that their church was on the "verge of an explosion" in numbers, she reportedly asked, "Which one of you is having the first baby?"[36]) Though the dual-headed arrangement caused some discomfort, there was much good that came from it.

The District Superintendent who succeeded Ford and Orphe, Ramonalynn Bethley, had a philosophy of leadership that fit well with the collaborative approach Hutchinson and Cottrill had adopted. Bethley's style is congruent with the ideas expressed by Rosamund Stone Zander and Benjamin Zander in *The Art of Possibility: Transforming Professional and Personal Life*. She liked the book so much that she bought a copy for everyone serving on the appointive cabinet with her.[37] Rosamund, a psychotherapist, worked with Benjamin, the conductor of the Boston Philharmonic Orchestra, to talk about a form of leadership drawn from Benjamin's experience as a conductor. The Zanders emphasize the necessity for the person who plays second chair to consider her or his contribution to the orchestra's performance to be just as important as that of the person who plays first chair, and for the conductor to share that viewpoint as well. Bethley says her own style involves asking what each person can contribute to the mission underlying any undertaking.

Another excellent work on leadership, Sally Helgesen and Julie Johnson's *The Female Vision: Women's Real Power at Work*, focuses on the fact

---

36. Tracy MacKenzie, telephone interview with the author, October 28, 2013.

37. Zander and Zander, *Art of Possibility*. The appointive cabinet consisted of the bishop and superintendents of the (then) seven districts in the Louisiana Annual Conference.

that not everyone sees situations the same way.[38] Because of their socialization, women tend to notice different facets of a meeting or conversation. These aspects tend to be relationship-oriented. Essentializing this as a female trait is too limited, however; male theologians and practitioners who adopt relationship-oriented leadership can bring the same gifts to the table.

That respect for relationships informed not just those who wanted to bring sanctuary for church members, but also those who wanted to use the opportunity to build new links with the community. Leaders had to draw on deep conviction as they encouraged churches to reach out to others. "Bring people into your circle. That's what the Gospel is about," the bishop said. "It took a while for some of them to see that."

Specialized Focus Congregations

Two congregations, El Mesias UMC and the Korean UMC, which would otherwise have been placed in a zone were deemed "Specialized Focus Churches." Presumably, the rationale was that English was not the primary language of the congregants and that this would complicate the kind of cooperation the designers hoped would occur. These congregations, along with other aspects of ministry with Latino/as developed since 2005, are included in a chapter devoted to them, Chapter 6.

The Roman Catholic Experience

Churches Occupied and Parishioners Jailed

A great deal of help in my analysis of the United Methodist response came from an unexpected source—the Roman Catholic archdiocese in New Orleans. The Roman Catholics did almost exactly the opposite of what the UMC did, and thus they created a scenario over against which I can pose the UMC results. It is extremely helpful to have evidence as to what could have happened had the UMC taken a different track.

Roman Catholicism is the only manifestation of Christianity that can serve as a genuine comparison to United Methodism in several respects: (a) the number of congregations and members in Greater New Orleans; (b) the extent of the racial and ethnic diversity of its members in New Orleans; (c) the kind of connectional hierarchy that holds title to property and assigns clergy with or without the approval of a congregation; and (d) the presence

---

38. Helgeson and Johnson, *Female Vision*.

of a deep bond among clergy and laypeople that includes an adherence to shared governance and a sense of spiritual belonging to and responsibility for one another.

Since Katrina, the Roman Catholic Church and the United Methodist Church have used their hierarchical authority in radically different ways. Very soon after the levees broke, the archdiocese issued a list of congregations it intended to close. One of them was St. Augustine, a thriving, mixed-race but primarily African American parish in Tremé served by an activist priest. St. Augustine is said to be the oldest African American parish in the United States. Because it was attended by free people of color, enslaved persons, and white people, the church also claims to have long been "the most integrated congregation in the entire country."[39] There was such an outcry about the closing of this congregation that the archdiocese actually backed down; however, they did replace the popular priest, Jerome LeDoux, who has written his own account of the events, *War of the Pews*.[40]

Geographer Trushna Parekh, who studied gentrification of the Tremé neighborhood, wrote about the situation at St. Augustine. "It is worth asking why St. Augustine Church was one of the seven parishes selected for closure when, in contrast to some churches that were completely destroyed, it had suffered only wind damage (losing part of the copper sheathing around its bell tower, and one of the walls of the church hall) and no flood damage." She said that St. Augustine had already been on a list the church developed in 2000, and that the "financial strain from the hurricanes prompted the archdiocese to move forward with greater urgency."[41] She thought that one possible reason was the increase in property value that gentrification had brought to the area. St. Augustine was not the only church that was threatened with closure, but it was the most prominent congregation on the list that the archdiocese released of churches that would be closed.

When other congregations made strenuous objections, the archdiocese announced that it would devote more time to considering the matter. After several years, during which congregations like St. Henry's and Our Lady of Good Counsel had faithfully met what they believed to be the benchmarks for their parishes' survival, the archdiocese issued the final list. It looked exactly like the first one, and St. Henry's and Good Counsel were still slated for closure.[42]

39. Living Cultures Project, "Sunday in Tremé."
40. LeDoux, *War of the Pews*.
41. Parekh, "Of Armed Guards and Kente Cloth," 141.
42. Bruce Nolan, interview by the author, July 8, 2008, New Orleans, LA.

The Process: Or, How the Church Decided to Decide

The parishioners at St. Henry's and Good Counsel were stunned to discover they had not been listened to, and were so angered by the archbishop's lack of response to their concerns that they organized protests. Elderly people showed up at their churches with toothbrushes and pajamas for sleep-ins. Still unswayed, the archdiocese closed the churches and changed the locks on the doors. Somehow, though, parishioners made their way back inside, and the occupation of the two churches continued for over seventy days and nights.[43] Finally, the archbishop sent the police and had the occupying parishioners arrested and handcuffed, put into police vans, and taken to jail for their defiance of the archdiocese. Print and electronic media gave extensive coverage to the arrests.[44] Videos posted on the internet were viewed all over the world. Supported by unnamed funders, Craig Kraemer produced a documentary recounting the story, *Swimming against the Holy See*.[45] Tens of thousands of New Orleanians were hurt and disillusioned by the actions of the archdiocese. The resentment on the part of many New Orleanians, Catholic or not, is profound. Many have not come to terms with these actions, and never will.

Archbishop Alfred Hughes told the New Orleans *Times-Picayune* in 2009 that he was "very disappointed" that he had come to a point where he was "persuaded" that he must "enforce the end of the vigils, as the parishioners called them, the occupations of the churches. What led to that really was growing concern about the risks." When asked what risks he referred to, he answered that there were risks "for the occupiers and for the archdiocese—risks for the people because they were overloading the electrical circuits." When asked how they were overloading the circuits, he responded, "They brought in microwave ovens and other electrical equipment that the wires, the outlets they were hooked up to were not equipped to handle."

When asked about the decision-making process for closing the churches, Archbishop Hughes said, "I recognize that [there are] people who disagree, and I recognize that there are people who claim that I have not listened. I find it very difficult to envision a process that would have allowed more listening, but if listening means, you haven't accepted my point of view, or my preference, well, I guess I haven't listened, but that's the challenge and the cross of leadership, to make those difficult decisions." When

---

43. The parishioners tended to call these events "vigils" and the archdiocese insisted they were "occupations." In truth, "occupation" seems more accurate. Rumor had it that parishioners re-gained entrance to one church through a hole in the floor in a utility room and by having someone hide inside the other church during the archdiocese's inspection after the lock changing. This rumor may or may not be correct.

44. Warner, "New Orleans Police"; Nolan and Finch, "Police Clear Out Church."

45. Kraemer, *Swimming against the Holy See*.

he declared himself "at peace" with himself about the decisions, his interviewer expressed surprise: "Really? Why?" The archbishop replied, ". . . this is not just organizational planning. We're involved in ecclesial discernment, trying to discover what it is God is asking us at this point in our history for the common good of the archdiocese. Now I indicated to people at the very beginning, to the priests and to the people, that this is going to involve sacrifice, to move beyond personal preference to embrace the larger good of the church and the archdiocese."

St. Henry and Good Counsel and a third church were merged into a single parish named Good Shepherd in 2008, and they held their worship at what had been St. Stephen Church at 1025 Napoleon Avenue, a quarter-mile from St. Henry's former building and a mile from Good Counsel. Monsignor Christopher Nalty became pastor of the merged parish. Archbishop Hughes expressed confidence that the new pastor had formed a good relationship with a number of the members of the predecessor churches, and said that he "continue[d] to pray that no one is permanently alienated."[46]

In 2009, when Hughes retired, he was replaced by Archbishop Gregory Aymond. A New Orleans native, Aymond holds a degree from Notre Dame Seminary in the city. He later served on the faculty and in administration at the school.[47] His return to New Orleans was greeted with optimism by many of the Catholic sisters who had known him during his tenure at Notre Dame. They felt he would likely be more willing to engage in dialogue with New Orleanians. And, after some time, Aymond reopened talks about the future of the Uptown churches which were closed.[48] In 2012, the archdiocese announced that daily masses would be held at St. Henry's.[49]

Hughes's prayer that no one would be "permanently alienated" has apparently not yet been answered in the affirmative. In late 2014, I snapped a photo of an SUV ahead of me in traffic; it bore a bumper sticker still in good condition that proclaimed, "We Survived Katrina! We Just Did Not Survive Hughes!"

Catholic Work for Justice

There is, of course, more to the story of the Roman Catholic Church than what I have presented here. The archdiocese produced a huge, coffee-table-sized book called *A Story of Hope in a Time of Destruction: The Archdiocese of New Orleans and Hurricane Katrina*.[50] However, it would be a mistake to say

46. Pope, "Exclusive Interview"; Pope, "Hughes 'At Peace.'"
47. Archdiocese of New Orleans, "Archbishop Gregory Michael Aymond."
48. Rodriguez, "Talks Reopen."
49. Nolan, "After Years of Struggle"; Rodriguez, "Three Years after Closure."
50. Maestri, *Story of Hope*.

that the book presents the "other side" to the matters discussed above. The closure of St. Henry and Good Counsel is barely mentioned, and then only in a rather oblique way. However, the book succeeds in offering information and photographs about other situations and work the church accomplished.

It is important to distinguish the policies and actions of the archdiocesan officials from the actions of other Catholics who worked to improve the lives of ordinary people who needed help of many kinds. I want to mention here just a few of the many who dedicated themselves to this kind of ministry.

William Quigley has been a legal advocate for New Orleanians who were evicted from their homes and several other groups taken advantage of during and after the time the city was closed down. Quigley is a law professor and Director of the Stuart H. Smith Law Clinic and the Center for Social Justice and the Gillis Long Poverty Law Center at Loyola University in New Orleans. He is well known for taking on difficult cases and taking unpopular stands. He is a devout Catholic layman and follows his understanding of Jesus' teachings as he chooses the cases and causes he will make his own.

Jane Remson, OCarm, affiliated with the Twomey Center for Peace through Justice at Loyola University, continued her work which included both advocacy at the national and international levels through the Carmelite NGO and Bread for the World, and local efforts of Catholic and non-Catholic ministries to feed those who needed food. Remson served as a tour guide and educator for a steady stream of groups who have come to the city post-Katrina. She spent a day with each class I brought from Phillips Seminary, sharing her deep knowledge of the city where she was born and putting aspects of recovery into local, state, and national contexts.

Other examples include Matt Rousso, the Maryknoll affiliate in New Orleans. A dedicated layman, Rousso is actively involved in many aspects of social justice work in the city. The staff and volunteers at Catholic Charities, a social service oriented organization of the church, have accomplished a great deal and continue to work on problems like homelessness, food insecurity and immigration.

The work of Sister Mary Daniel, OP, in restoring the look of the Domincans' school was described earlier; she was one of many sisters who endeavored to help and comfort and educate returning children. She was also director of the Dominican Conference Center which was able to reopen just a few months after the storm. My students and I stayed there during the first two Katrina-related classes I offered. Many volunteers who came to the city were the recipients of the sisters' hospitality.

Other groups suffered so much damage that they could not return themselves. The Congregation of St. Joseph's mother house was destroyed, and they wound up moving to a location in Ohio. Helen Prejean, author of *Dead Man Walking*, is probably the best known member; she and other sisters had lived next to the St. Thomas housing development, working with residents there. The cost to the city from the loss of professional religious workers is immeasurable.

Results

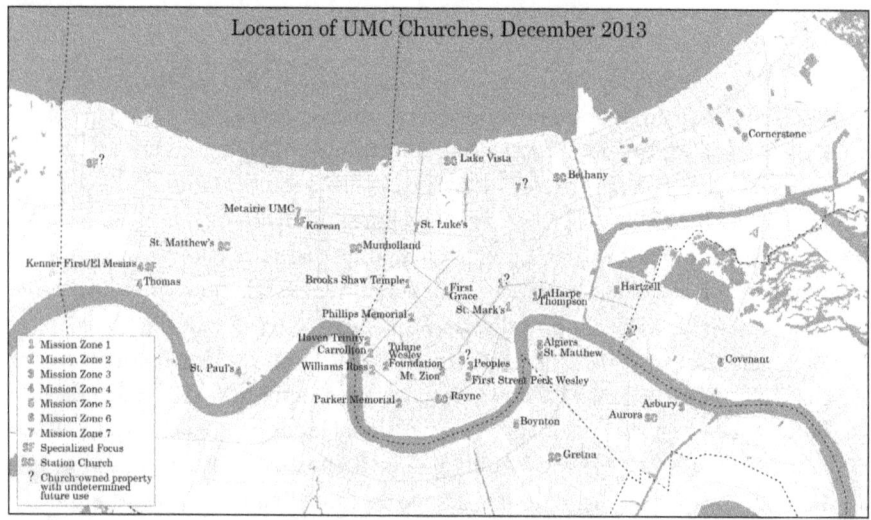

Evaluating the UMC process for congregational reorganization described above is the task of the next several chapters that provide narrative and some analysis of results in various churches. Chapter 5 tells the story of First Grace UMC, a successful merger of an African American congregation (Grace UMC) and an Anglo congregation (First UMC) that would never have succeeded had it simply been mandated by the bishop. Chapter 6 looks at ministry at the "specialized focus" congregations, the Korean and El Mesias UMCs, as well as other ministries with Latino/as in Greater New Orleans, some of it conducted at First Grace. Chapter 7 is a discussion of four congregations that have engaged in various kinds of cooperative ministries since the storm. Rayne, Mt. Zion, Parker, and People's each remains a separate congregation, but by working together, they have been able to address needs that would otherwise have remained unmet. The fourth results chapter, Chapter 8, profiles Bethany, Hartzell, St. Mark's, First Street Peck Wesley, and Ross-Williams churches.

5

First Grace UMC: Where the City Worships

Nothing in the world is as soft and yielding as water. Yet for dissolving the hard and inflexible, nothing can surpass it.
—Tao Te Ching[1]

The consensus among United Methodists in New Orleans is that a merger between the Anglo congregation at First UMC and the African American congregation at Grace UMC would not have happened if it had not been for Katrina. In fact, it would be fair to change the word "not" to the word "never"—the opinion is that the merger would *never* have occurred had it not been for Katrina. I agree that the merger would not have occurred during my lifetime, and without the merger, Grace and First UMC would both have ceased to exist. But the fact that the legacies of the two congregations still live in First Grace UMC is less important than the fact that something entirely new, something perfect for the context of New Orleans, and something making a true contribution toward improving the city is happening.

Material about how the unexpected and difficult merger occurred is included in this chapter. This involves a consideration of how worship practices that were right for the new congregation were hammered out. New ministries developed by young people who lived in intentional community in the First Grace building are discussed.

The significant ministry with Latino/as that occurs at First Grace is detailed in the next chapter. That chapter also includes information about

---

1. Mitchell, *Tao Te Ching*, 78.

the Spanish speaking congregation, El Mesias UMC, and its merger into 1Love UMC in Kenner, and the newer Hispanic ministry at Gretna UMC.

To Be in Love with "The Holy City"

Recall from the previous chapter that the bishop and cabinet had decided not to send anyone to the Mission Zones who did not actively want to be in New Orleans. The result was that many of the individuals placed there deeply loved the city. Shawn Anglim and his wife, Anne Daniell, were among them.

Anglim is a native of Ohio. He earned an MTS at Harvard Divinity School and an MDiv at Drew University, a United Methodist school in Madison, New Jersey. At the time the floodwalls broke, Anglim was campus minister at LSU in Baton Rouge and affiliated with the nearby University UMC. Anne Daniell was within two months of defending her dissertation for a PhD in theology at Drew, and her topic was theology of place. The place she was writing about was New Orleans, and some of her ideas are discussed in Chapter 9.[2] Doctoral dissertations are not developed quickly, and the couple had been deepening their relationship with the city for some time.

In fact, three years before Katrina, in July 2002, Shawn Anglim wrote a lengthy letter to Bishop Bill Hutchinson about the UMC in New Orleans "and the possibilities for ministry in that wondrous, troubled and vibrant city, one of the defining cities of this country and perhaps the world." A copy of the letter was still among the bishop's Katrina materials in 2005; since Anglim said he did not re-send it, Hutchinson evidently remembered the letter and pulled it out when he was thinking about post-storm possibilities.

Although letters do not usually have epigrams, Anglim set off a quote at the top of the page: "The most effective and fulfilled pastors I've known are those who, like [Francis] Asbury, are in love with the land and inhabitants they've been given to serve." Asbury was the bishop most responsible for shaping Methodism on this continent, and the quote came from Thomas Frank, the man who literally wrote the book on UMC governance.[3] Note the reference is not "who love the land and inhabitants," but rather "who are in love with the land and inhabitants." The connotation is different, and "in love with," which Frank chose and Anglim quoted, implies a lure and a response, an excitement, a reciprocity in relationship

---

2. Daniell, "Incarnating Theology."

3. The exact source of this quote was not recorded in the letter, and neither Anglim nor Thomas Frank remembers its location.

which "who love" lacks. Readers acquainted with multiplicity of words for "love" in the Greek language may be thinking of *eros* versus *agape*, and that is indeed what I intend.

Anthropologist Martha Ward said she was attracted to First Grace by the spiritual openness of the church to the city, and it is something many other members find appealing.[4] She likes Anglim's repeated assertions that New Orleans is "the Holy City." While that language does not appear yet in his 2002 letter, the idea was brewing in Anglim's soul in a way that prepared him for his post-Katrina ministry. He wrote that he hoped the churches in New Orleans could "provide spiritual vision to the city" and "participate in the city in such a way that they shape its renewal for the Kingdom of God."

The tag line for the church is "Where the City Worships." Anglim calls it "an incredible line. It is bold, and it is prophetic, and it makes people feel really welcome. And [it means] your work is never finished. It's always in front of you." Anglim's 2002 letter spoke of his dream of pastoring a church "that has a vibrant ministry and claims a prominent voice for the city by speaking directly to the issues of that community and leading it, shaping the movement of the spirit in that place." He said, "I believe ministry is ultimately organic: it emerges and grows out of the people and place."

He wrote about the potential of various UMC locations, and had a special interest in the Mid-City area. First UMC, for instance, could "be a major voice" in the city. "Because of its location, thousands of people drive by First UMC *every day*." Further, its "unique" placement at 3401 Canal Street put it at the intersection of three neighborhoods with varying socio-economic make-ups. He dreamed of a time when "the big blue sign" out front would bear a message "that stirs a whirlwind of a spirit in people and in the city; a message that spiritually addresses people by catching their attention and catching them off-guard, by asking and addressing who they are as a community." The sign, he hoped, "would become the *sign* of a congregation and a city renewed in Christ."[5]

Indeed, the site he described has become some of those things, but not as First UMC. It has instead become First Grace, a merger of First with Grace UMC.

---

4. Martha Ward, interview by the author, March 20, 2009, New Orleans, LA.

5. Shawn Anglim, letter to Bishop William Hutchinson, July 9, 2002. Copy in the Louisiana Annual Conference's Katrina files (emphasis Anglim's).

Visionary Young People Shaping the New Church

Four young adults—Angela Davis, Sarah Fleming, Eric Gremillion, and Jennie Hammatt—were deeply involved in the shaping of what First Grace would become. When Anglim left the LSU campus ministry to become the leader of one of the Mission Zones, young people followed him and began to live in intentional community in the huge but badly damaged First UMC building at 3401 Canal Street. They were joined by other young people who wanted to be part of the recovery of the city and who were drawn to the work happening there.

In all, there were seven residents. They turned a large room on the second floor into a kitchen and community room. Small Sunday school rooms were converted to bedrooms. A couch in a nook in a hallway became a sitting area. Bathroom space was not what one would hope for. There was no hot water for many months, and no electricity on the first floor of the building. They had a community meal each Sunday. They had devotions together each Monday. They adopted a dog who belonged to the community as a whole. The experience of living and working together was immensely valuable for the young people and contributed to the creativity of their work.[6]

Some in the community were paid a stipend through the United States government's AmeriCorps program at first, and therefore they were not allowed to spend all their time in overtly religious work. They were to ascertain needs and develop plans to address some of them. They rode their bikes around the neighborhood as it slowly resettled and talked to people, learning the community's day-to-day situation and what tasks needed doing. They painted the music room at Warren Easton High School, some four blocks down on Canal Street. They worked with the reading program for fourth graders at John Dibert Community School. They created a community garden which had twenty-two participants.

Since everyone needed pretty much everything, isolating the issues that they could address effectively was not a simple process. Because of the scarcity of resources, they took "the logical path of partnering with other groups" to accomplish both ministry with individuals and broader social change. Like both Anglim and Anne Daniell, Angela Davis uses the term "organic." She said, "It was really organic, all tied together."

---

6. Ten years later, there is still an intentional community of seven people in residence there, though the make-up of the group has undergone change throughout the years. My student Janet Barrow completed a practicum in the summer of 2014, living in this community, and her experience was helpful for me in understanding the difficulties such a setting involves.

Davis was in seminary at Princeton in 2005 and came to New Orleans after graduation in 2007. She had also spent a year doing mission work in Ethiopia. She said the people who were in the First Grace community before her had done a great deal of the thinking and talking required in order to choose a place to start. "By the time I got here, we were ready for action."[7] The work they chose for First Grace included the establishment of a home for women and children in transition toward housing (see Hagar's House, below). Davis later earned a law degree at Loyola University in New Orleans. Along with her work at Hagar's House, she has more recently established a legal clinic to help young people with immigration issues; this project is discussed in the next chapter on ministry with Latino/as.

Several of the residents also played pivotal roles in designing worship and providing music. Jennie Hammett was in place early on and contributed in many ways. At one point, she was considered the artist-in-residence, and she painted murals throughout the building. In a city still overwhelmingly brown from the flood, it was a gift to see color in the halls. She worked on the music committee (a topic discussed below) and sang solos or in duets most Sunday mornings. When she left the city, Hammatt went to Germany for further language study, and then moved to Santiago, Chile, to teach German.

Sometimes Hammatt sang with Sarah Fleming. Fleming, whose mother is Rayne UMC pastor Callie Winn Crawford, later moved to Denver for theological studies. She has since graduated from seminary at Iliff University, and now works at a non-profit in Denver.

Eric Gremillion earned a graduate degree in film production at the University of New Orleans, and he has used his talents to tell the story of First Grace in several videos. He has documented events like the decommissioning of Grace UMC and the opening of Hagar's House.

Approaching a Merger of First and Grace UMCs

> First Grace is the story of two congregations—one black, the other white—that merged in the aftermath of a great storm and proved that King's dream of "the beloved community" remains a possibility. In the chaotic aftermath of Hurricane Katrina in 2005, a circuit-riding pastor and several brave laypeople decided to take a chance. They would merge these two churches. First Methodist and Grace Methodist would become First Grace.[8]

7. Angela Davis, telephone interview by the author, November 19, 2013.
8. Thomas, "New Orleans Church."

So wrote Oliver Thomas in *USA Today* in 2013, describing the remarkably multiracial turnout for the funeral of Marguerite Washington, a young woman who was a beloved member of the church. But this brief description hardly begins to capture the process that brought these two churches to come together as one.

Nothing was easy after Katrina. Unless you've spent time in a place devastated by war or a massive earthquake, you have no frame of reference to let you imagine what life in this American city was like. For months on end, there was no electricity. No safe drinking water. No health care. No mail service. No functioning schools.

But cultural challenges were nearly as difficult as physical ones. When members from First UMC and Grace UMC first gathered to discuss possible merger, those from Grace could not help but notice that the First UMC members would not eat the food their African American hostess served. Even those white people from First UMC who were open enough to the idea of merger to go to a mixed-race meeting held in the apartment of a black woman were still too uncomfortable to eat food while they were there. Having been brought up in an environment which left me as a young adult uncertain how to behave in a similar situation, I unfortunately understand their dilemma.[9] The cultural journey that the two congregations had to make in order for First Grace to be born was long indeed.

First UMC had declined dramatically in membership before the storm. Although the building was not in perfect condition and needed some updating, it was quite large. It had taken on six to eight feet of water after Katrina, but one of its few remaining members had the drive and expertise to see that repairs were well started very early on. Occupying a very visible

---

9. The first time I attended a meeting of an African American political caucus was in the early 1980s. I was in my early thirties and running (successfully) for a minor office. I went to ask for their support and to show I was willing to stand over against the culture of north Louisiana enough to drive myself to an all-black political meeting held in an African American-owned establishment in an all-black neighborhood. Everyone I knew perceived this as a radical act. Yet I didn't know whether to eat the food. The caucus served lunch, and a woman there whom I knew advised me to be sure to eat, because people would watch to see whether I did. This may sound strange to non-Southerners, since many prosperous white families have black cooks, and whites thus eat food prepared by black people all the time. However, for whites to eat in places where blacks have prepared food for other black people is "different" in a way for which I cannot find any logical explanation. These kinds of dehumanizing customs were developed and maintained to prop up Jim Crow segregation, and people who were brought up with them usually absorbed them in an uncritical way. Having lived in a thoroughly racist environment, I honestly was not sure whether I would be expected or even welcome to eat. I was deeply grateful for the advice the woman gave me. Thus, the discomfort the white members of First UMC felt is something to which I can relate.

location at the corner of Canal Street and Jefferson Davis Parkway, it offered great potential for ministry in the Mid-City area.

Grace UMC's building at 2001 Iberville was a little more than a mile from First UMC. It sustained severe damage, including a large hole knocked in a wall of the sanctuary. Although they received a significant insurance settlement, none of its members was able to take immediate initiative to limit the damage. What they had, Martha Orphe, director of the Mission Zone program, observed, was "a good group of people" who could be the nucleus of a merged community.[10]

Orphe said she kept having lunches with Shawn Anglim, the lead pastor of the zone that encompassed both First and Grace churches, and asking, "What could happen here?" Anglim says he was well aware of the mysterious ways in which God works in the midst of crisis, and that sometimes "the Lord just opens up things." He considered one of those things to be the relationship he had developed with two women from Grace, Margaret Washington and Gwen Anderson. When the pastor who had been serving Grace left midyear, "[Washington and Anderson] picked up the phone and called me, saying they needed some pastoral leadership."

When Anglim began to understand the opportunity that Orphe was imagining, it was Anderson and Washington whom he approached. "It was very clear to me the question that I was given to ask," he said. "But once you ask this question, there's only one answer to it. If you say 'no,' it's like you are saying 'no' to the Holy Spirit, and [the Spirit] will go somewhere else. You missed your moment. You'll get other moments but you won't get that one." He believes that such moments are God-given, "and they're very real. If you recognize them, that's the first thing." When people can answer "yes," Anglim believes, "there will be consequences. They'll be powerful, but it doesn't always mean that it's all roses all the way through. And so, I asked Gwen and Margaret, 'Do you think that we could do more for our city as one body of Christ than we'll ever do as two bodies?' Everybody knows the answer, and they just started crying. That's when I knew I had asked the right question."[11]

Orphe hosted the gatherings where the initial conversations between laypeople from the two congregations occurred. They met in her apartment near City Park; she invited them there to provide "a neutral location," one not affiliated with either church. "At first," she recalled, "the blacks would sit on one side of the room and the whites on the other." As Anglim put it, "It was cordial, but you know, some people don't cross boundaries very often."

---

10. Martha Orphe, interview by the author, January 28, 2009, New Orleans, LA.

11. Shawn Anglim, interview by the author, June 25, 2013, New Orleans, LA.

But the issue of sharing food was not the only boundary that would need to be crossed.

A week after this first gathering, Anderson and Washington came back for a discussion with Anglim. "They asked some pointed questions that I didn't necessarily have a clear answer for, other than, this is a new body and it will have a new identity that we will figure out together. It was in my mind that while First had the building, Grace had a chunk of money. Grace didn't have to do this. They could have merged with a black church. They had options."

First UMC had more than its share of doubts and resistance as well. When it came time for a second gathering, the chair of the church council called Anglim and said that he had cancelled the meeting. Anglim said, "We had a difficult moment, and I said the meeting was going to go ahead. He said, 'I've already called the council members and cancelled, and no one's attending.' And I said, 'The meeting's going to go ahead.'"

Anglim called Mary Elizabeth Shaw, whom he describes as one of the "back-row ladies" at First UMC. "I said, 'Mary Elizabeth, here's the deal. I'm not sure if you are aware that there have been these conversations.' She said, 'Well, I've heard a few things.' And I said, 'I really need you to attend this meeting.' She said, 'What time will you pick me up?' And I picked her up, [along with] one of the only African American members of First, Audrey Gates, who is now deceased. . . . So, it was Mary Elizabeth and Audrey Gates and Tommy Gilbert, who was a new member of First, a man in his fifties. After that second meeting, I said, 'I think we need to tell people we're having this conversation if we're going to go for it, because I believe the word is going to get out.'" So, the following Sunday, he told the worshiping congregation at First UMC what was going on and, shortly after that, the Grace congregation.

Despite the ongoing discomfort, the people kept meeting and eventually one black woman from Grace asked a younger white person from First to go to her car for something she had forgotten, and the key ring she handed over had a Mercedes emblem on it. Orphe said that at that moment, the First UMC members began to recognize that they had things in common with the Grace members. Orphe told me this story several times in different interview settings over the years. She never used the words "class" or "socioeconomic status," but she did say, "They recognized that they were not poor people and rich people, but people with things in common." Soon, the groups found other commonalities: "Oh, your son is in the military? My son is in the military, too," was an example Orphe used.

They also discovered differences. They decided to have an initial worship service together just to see how it went. Some noticed that the first date suggested would fall on Mother's Day. The First UMC members said the date was fine, but the Grace members were silent, Orphe said, until she drew them out, asking, "Isn't Mother's Day second only to Christmas in your church?" Pressed, they explained that it was a particularly important time for people to return to their own church homes to honor the women of their families. First UMC folks could understand that, but they noticed the alternate day would fall on Father's Day. That was fine with the Grace members, which then required a discussion about why Father's Day did not carry the same weight for the group.[12]

Coming Together as First Grace UMC

On the first anniversary of Katrina, in August 2006, the two congregations came together again at First UMC for worship. Anglim remembers,

> There was no heat, no air conditioning. I'm not even sure we had a front door. But we had a back door. I can't remember the count; I think it was seventy-five or eighty-five people that were here. People had traveled far and wide; people brought their grandchildren, the District Superintendent came, the construction workers came.

The next Sunday, however, the numbers dropped to about twenty-five. With no air conditioning or heat for about a year, it was clear to people that the church had no amenities.

Within a few weeks, there were about seventeen people who decided they were sticking around. Anglim said,

> If you look from the time we started worshiping together . . . things were very discombobulated, because we really did take two different worshiping congregations and put them together, and nothing's the same. Now, the way God has blessed us, we had had a worship service two or three months prior to that. Just one. We came together, and it was magical. Everything about it was magical. And we were blessed with that. You know, we were just given this moment, as difficult as it might be later.

The two churches continued to worship together, but still as First and Grace, not as a merged congregation. Anglim's brother belongs to a United Methodist congregation in Maryville, Tennessee. One Sunday, a group from that church had come down to New Orleans to do a volunteer mission

---

12. Martha Orphe, interview by the author, January 28, 2009, New Orleans, LA.

project. Describing the worship service they attended, Anglim said, "There were about sixty of us, and there were a hundred white folks on a mission project. They built these walls. They painted. They did grounds work. They built the chancel stage that the choir sits on. My brother is a contractor, so they brought several people like him. And there were bunch of high school kids. So that first worship service, there were a hundred purple shirts and a little smattering of us."

That first visit has resulted in enduring relationships between the New Orleans and Maryville churches, Anglim reports.

> Gwen Anderson was one the first two women at Grace that I spoke to; they connected with Gwen somehow and got to know her and found out her story, and they have raised the money and rebuilt her house in New Orleans East. They have been working on Stephanie Martin's house which needed a couple of boards replaced. And next thing you know, they had every other board off the place. They've come back three years, rebuilding it.

Martin, the administrator at First Grace, told my practicum students in summer 2014 that she was there because First Grace had loved her and thereby saved her life

The relationship with the Maryville church has continued for more than seven years. Anglim said,

> They've come back every year now. So this past year they came back for their seventh trip. There were thirty-five of them and 220 of us. . . . So it has been powerful for them to see that transformation. And the scripture becomes very alive when we go through these transformations.

When First UMC and Grace UMC merged, they counted only about sixty members between the two congregations. But Anglim noted that, "There were really three groups that came." First, he counts about twenty-five people who had returned to New Orleans after Katrina and who were worshiping at Grace. Second, he said, "My official count of the old members of First UMC is seventeen. Imagine this big sanctuary with seventeen people." The third group included about fifteen new people who joined First before the formal merger, and four young people "that followed me from LSU and joined the church. There was just something bold going on here that you could sense."

Anglim is still astounded that "no one from Grace Church left at all." One family of five no longer attends, because one of them is now pastoring another church. "Some people moved and some have died, but none of the original group who moved from Grace to First Grace has left, which is unheard of. Usually when two churches merge, only a small percent of the members that leave their physical place stay. I think it says a lot about the faithfulness of the people of Grace, and about what happened here, that people felt like this became their church. They did have to let go. But this became their church, and I became their pastor."

Anglim continues to sit down regularly in his home with the former members of Grace and ask, "How are you feeling about the church?" He recalls,

> Early on, that was discombobulating. Like everybody, they were losing so much. Some of them had lost their homes, some of them lost their loved ones, they lost their church, they lost their style of worship.

First UMC had less human capital to bring to the merger, but Anglim praises those who stayed through the process. "They were all faithful. They all really wanted to be that. That handful of people, the members from First—we're talking six or seven women in their eighties and some in their nineties—their faithfulness provided this opportunity. If those women had left three months earlier, I'm not saying we wouldn't exist, but they did their part, and we will forever be in debt to them."

In June, just a few months before the merger in October, First and Grace UMCs were worshiping together regularly, but there were still some hard conversations to be had, particularly with the people at First UMC. Anglim recalled,

> I frankly said to these women, "You cannot leave. You need to be faithful to your church and this process that we've started and you need to see this through," and I never asked them to say okay to that, but they're good old Southern women. They don't need to say it. [Their silence] was their way of saying, "You understand this is our church, and we're going to see this through." And they did see it through. They were here till we merged.

But shortly after the merger, Anglim went on vacation, and upon his return, a few of these women had departed. He laughs, "Not all of them but a couple left and then a couple others left. But I will tell you, one of those women [who stayed] is Mary Elizabeth Shaw, who is still here."

Shaw's steadfastness has continued to impress Anglim.

> Mary Elizabeth Shaw continued and another woman joined her, and she drove herself here until she was ninety-five years old, [when] her children took her car keys. And now, a member of

the church who lives in Lakeview drives all the way Uptown, picks up Mary Elizabeth and brings her here to church. This is someone who's grown up in tradition; however, she's also grown up learning, "This is my church, and I'm staying at my church." And she appreciates, respects, and knows what has happened here has been beautiful and very important. But it is the worship . . . she would look around and say, "This is about how it should work."[13]

Worship—"This is about how it should work"

I attended worship at First Grace many times through the years, but I will never forget the services I went to when the merger was still brand new. I was fascinated by the white people there. When the music was in a style more associated with African American worship and the black people there were moving with its rhythm, the white worshippers had one of two responses. Some were clapping and moving and had big smiles on their faces. Others were standing rigidly with their arms crossed in front of them—the classic defensive posture. They were not singing or humming, and they were most decidedly not smiling. Whether those particular individuals were former members of First UMC who later left, former members of First UMC who learned to thrive in the new worship atmosphere, or visitors who were unlikely to return does not really matter. Imagining the experience of leading worship where some people are obviously appreciating what is happening and others are demonstrating with their whole bodies that they find the experience positively distasteful can help put flesh on the idea that "merging these two worship forms will be difficult."

It was not only First members who were bemused by the new worship but learned to adjust. Anglim said,

> Some of the people in Grace who maybe weren't directly involved in planning worship thought, "Why aren't we singing *these* hymns?" There was that kind of classic stuff. But the only way to honor what we've done is to keep moving forward and to keep figuring it out and honor the Spirit until you finally get it. It took months to achieve the feeling that people now have in our worship.

Writing about the complex topic of religious music in multiracial congregations, Gerardo Marti discusses ethnodoxology, an emerging field that

---

13. Shawn Anglim, interview by the author, June 25, 2013, New Orleans, LA.

considers race and worship. Through theological and anthropological study, as well as practical application, scholars consider how a cultural group "might use its unique and diverse artistic expressions appropriately to worship the God of the Bible." Their academic exploration of the problems that emerge in multi-cultural worship acknowledges the lived struggle that the pastors and members of congregations like First Grace have experienced. Marti wrote, "Over the course of my research, I came to realize that when a person is recruited to serve in a choir or worship team, they take on a concrete commitment to the diversity goals of the congregation." [14]

Jennie Hammatt said that at first, the music committee at First Grace met every single week to choose music for the next Sunday. They asked congregants what they would like to hear, and took the inclusion of their requests very seriously. Each week, they chose one secular song in order "to point out the lack of boundary between what's sacred and secular. For my generation, it's an important bridge," she said.

The music director then was an expert at gospel music (as is the music director now), but modern black praise music, operatic numbers, hip-hop, bluegrass, and folk are all included. "Everybody can feel they are spoken to in some way," she explained. That means, of course, that no one is spoken to all the time. With much wisdom, she said, "If we really want diversity, we have to let go of things."[15]

Though for some readers it will restate the obvious, it seems necessary to point out that not all African American Christians worship alike. Even within the same denomination, all African American congregations do not worship alike. There are large differences and widely divergent degrees of formality in liturgical practice. Some African American United Methodist churches lean toward "high church," and services are complete with a formal choir processional and liturgical elements repeated without change from week to week. Others have far more informal services, with music that stirs strong response of a physical kind.

Nevertheless, there are also similarities from group to group and congregation to congregation, and Cheryl Sanders, author of *Saints in Exile: The Holiness-Pentecostal Experience in African American Religion and Culture*, has produced an excellent analysis of some commonalities in African American worship. Sanders described the "holy dance" which is common in many churches. This is not the same as liturgical dance, a choreographed performative event in which a limited number of people participate. Rather,

---

14. Material from the website of the International Council of Ethnodoxologists, cited in Marti, *Worship across the Racial Divide*, 13, 191.

15. Jennie Hammatt, interview by the author, February 24, 2008, New Orleans, LA.

she means the movement in which most or all of the congregation will engage when the music has brought them to the desired state of worship. The most common manifestation is the "resting step," a simple movement of one's weight from one foot to the other, performed in time to the music.[16]

In my own experience, hand clapping often accompanies this step. The degree of movement of the shoulders and the head can vary significantly. Worshippers feel free to lift their hands and arms and to wave them, but (to speak in a generalization) this is not as routinely done as it is in an Anglo charismatic church.

Theologian Karl Barth insisted that anyone who comes to church has come, knowingly or not, because they desire an encounter with God.[17] It is the job of the pastor, musicians and worship leaders to facilitate that encounter. The encounter itself is a genuine recognition of being in the presence of the Holy. Worship at First Grace often allows such an experience, through the music, the sermon, and through the opportunity to see God in the face of the city around you. There is a weekly observance of Holy Communion, or Eucharist, where the children come and partake first. In more formal settings, each time the Eucharistic elements are consecrated, we pray, "Pour out your Spirit on us and on these gifts of bread and wine." However, as ritual studies scholar Tom Driver says, we don't wait for that to happen.[18] Indeed, in much Anglo worship, the idea that the Deity might manifest in any form is never even considered.

Sanders addressed the issue of God/Spirit encounter, noting that "the ultimate objective of worship in the Sanctified church tradition is some form of spirit possession." Addressing the "aesthetic and ethical norms" that are "derived from the Bible and black culture," she said, "The distinctive song, speech, and dances of the Sanctified church symbolically 'usher' the saints 'out' of this world and into a more authentic one discerned within sacred time and space." The inauthentic nature of this world is constantly brought home to the worshippers because "they are themselves 'rejected' by the dominant host culture because of their race, and sometimes their sex and class." They believe it is the Holy Spirit who "has freed at least some of them from the pressure to conform to the worship styles of the dominant culture."[19]

Anne Daniell has written that all public rituals occur in a context. That context always includes countless other events and countless relationships

---

16. Sanders, *Saints in Exile*, 64–65.
17. Barth, "Need and Promise."
18. Driver, *Magic of Ritual*, 84.
19. Sanders, *Saints in Exile*, 63–64.

from every participant's life. Enactments of similar rituals in the past serve as rehearsals for the current one, and the "mental anticipation, imagination, and pre-ritual social gatherings may all be counted as their preparation." Yet cultural performances emerge not only from the collective memories of those present, but also from their imaginative and spontaneous embrace of the present moment.[20] It is that spontaneous embrace of the moment where New Orleans excels.

Configuring the space at First Grace to welcome both its new members and others from the surrounding community has been an ongoing challenge. As Anglim explains, "Part of your life blood as an urban church is checking: 'Are the other among you?' You always have that. It's not like it ever goes away completely. The question is, 'Do you make space to figure out how to get comfortable and to engage in what we're doing?' So when we remodeled the sanctuary, here were my directives: There's a flow to the sanctuary that creates this open space. So from the chancel to the stairs, it is open. There's an altar there, but it doesn't obstruct this movement of the Spirit as I would call it." They used leftover money from their Katrina recovery funds to paint the elegant sanctuary and upgrade the sound system, but kept the same chairs that other churches donated to them during the rest of the remodeling.

However, welcoming is not just a matter of smart remodeling, a fresh coat of paint, and a decent sound system. Anglim explains,

> If we make the poor feel uncomfortable, we have failed. So, everybody thinks the coffee pot [always present on a table in the back] is cute; well, you know, the coffee pot is there in part because people who are cold or hot and they don't have any place to go, they're here at 10 o'clock in the morning cause they're looking for some place to go and the coffee pot says, just like at an AA meeting, you are welcome. You're welcome to be here.

First Grace has recently adopted a new affirmation that is mentioned in the section on diversity below. But when Aziza Bayou was researching her thesis on First Grace in 2008–9, another affirmation, written by Anglim, was in use. It ended with the declaration, "And we believe that by seeking the welfare of our city, / As peace comes to it so shall we find our own."[21] She saw the Statement of Faith as a portrayal of "First Grace's congregant community as a non-judgmental, forgiving, and loving group." It also

---

20. Daniell, "Incarnating Theology," 136.
21. Bayou, "United for the City," 82–83.

"emphasized that First Grace's congregation believes in a universal human spirit that transcends socially constructed differences."[22]

The ways that multicultural worship can go wrong are seemingly endless. The devotion to the city as a whole, and a remarkably eclectic city at that, have helped those who worship at First Grace to cohere around an identity as New Orleanians. Furthermore, the payoff for successfully navigating the difficult path to transformative multi-cultural worship is huge. In the "growing literature on racially diverse churches" worship is increasingly credited with "potential for removing racism in the church."[23] If racism can be removed—and I think that following Jesus requires hoping that it can—worshipping together will certainly have to be a part of the process.

There is one more aspect of worship at First Grace which has not been addressed here. Bilingual worship in a city with an exploding Hispanic population is yet another layer of complexity to be worked out, and the Spanish speaking congregation at First Grace, *La Gracia*, usually meets separately from the group which attends the English service. There are native Spanish speakers in both groups. The worship in Spanish and its leader, Oscar Ramos-Gallardo, are discussed in Chapter 7 which addresses UMC ministry with Latino/as in several locations around Greater New Orleans. This placement is not meant to diminish its importance to First Grace. It is rather to emphasize that the commitment of the UMC to Hispanic ministry needs to be thought about in terms larger than individual congregations (though in truth that narrowing of focus seems to be the direction the larger UMC is currently taking).

Finding Support

Bishop Bill Hutchinson was instrumental in providing necessary support to ensure the success of First Grace. Anglim said,

> I told the bishop, "Whatever flack you take and whatever your shortcomings are, First Grace will be your legacy because you gave me the space to figure it out." And the truth is that everything I've asked for, he gave it.

Immediately after the storm, there was a general understanding in the city that people were doing the best they could with what they had. All sorts of regulations were ignored because in the chaos and devastation, no one had the capacity to obey them and furthermore, there was no one with time

---

22. Ibid., 83.
23. Marti, *Worship across the Racial Divide*, 23–24.

and resources to enforce them. In time, however, some of the make-do solutions were deemed unsuitable, and the church had to scramble just to stay in place. "See this sprinkler system?" Anglim asked.

> Just as we really got on our feet, the fire marshal walked in and said he was going to shut us down in five days, because we had people living here, we had a clinic upstairs, we had a day care downstairs. The only way we could go on was to put in this $100,000 sprinkler system. I went to the bishop and said, "We need some help." And so, over the next two years, he gave us support to keep going.

The bishop had not actually been to First Grace, and the staff decided to give him an award to insure that he would experience worship there firsthand. It was a joyful occasion. The congregation demonstrated their appreciation for the bishop's help, and Hutchinson blossomed in the freedom and authenticity of the worship. I was present that Sunday, and his body language made clear that he thrived on seeing how meaningful the service was for people of different races, ethnicities, and circumstances. Anglim says,

> I knew after that day, there would be no question about things. And that's exactly what happened. A year later, when the fire marshal stuff happened, I said, "This is what's going on, and I need your support." And he said, "Write it up for me." So I did, and basically they gave this church what we asked for. They also gave us all that space when things were discombobulated, and no one shut it down.

The affirmation of Hutchinson's leadership is particularly significant because Anglim is one of several pastors quoted in Chapter 4 who maintain that they would have proceeded differently than Bill Hutchinson did and seized the opportunity to close some churches. However, while some others still believe Hutchinson was wrong, Anglim recognizes that the bishop's strategy of supporting all congregations for a time so that each had an opportunity to flourish is precisely what allowed First Grace the time to develop and thrive.

Strong lay leadership within the congregation has been an equally important factor. Anglim believes,

> There's real leadership here. The leadership at First Grace, it's a strong group of people. When I sit down with the church council or the trustees or the staff-parish committee . . . they are very capable. And they make me stronger, and they make the church stronger. We've established something. We're five-and-a-half

years old. We're not a toddler, but we're in kindergarten. And there's a lot left to happen, though we don't know what that is.[24]

Building New Ministries

Margaret Washington, one of the stalwarts from Grace UMC, served as chair of the council at First Grace for several years. She has been a crucial part of holding the church together and of helping it to make decisions to reach out to the community. It was the funeral of Margaret's daughter, Marguerite, that Oliver Thomas wrote about in the *USA Today* quote cited earlier.

Thomas' article went on:

> When Marguerite La Joy Washington, a freshman at Dillard University, was gunned down in New Orleans, it had all the appearance of business as usual. Thousands of young blacks are killed in America each year. But if you had attended Marguerite's funeral at First Grace United Methodist Church, where she taught Sunday School, you would have realized that something was different. Instead of the nearly all black affair you would expect in too much of America, the crowd—so large that it spilled out into the streets—was half white.[25]

Shawn Anglim remembers the profound effect of Marguerite La Joy Washington's murder on First Grace.

> What happened was Marguerite's death. She was known by everybody. She was very quiet, but she was in every corner of the church. She was in the nursery. She was in the kitchen. She was from the Grace church. We didn't have any youth. She was a prominent youth. She was passing out the pew pads. She was helping in communion. Everybody knew her. And so, when she died, everybody was connected to that. Basically, the entire worshiping congregation was at First Grace for her funeral, along with 750 other people. There was not a space anywhere. Many of the people had joined this church in the past four years, many of them in the last two. But when that event happened, they realized they were much more part of a church than they had realized.

Marguerite was a driven, hard-working first-year nursing student, killed when someone fired several rounds into a bedroom where she and

---

24. Shawn Anglim, interview by the author, June 25, 2013, New Orleans, LA.
25 Thomas, "New Orleans Church."

her boyfriend were sleeping.[26] As Anglim told the New Orleans *Times-Picayune*, "It was a defining moment for our congregation.... The whole church was there. It was like they were saying, 'This is *our* family. *Our* child.'"[27] Marguerite's funeral was on a Saturday. The next day, Beretta Smith-Shomade, department chair of the Tulane University communications department and a member at First Grace, approached Anglim after worship and said, "Pastor, I've been in this church a year. I only know nine people. I know *nine people* from my church." And she said, "We need to do something about this."

First Grace had put together a program called the Common Conversation, which had more or less run its course in about two years, a phenomenon not uncommon in small groups. Beretta's comment prompted Anglim to see that it was time to put together a new structure. He told Beretta and her husband, Salmon Shomade, a political science professor from Nigeria, "I'm calling this the Shomade Groups because that was where my inspiration came from." As it happened, the Nigerian name "Shomade" means "Are you coming?," so Beretta and Salmon were glad to give permission to use their last name. Anglim remembers, "And so, her coming up to me was her way of saying, 'I'm a part of the church and I realize this is my church.' The people need a place to connect." The essential thing was to create a doable form to accommodate the needs of First Grace's large number of parents. That meant a once-a-month commitment, and every member of First Grace was assigned to a group.[28] They continue to meet in 2015.

Hagar's House

Scholar Brenda Phillips observed, "Social problems, particularly those associated with gender, compound disaster consequences. We cannot afford to move emergency management forward without acknowledgment of and action on gender issues." She was referring to "thorny, entrenched issues" such as "housing, poverty, equity, accessibility, violence, child care, employment, health care, and more."[29]

In the fall of 2007, about a month before the planned closing of Tent City, an area in front of the New Orleans City Hall where hundreds of people were living, some personnel from another agency that advocated for homeless individuals came to First Grace to see whether the church might

26. Martin, "New Orleans Murder Victim."
27. Thomas, "New Orleans Church."
28. Shawn Anglim, interview by the author, June 25, 2013, New Orleans, LA.
29. Phillips, "Gendered Disaster Practice and Policy," 233–34.

be able to help. Since the 2008 Sugar Bowl was approaching, the city also wanted to clear out the hundreds of people who were living under the raised portions of I-10 alongside Claiborne Avenue. The issue of housing—or lack thereof—was also being brought to the forefront in the city by ongoing protests against the demolition of public housing.

Although homelessness affected a broad sweep of populations after the storm, women and children affected by domestic abuse had a special need for both advocacy and housing. Four of the young people living in community at First Grace decided to focus on that need, and they were involved in establishing Hagar's House which its website calls a "sanctuary for women and children . . . that provides an open and empowering residential community" and "a safe space to transition into sustainable housing." The four were Angela Davis, Sarah Fleming, Eric Gremillion, and Jenny Hammatt. Davis became the director of the facility that emerged from their vision when it opened in late November 2007.

Hagar's House is named for the woman whose story is told in Genesis 21. Hagar was the servant of Sarah, Abraham's wife. Sarah and Abraham were childless, and although the couple received a message from God that they would have a child despite their advanced age, the promised child did not appear. Taking matters into her own hands, Sarah offered Hagar to Abraham to bear a child which she, Sarah, would take as her own. Hagar gave birth to Ishmael, Abraham's first-born. Then, several years later, Sarah herself became pregnant and gave birth to Isaac. The Genesis writer depicts Sarah as consumed with jealousy on behalf of her own son and says she insisted that Abraham send Hagar and Ishmael away. The "father of the faith" does just that, not sending them somewhere else so he can provide for them there, but rather casting them out into the wilderness alone with just a skin of water and some bread. They were near death when they were divinely rescued. Thus, the name Hagar's House seems very appropriate, since the women and children who find refuge there were not properly valued by those around them, either.

In the fall of 2008, First Grace incorporated a 501(c)3 non-profit organization, First Grace Community Alliance, to operate Hagar's House. Its purposes include working "with and for people in need" through both mercy and justice-type ministries, providing "food, housing and other emergency needs, while simultaneously challenging systemic poverty" in the area. The Alliance's webpage describes Hagar's House itself as "a beautiful, clean, safe place to rest and call home." They see themselves as forming an "intentional community that is actively engaged in undoing the root causes of poverty." Holistic programming focuses "on physical health, emotional/

spiritual health and social justice," healthy food, and a space for planting in the community garden.

Residents are required to participate in a savings program that lets those who are employed save 70 percent of their income, with the goal of having accumulated $3,000 by the time they move. Davis says that the program is "a concrete piece" of their work. "It's mandatory. We're flexible, but not very flexible." It is always, she said, a struggle to help the women get jobs "that will let them pay rent and child care."[30]

Establishing a Legal Clinic

Another issue that is fast becoming more volatile is immigration. In New Orleans, where the percentage of Spanish-speaking residents increased perhaps tenfold after the storm, immigration is very much a justice issue. First Grace, and particularly staff member Angela Davis, have responded by establishing a legal clinic which focuses on assisting children and young people affected by immigration issues. This particular ministry of First Grace, along with other aspects of UMC ministry with Latino/as in the city, is addressed in Chapter 6.

The Gift of Diversity

As noted in the previous paragraph about the legal clinic and the earlier discussion about bilingual worship, the aspects of First Grace's ministries that primarily involve people who are Spanish speakers are a part of the next chapter. I made that decision in order to point out that the UMC's work with Latino/as needs to be considered as a whole. There are a number of people whose first language is Spanish who nevertheless attend the English service at First Grace, and the attempt to isolate which ministries are Latino-focused is not, in and of itself, helpful; yet the alternative, separating the work at First Grace from the work done in other locations around the city, is not intrinsically helpful either. I chose to combine these ministries in one chapter to provide a better opportunity to comment on the UMC's efforts overall. Despite this decision, it is important to remember that the discussion of race and ethnicity at First Grace is far more complex than "black and white." The Creole identity of the city is explored in Chapter 9, and even in apparently homogenous local congregations, there are layers of lineage which add to the richness of the culture.

30. Angela Davis, telephone interview by the author, November 19, 2013

"Homogenous" is in fact one of the more important words in this discussion, because the homogenous units principle has for decades been accepted as a hallmark of church growth strategy. "Church growth books have been written advocating the concept that bringing in people highly similar with regard to characteristics like race is the fastest way to grow congregations, that congregations using the principle run more efficiently, and that people in homogenous congregations find them more fulfilling."[31]

In his book on multiracial congregations, Michael Emerson went so far as to observe, "Multiracial congregations do not fit well into the dominant paradigm. In fact, they are violations of it, or at best, aberrations." He noted, "For some, multiracial congregations are a reminder of the older, outdated model of integration (read assimilation and control). For others such congregations simply are attempting to do the impossible. The reality . . . is more complex."

Emerson went on to argue, "These congregations may be harbingers of a new stage of US race relations."[32] I am intrigued with this idea because of my own experience in a cross-racial appointment. My first pastorate was at St. James UMC, an African American congregation in the deteriorating downtown section of Monroe, Louisiana. The local media was captivated by the idea that a white woman would serve there. Black-owned newspapers ran headlines that called me a "white pastor," making clear to me that my race was more newsworthy than my gender. A white television reporter interviewing me asked bluntly, "What makes you think this will work?" I replied,

> The members asked for me, because they knew me. I've worked with them for years in civic groups, like the Mayor's Commission on the Needs of Women, and in politics. They already know who I am. But it's sad that I'm saying we can be the church together because we know each other from politics and civic clubs. What I ought to be saying is, "We can work together in a civic group because we know each other from church."

Michael Emerson noted that when public institutions integrate, it does not necessarily follow that private institutions will do so, too. A religious congregation is "a *mediating institution* between the small private worlds of individuals and families and the large public worlds, such as politics, the educational system, and the economy."[33] He wondered whether racially

---

31. Emerson, *People of the Dream*, 3.
32. Ibid., 193.
33. Ibid., 5–6.

mixed congregations might therefore have specific things to reveal about larger issues of race and ethnicity or of religion in society.

> I find that multiracial congregations are atypical, more racially diverse than their neighborhoods, places of racial change, and filled with people who seem to flow across racial categories and divisions. They are filled with a different sort of American.
> ... and they may be harbingers of what is to come in US race relations.[34]

Bayou said she hopes, "First Grace's growing membership may set the stage for other religious and social institutions to actively seek community-based integration rather than condone *de facto* segregation."[35] She found that, "In the case of First Grace, belonging is not engendered by a homogeneous ethnic identity, but by a shared system of values and goals that are imbued with greater meaning in the particular context of post-Katrina New Orleans."[36] She noted that a worshipper in the First Grace sanctuary would find themselves not just among people of differing ethnicities but also among "people from the educated upper middle-class, homeless people, working class people, young adults, gay couples, middle class people, heavily tattooed people, children, and elderly people. People from all spheres and strata ... [reflect] the diversity of the city of New Orleans."

She wrote, "Equality and common humanity are at the forefront of First Grace's messages," and in fact, "At multiethnic First Grace, assertions of differential ethnic identities are deemphasized, as a common New Orleanian identity and shared values are emphasized."[37] Whether First Grace would remain racially mixed was a real question at first, as white flight is always an option. At first, the newly merged First Grace managed to attract only black members. Shawn Anglim reflected:

> From the time we merged until that first Easter, my memory is that the only people who joined the church were black people, and I find that fascinating. I don't know what that means but that's the way it went, and then a white woman, Paula Eagan, joined. And I thought, "I'll be darned. Some white people might join this church." And then all kinds of people started joining.
>
> [One] Sunday, eleven people joined the church. There was an African American couple, thirtyish, husband and wife, two little

34. Ibid., 193.
35. Bayou, "United for the City," 12.
36. Emerson and Woo, *People of the Dream*; Bayou, "United for the City," 34.
37. Bayou, "United for the City," 79, 81.

kids; two young African American lesbian women; a mother with her two children, a white child with blonde hair and one with a very dark skin; and a couple that you don't know if they're black and you don't know if they're white, you don't know if they're Hispanic. Like most of the world now, these young people just don't fit into any of those [categories], and you know that's our church right there. What other church are they going to join?[38]

He is right in his observation that the city itself has become more and more open to diversity. Marti and others talk about the tendency of creative people to "cluster" in cities that offer stimulation and openness to various lifestyles.[39] This is an excellent description of post-storm New Orleans, a city that was a magnet for people who wanted to be part of the recreation of a vibrant urban area.

The variety of people that join First Grace reflects the way in which Holy Spirit has prompted the congregation to expand its vision of diversity, particularly as concerns New Orleans's large gay/lesbian/bisexual/transgender population. Speaking to the church council, Anglim said,

> I believe in the power of relationships, and if you pay attention, God will give you the opportunity to be in relationships. That's how you grow. That's where you feel the tension, and the discomfort, and the gospel. I'm not happy with the answers I'm giving to gay and lesbian folks. I've had two different people ask me the same question—whether it's me who's open and affirming or the church that's open and affirming? They say they hear the way I preach and the way I invite people to communion, but they still have a question about the church. It got me thinking that we should talk about it.

First Grace's council, Anglim says, was "extremely affirming and said we should do this." They decided to hold open church conversations, hosting an all-church gathering on two Wednesday nights to discuss their status as an open and affirming church. On the Sunday morning when Anglim was to announce these gatherings, he came into the sanctuary later than he usually does because he had met with some small-group leaders.

> So, I wasn't in the sanctuary till five minutes before worship—thank God!—because what would I have done? Hopefully, not something stupid. But I walk in, and sitting in the front row of the choir is a transgender person who identifies female, looks

38. Shawn Anglim, interview by the author, June 25, 2013, New Orleans, LA.
39. Marti, *Worship across the Racial Divide*; Baker, *Hybrid Church in the City*.

very masculine, has a spectacular green dress on—I mean spectacular with cleavage down to here—a little bit of a scruffy beard, and a "Who Dat?" forehead tattoo.[40]

The assistant choir director came up to Anglim and said, "Did you know [name redacted] is sitting on the front row? What should I do about it?" Anglim replied, "Was [name] there at choir practice last Wednesday night?" The answer was affirmative, so [name] sang in the choir.

> And so, here we were, and here I was, making this announcement. It looked like it was a plant. There's no way this could have happened unless you planned it this way. So, there we went. We went forward, and you know, we're still alive.[41]

In fact, First Grace has adopted this affirmation which appears in its bulletin every week: "First Grace is an urban community of faith embracing all of God's children as persons of sacred worth, regardless of station in life, race, ethnicity, sexual orientation, or gender identity. We invite and welcome all persons to join us as disciples who believe in the transforming love of God revealed in Jesus Christ from which nothing can separate us."[42]

Reflecting on the Emergence of First Grace

It was July 23, 2012, a Monday. Because it was midsummer in the subtropics, there was still plenty of natural light to shoot a video at 6:30 pm. That was fortunate, because there was no electricity to power artificial lights, and Eric Gremillion's only equipment was a handheld video camera.

His footage shows Shawn Anglim standing in front of the altar area in the sanctuary of the former Grace UMC. Anglim wore black pants, a long-sleeved white shirt, and a striped tie, and a white stole hung around his neck.

He stood on the red carpeting that was still in place almost seven years after the storm. Behind him were an ornately carved communion table, reredos, and pulpit. Huge splotches of mold were visible on the wall. High up, a round stained-glass window depicted Jesus wearing a crown of thorns. To the window's right, there was a huge, gaping hole in the wall.

---

40. "Who Dat?" is a slogan associated with the local professional football team, the Saints; it originated in a song written years ago, "Who Dat Say They Gonna Beat Dem Saints?"

41. Shawn Anglim, interview by the author, June 25, 2013, New Orleans, LA.

42. Statement of Affirmation adopted by First Grace UMC which now appears in the Sunday bulletin each week.

The pews were not packed but comfortably full. Everyone was fanning themselves with their bulletins to circulate the air. The odor isn't conveyed on the video, but the room must have smelled somewhere between musty and horrible. The front door was left open, both for light and also, no doubt, in hopes of getting a breeze.

The people followed along in the liturgy, participating in the prayers. They sang "I've Come This Far by Faith" without accompaniment and with a leader lining out the words for them. Several people from the Grace congregation spoke about their memories of the church. One woman was dressed in a white suit and a hat, but most people were casually dressed, perhaps for some as a concession to the heat.

A small, elderly African American woman sitting on the back pew got up, with someone on either side assisting her so she could remain standing without the aid of her walker, which had had to be left outside her pew. Her voice, though, was strong, and it was clear she thought that what she had to say was worth the effort of rising.

"This church was my life," she said. "I spent more time here than I did at home. But I thank God for enabling us to be united with a new family that's so precious."[43]

Reflecting on the successful family that First Grace has become, Anglim said,

> Sometimes, even if we do want to go back to Egypt, we honor what we did in faith, which was to form a new life, and that means to move forward in love, even while we know there's going to be tension and difficulty. You don't always know what needs to happen, but you know that you need to be creative enough and bold enough to keep trying.[44]

---

43. Eric Gremillion provided me with a copy of the raw video footage he shot at the decommissioning of Grace UMC, July 23, 2012.

44. Shawn Anglim, interview by the author, June 25, 2013, New Orleans, LA.

6

"Specialized Focus" Ministries

In a sense, 30 percent of the population is invisible.
—Ralph Ford

For Latinos, it became impossible to live a normal life in St. Bernard Parish.
—Oscar Ramos-Gallardo

When the Mission Zones were created, a number of congregations in the city were not included in any of them. Seven of these were the station churches which were designated as "stand-alone" ministries. Two of them were deemed "Specialized Focus" ministries. These were El Mesias and the Korean UMCs. Their stories are included here.

Since the storm, there have been other significant ministries with Latino/a people established. Those are a major focus of this chapter.

Latino/a Ministry

The huge influx of construction workers from Mexico and Central America after the storm changed the ethnic makeup of the recovering city dramatically, and it was not a change the church was prepared to deal with effectively. The route required to establish Hispanic ministry in mid-city New Orleans was long and circuitous, and the future of the work is in doubt as I write. Nevertheless, some prophetic work has been accomplished in a place where much is needed. On the way, a ministry in Kenner took root, along with multicultural work in Gretna.

This chapter will sketch out some of the church's successes and failures in providing hospitality to Latino/as in New Orleans. The ministry that began in the late 1990s at El Mesias UMC, located near the intersection of West Esplanade Avenue and Loyola Drive in Kenner, is briefly discussed, along with its much more recent merger with First UMC in Kenner. The new church is known as 1Love UMC.

Post-Katrina, two additional missionaries were assigned to the city. Oscar Ramos-Gallardo works at First Grace UMC, the church described at length in the previous chapter. Juanita Arrieta Ramos was based for a time at Covenant UMC in Chalmette in St. Bernard Parish but has more recently begun to develop ministry at Gretna UMC, on the West Bank of the Mississippi River in Jefferson Parish.

Ten years out, as construction has slowed, the welcome foreign workers experienced has ebbed, and the US Immigration and Customs Enforcement agency (ICE) and local authorities are actively engaged in deporting undocumented workers. The church's response to a new wave of deportations has included the establishment of a legal clinic affiliated with First Grace. However, the withdrawal of support in 2015 for the missionaries who are serving in the city leaves the status of other kinds of ministry with Latino/as in serious doubt.

How UMC Ministry with Latinos in New Orleans Began

In March 2006, one of my students asked Bishop Bill Hutchinson how to prepare for ministry in the future. He responded with two words: "Learn Spanish."

In January 2007, then District Superintendent Ralph Ford said it was estimated that the Hispanic population of the city had risen from 3 percent to as much as 30 percent since 2005, in large part because of the demand for construction workers. Contractors often exploited Hispanic workers. Available laborers would gather at certain locations, like home improvement stores. Sometimes contractors would hire workers there on Monday morning, promising that if they worked all week, they would be paid on Friday, but when Friday came, the men who did the hiring were nowhere to be found. Others would promise workers twenty dollars per hour, but when payday arrived, they'd pay only five. Undocumented workers felt they had no recourse.

Ford told my students that there was an extreme need for Hispanic pastors in the city. To those who think Latin America is still monolithically

"Specialized Focus" Ministries

Catholic, this might sound like a plea for priests. In fact, Honduras and Guatemala have more evangelical Protestants than actively practicing Roman Catholics now. Other countries in Central America such as Guatemala are seeing substantial rises in Protestantism, as well. Latino immigrants in New Orleans come primarily from Honduras, with people from Nicaragua, Guatemala, and Mexico running second, third and fourth.[1]

There were occasions in the late twentieth century when the UMC recognized a need for Spanish-speaking ministers. In the late 1990s, I was serving a congregation in Greater New Orleans when the General Board of Global Ministries (GBGM) sent a missionary to the city. Maribel Mojica-Molina was a native of Puerto Rico who had been serving in Brazil, focusing particularly on ministry with women there. Information that circulated among pastors in the district was that she had been sent to the city to do ministry with a growing Latino population in mid-city, specifically from the underused First UMC building on Canal Street. Then, information circulated that First UMC had pulled out of the agreement at the last moment.

She wound up working instead at Messiah UMC, a small Anglo congregation in the suburb of Kenner that decided it could share its unusually small building with a Latino congregation. Messiah UMC eventually dwindled away, and the Latino/a congregation, called El Mesias, wound up with the building. El Mesias was served by Rev. Samuel Calvo, who had been a high-ranking official in the Methodist Church in Costa Rica. He and his wife moved to New Orleans because their son, Esteban, a chemist, lived there. Eventually, Esteban and Maribel fell in love, married, and had a child. When Esteban accepted a position in Arizona a few years ago, Sam retired, and the entire family moved there. Sam has since died.

In the fifteen or so years they spent in New Orleans, Sam Calvo and Maribel Mojica-Calvo worked constantly to serve Spanish-speaking people who needed not just a place for worship and Bible study, but also instruction in English, help with applications for citizenship, and advocacy against deportation. The tasks were overwhelming, but no other personnel were sent to help them until after Katrina.

Creating 1Love

In mid-2013, after Sam Calvo and Maribel Mojica-Calvo moved to Arizona, the congregation at El Mesias began worshipping with the people at First

---

1. Oscar Ramos-Gallardo, interview by the author, August 12, 2014, New Orleans, LA.

UMC in Kenner. In time, they decided to merge and form a new congregation and chose the name 1Love UMC for it.

Kenner First UMC

Kenner FUMC was established in the mid-twentieth century. According to Tracy MacKenzie, the leader of the Mission Zone that included Kenner FUMC, "In the early seventies, Kenner had the highest attendance in Sunday school in the New Orleans district. They averaged more than 500. They have more than 10,000 square feet in educational space."[2]

One of the storm centers the conference established was housed at Kenner UMC. "About a third of the volunteers who came through stayed in the Kenner facility during the time I was there. In those two years, 2006–2008, there were about 46,000 volunteers in the city and around 15,000 stayed at Kenner." Every team that came in paid a fee to the church. "I kept pushing them to realize, 'These folks will leave and you won't have that income.' They could not have afforded a full-time ordained elder if they had been autonomous from the Mission Zone program which was funding all of my salary at that time."

After she had been there a year, she gave a "state of the church" report and told them, "If you continue on the course you're on, you can merge your church or close." MacKenzie says she is always "big on current reality. I see a blonde bombshell in the mirror, but reality may be a little different. And I told them that when I left, I didn't want to hear, 'Oh, Lord, we had no idea.'"

The population of Kenner in the area where Kenner First is located had become about 30 percent Latino. Even before the storm, the church had made some attempts at hosting English as a Second Language (ESL) courses, with some success. Nevertheless, the suggestion of merger caused much controversy at Kenner, MacKenzie said, and it took several more years before it happened.[3]

El Mesias UMC

When the Mission Zones were created, El Mesias was not included in any of them, nor was it deemed a Station Church. It and the Korean UMC were considered "Specialized Focus" congregations, and each operated on its own.

---

2. Tracy MacKenzie, telephone interview with the author, October 28, 2013.
3. Ibid.

El Mesias operated in one of the smallest UMC church buildings in the city, located about five miles from Kenner FUMC. After the storm, while the Calvos were still there, the ministry remained essentially the same, except that the huge influx of Spanish speakers increased the needs and problems tremendously. The space at Kenner FUMC would obviously be of benefit to the membership, but there was a lot of hesitancy among the El Mesias congregation about picking up and moving into a largely Anglo membership church.

Beth Love Tu'uta was appointed as the pastor at Kenner FUMC. She was in some ways an excellent choice to pastor the churches toward merger; she is married to a man from Tonga and deeply and genuinely appreciates the gift that intercultural experience brings. However, she spoke no Spanish at the time El Mesias began to worship with Kenner. In order to address this lack, she went to Costa Rica for an immersion course in 2014 and is said to be doing very well at picking up the language.

Tu'uta said that El Mesias and FUMC began meeting together on June 1, 2013 to vision together about becoming a multi-cultural, multi-lingual congregation. "Then, in May [2014], we approved and submitted an official resolution to merge with the purpose of creating just that." The conference approved. Tu'uta wrote an announcement to explain the merger:

> El Mesias will be officially closed by the conference, followed by legal closure, and we will be one congregation. I intend to push for some sort of acknowledgment that FUMC is also no longer existing.

It was important to her that no members of El Mesias feel that they had simply been absorbed into First Church.

> It's a delicate, sensitive journey. The conference has never done anything quite like this, with all of the intricacies we have, so it has not exactly been a smooth journey.[4]

1Love

To help clarify the nature of the merger, the merged body chose a new name which was different from either of the former congregations' names. In a meeting with folks who would be affiliated with the new church, Tu'uta asked for ideas, and a child who was there suggested "Love." The pastor was

---

4. Beth Love Tu'uta, Facebook message to the author, September 4, 2014.

uncomfortable with that at first, because her birth name was "Love," but finally accepted that it was the right thing to do.[5]

I attended worship at 1Love one Sunday, and a layman from El Mesias interpreted the sermon, prayers, and other worship elements into Spanish or English, as needed. It went quite smoothly. One thing Maribel Mojica-Calvo was particularly good at was developing lay leadership within the congregation. It was in part a necessity because of the overwhelming number of needs which the ministry professionals had to address, but it was also a part of her theological approach to ministry to see that laypeople had as much training and as many opportunities for growth in leadership as possible.

The interior and spiritual strength of the Latino members of 1Love will play a pivotal role in whether the new church flourishes in a place where white privilege still dominates the local culture. It is an important moment of growth that Katrina helped to enable.

Two New Missionaries Begin Ministries in the City

In response to the need that Ford and others articulated, the General Board of Global Ministries sent two additional Spanish-speaking missionaries to New Orleans in 2007. They are a married couple who have two children.

Oscar Ramos-Gallardo was born in Tamiahua, Mexico. He studied in Monterrey at Juan Wesley Seminario, and then earned an MDiv from Garrett Evangelical Theological Seminary in Evanston, Illinois. He received a DMin from Drew University, specializing in Hispanic/Latino leadership. He is an ordained elder in the Indiana annual conference. He pastored for seven years and then served as coordinator for Hispanic/Latino ministries for six years in what was formerly the North Indiana conference.[6]

Juanita Arrieta Ramos is a native of Monterrey, Mexico. Like Oscar, she studied at Juan Wesley Seminario in Monterrey and then earned an MDiv from Garrett Evangelical Seminary. In 1997, she was ordained an elder in North Indiana, and she served in pastorates in that conference for thirteen years.[7]

As GBGM missionaries, both of them work with *La Semilla*: Hispanic/Latino Center for Educational Development, which is a non-profit organization that "seeks to increase the number of Hispanics/Latinos in college, increase the number with English-language proficiency, create a culture

---

5. Beth Love Tu'uta, interview by author and students, January 9, 2015, Kenner, LA.

6. "Oscar Ramos," Missionary Profiles, UMC General Board of Global Ministries.

7. "Juanita Arrieta Ramos," Missionary Profiles, UMC General Board of Global Ministries.

favorable to education in the community, and help families navigate the US educational system."[8] They prepare students for GED exams. On class nights, volunteers help people prepare applications for universities. "It's an eternal fight to get parents to understand the need for their children to continue their studies," Oscar Ramos said. *La Semilla* has provided education about and engaged in advocacy for the Dream Act, legislation that would allow a path to citizenship for students brought here as children.

La Semilla has been housed at First Grace UMC, the subject of the previous chapter. Worship in Spanish is also held at First Grace; that congregation, called *La Gracia* and led by Oscar Ramos, is discussed later in this chapter.

From St. Bernard to Gretna

One of the question marks on the 2013 map (Figure 2) is the location in Arabi that was one-half of Covenant UMC, a church formed in 1995 when St. Bernard UMC in Chalmette and the UMC in Arabi merged and took the name Covenant. However, Covenant continued to operate and hold services in both locations. The Arabi church was founded in the late 1930s, and St. Bernard UMC began in the early 1950s.

The location in Arabi was used to house volunteers after the storm, but by 2013 it was no longer needed for that. They explored converting it to a day care facility, which would have been a help to the congregation and the community, but the cost of modifications required to meet regulations for child care facilities were prohibitive. Instead, it is going to reopen as a church, pastor Jeff Duke said. He plans to center the church's outreach on the arts and to move toward its use as a performance space.

Attendance at the Chalmette location is "picking up a little bit," Duke said. "Our goal was to average forty in worship this year, and we're going to do that." The structure sustained damage during Hurricane Isaac in August 2012. More damage occurred when "a candle was left burning on the altar, and it burned the top of the altar and the carpet around it, and there was smoke and soot damage." Altogether, the costs from the fire amounted to $76,000, "and that's been repaired," Duke said. They also had to redo and repaint the north wall after windows leaked and mold formed on it. "So physically, it looks pretty good."

---

8. "Oscar Ramos," Missionary Profiles, UMC General Board of Global Ministries; "Juanita Arrieta Ramos," Missionary Profiles, UMC General Board of Global Ministries.

In 2007, the church was chosen as a site for Spanish-language worship, and Juanita Ramos began leading services on Sunday evenings. Duke said that because of Oscar's enthusiasm for ministry at First Grace in mid-city, Juanita's focus had also been drawn in that direction. Spanish services are no longer being conducted at Covenant. "It's been effectively killed," Duke said.[9]

However, the lack of hospitality in the larger community must be considered, too. In 1960, St. Bernard Parish opened its schools without any residency requirement to white children whose parents removed them from the first two integrated elementary schools in New Orleans. This allowed white parents who could not afford Catholic school a free alternative, and prevented integration from truly succeeding that year. It was a deliberate decision on the part of parish leaders.

Then, after Katrina, the parish's "blood relative" law made national news. The parish enacted an ordinance which said that no one could rent or loan their property to anyone who was not a blood relative unless they obtained a permit. The parish also imposed a moratorium on reopening any apartment complexes or developing any multifamily dwellings. This was widely seen as an attempt to keep African Americans and others of ethnic minority descent out of St. Bernard. Parish officials insisted that they were just trying to maintain the "single-family character" of parish housing and that there was nothing racist about the policy. Lawsuits were filed alleging discriminatory housing practices, and eventually the parish had to pay millions in fines and attorney's fees for the plaintiffs.[10]

Oscar Ramos said that until 2013, Juanita and he had worked hard to connect to the church in Chalmette, but continued to feel "like an appendix." He said that ICE and the local police had arrested so many people that "For Latinos, it became impossible to live a normal life in St. Bernard Parish." The people of First Grace protested on more than one occasion the arrests of members of the congregation. Finally, the language classes offered by the ministry began to feel like a dangerous place for undocumented individuals.[11]

For these and other reasons, the decision was made to move the focus of the work to Gretna, a suburb on the west bank of the Mississippi River. There, eighty to ninety students enrolled in English as a Second Language (ESL) classes, and Juanita also teaches Spanish. Ramos showed me a photo

9. Jeff Duke, telephone conversation with the author, December 11, 2013.

10. Alexander-Bloch, "St. Bernard Multifamily-Housing Battle"; Alexander-Bloch, "In Post-Katrina Housing."

11. Oscar Ramos-Gallardo, interview by the author, August 12, 2014, New Orleans, LA.

of a group of fourteen young people who appeared to be middle-school aged who are part of the ministry.

During the years that Tim Smith was appointed as senior pastor at Gretna UMC, he put emphasis on working to establish multicultural ministry there. He had some success with his endeavors. As Ramos put it, when people begin to have multicultural encounters, "they get addicted to it." When Smith was later appointed to Munholland UMC in Metairie, an African American pastor, Bertrand Griffin II, replaced him as senior pastor at Gretna. There is a steering committee of six or seven laypeople which includes Latinos and African-Americans; they are leading the congregation to do meaningful multicultural work. "It's God's idea," Ramos said, "and it's something we should work toward."

La Gracia—Ministry at First Grace UMC

The story of the First Grace merger was recounted in the previous chapter. Opening itself to the Latino community has proven to be tougher for First Grace on some levels than the Anglo/African-American work, but fortunately there has been strong leadership and commitment, particularly from Oscar Ramos.

Shawn Anglim, First Grace's senior pastor, said, "Oscar has done a really incredible, important work, and as far as I can see it's endless. It's difficult to figure out because in part it's missional, and there are a lot of people with immediate needs." First Grace offers language classes two nights a week, teaching both English and Spanish, though far fewer study Spanish. The English classes "are packed," with sixty to eighty students a semester. "People want to learn English. It is very clear."

Both Tulane and Loyola Universities are involved, sending students to help. "They are a group of dedicated teachers," Anglim said. "They just love it. They've been doing it for years now." *La Semilla* volunteers also attend those evenings to help high school students with college applications. "They are here just to help young folks figure out that path."

First Grace's growing pains came when Ramos came to Anglim and said he wanted to start another worship service. Anglim remembers, "I was against it but I knew we needed to do it. He said, 'Look, I have so many people that don't speak English.'" Although they were about to make the decision to have a bilingual service every Sunday, Ramos convinced him that there were Spanish speakers who would never come to that service.

Ramos decided to hold this new service, *La Gracia,* on Sundays at 2 pm, a time that Anglim was skeptical about. Despite Ramos's faithfulness to this service, "it never really went anywhere. Some Sundays, twenty to thirty people would show up, but having only about ten was more common." They decided to move the service to Sunday mornings, concurrent with the other service.

The Spanish-speaking congregation meets in the chapel, and Ramos said they average about sixty in attendance. Music is provided by a praise team whose members are writing bilingual music for worship.

Anglim noted, "So, now, there's the Spanish service and the English service at the same time, and [both are] First Grace. Does it feel sad that people don't know each other? Yes, but I also know that in a year or so, First Grace is going to start a third worship service. And those 9 o'clock people are going to feel like they don't know the 11 o'clock people. Everybody has different ways that they think that you solve that."

Since they have found bilingual worship impractical, the goal at present is for the two groups to blend in other ways, such as having meals and language study together. Spanish is the first language of three of his trustees, he says. "You do need to keep working at this relationship. We had magical bilingual worship services and then they became not so magical. I don't know why that happened. I just know it did. . . . You have to figure out how to be one body. You keep figuring out the way forward. The commitment is to keep figuring it out."[12]

Justice for Our Neighbors

One historian recently wrote, "Latinos have contributed both directly and indirectly to New Orleans's social, cultural, political, and commercial development. . . . Following the storm, however, Latino/Hispanic migrants have experienced significant scrutiny and outright hostility." Worksites are no longer the only places where challenges abound; problems "have expanded to the communities and homes where they live. For instance, recent research finds Hondurans are deported at rates that exceed their representation among undocumented immigrants."[13]

In response to having a number of their own members arrested and deported, First Grace has conducted protests and demonstrations. More than fifteen of their members have already been deported, according to Oscar Ramos. "I deal daily with families that have been broken because of a broken system."[14]

12. Shawn Anglim, interview by the author, June 25, 2013, New Orleans, LA.
13. Trujillo-Pagan, "Recovering Latinos' Place."
14. Lawton, "New Orleans Church."

Angela Davis, former director of Hagar's House, spent several years establishing a local office of Justice for Our Neighbors (JFON), a UMC ministry dealing with immigration, which opened in September 2014 under the auspices of First Grace. A group of attorneys volunteer to handle approximately one case a year that deals with juvenile immigration rights.

In preparation for this work, Davis, a graduate of Loyola Law School, took leave from Hagar's House, and went to Chile to work in a legal clinic there and perfect her Spanish. Anglim says,

> Much of that ministry will probably be to children who are in situations of being citizens but their parents get deported or they're not citizens. . . . Loyola is very interested in a place like that being formed.

Davis herself says,

> There are few places in New Orleans where children and their families can receive health care, food, housing and legal resources all in one spot. With the opening of the legal clinic, First Grace will provide a place.[15]

On December 11, 2013, the church held a press conference and demonstration on the front steps to protest the deportation of two of its members. The press release read,

> First Grace Church has become known throughout the country as one of the most racially and economically-diverse religious congregations in the South. A post-Katrina merger of two predominantly white and black churches, the church also has a growing Spanish-speaking membership. "Our diversity now has brought our church community face to face with an intolerable form of injustice, one that is a daily reality for thousands of our brothers and sisters," Anglim said.[16]

News coverage indicates that about sixty members of the congregation attended the press conference and demonstration.

An Uncertain Future as Resources Are Withdrawn

The National Hispanic/Latino Plan developed by the UMC calls for each conference to have a coordinator. Oscar served in that position in North

---

15. Backstrom, "Church Ministries."

16. Hagar's House, "Please join us this Wednesday," Facebook post, December 9, 2013.

Indiana for seven years. He had hoped to serve in that capacity in Louisiana, "but the Louisiana conference did not have the same idea."

Bishop Cynthia Fierro Harvey herself is a Latina, and there were hopes that she would be especially supportive of Hispanic ministry. However, Ramos says that she changed what had previously been three-year contracts between the conference and GBGM to one-year contracts. In 2013, Ramos was informed that after one year, the contract would not be renewed. He says that many people in New Orleans wrote to ask that the decision be reversed, and they were given a reprieve of one year. However, June 30, 2015 would be the end of support from the conference. He sees the letters that added a year to their tenure as a gift—"the voice of God is the voice of the people"—but knew that the tactic would not succeed again. In 2015, Ramos presented a plan to Harvey to become a coordinator for the state, but in the end, it was not accepted.

Yet, he said, "We are called by God, not the bishop. Our ministry is here. There are lots of needs in the city." Furthermore, Oscar and Juanita bought a house in New Orleans. Another factor that continues to impact the family is that Juanita was diagnosed with cancer and has had to undergo extended treatment. She is still in treatment with three doctors in the city.

There are sixteen to eighteen agencies with whom the church has been working, and Oscar Ramos hopes that one of those will be able to provide secular employment for him. It continues to be his goal "not just to receive, but to produce theology" through sermons at *La Gracia* and through relationships with the people with whom he is involved.

This decision on the part of the Louisiana conference to lessen support is by no means unique. It is the common experience everywhere that Latino congregations have difficulty becoming self-supporting, and many conference officials are therefore often lukewarm in their support. Due to membership decline and overall budgetary pressure, the idea that the primary support for Latino ministry must come from local congregations who are committed to the ministry is gaining wide acceptance and being put into practice across the UMC. But no matter how the work in mid-city progresses, the situation has the feel of an opportunity partly seized and partly lost.

On June 26, 2015, Oscar Ramos-Gallardo made a public post on his Facebook page. It was in Spanish, and this is my own translation:

> This Sunday, June 28, 2015, is our last Sunday as missionaries of the General Board of Global Ministries assigned to the Louisiana conference of the United Methodist Church. This does not mean that we are leaving New Orleans, or that we want to leave La Gracia and La Semilla. It does mean that we will not receive a salary and that we will seek a job outside of the church in order

to continue to attend to those ministries. We decided to remain in the city for several reasons; two stand out as most important. The first is to continue cancer treatment for my wife, Juanita. The second is to continue leading the ministries of La Gracia and La Semilla which have not yet reached the maturity we would want. We ask for your prayers and your help. We appreciate the GBGM and the Methodist Church and will maintain our connection with the church. We hope in God and in God's grace and love. People of New Orleans, we will see you Sunday at 10 and at 11 am to praise our eternal Creator and Sustainer of life.[17]

Korean UMC

Members at one of the churches I pastored in Greater New Orleans in the late 1990s told me that the local Korean UMC congregation had approached them about renting space in their building. They never articulated the reason they refused, but I knew from my seminary studies with Dr. David Maldonado that the potential for problems in such arrangements is extremely high, even if both congregations seem committed to the idea. One of the case studies I wrote for *Attentive to God* centers on a regional executive's dilemma when an Anglo congregation decides to share its church with a congregation of another ethnicity but then wishes it hadn't.[18] Such an arrangement can work, but more often than not, it doesn't, and it can leave smoldering resentment when it falls apart.

The Korean congregation wound up meeting at Rayne UMC, almost ten miles away from the church that they wanted to rent. The storm damage to Rayne (see Chapter 7) ended that arrangement, because the much larger Rayne congregation was unable to worship in its sanctuary and needed space that had been used by the Korean church.

Although I attended worship at the Korean church and visited the pastor, there was little communication, as I speak no Korean. Fortunately, one student who took my Katrina class is a Korean American, and while the rest of us attended an African American congregation's service, Samuel Lee worshipped with the Korean congregation. It was held in their new building in Metairie, a major suburb immediately west of New Orleans. He reported that afternoon what he had learned.

The Korean congregation, he said, was in better shape as a congregation (not as individuals) than it had been before the storm. Congregants told him that Korean-American United Methodists from around the

---

17. Oscar Ramos-Gallardo, public Facebook post, June 26, 2015.
18. Wood and Blue, *Attentive to God*, 99–102.

country quickly sent funds to the New Orleans church to help them recover. Local members placed a high priority on procuring adequate space for their church right away, in many cases devoting more resources to that goal than they did to their own living situations. They were able to purchase a former Lions Club building located less than a quarter-mile from the congregation that had decided not to share its space with them. The Lions Club building was larger and offered better space for a worshiping congregation and for their children's Christian education program.

When I attended worship there a couple of years later, the building seemed very suitable for the group. A former meeting room had been transformed into a peaceful sanctuary with plenty of space for those gathered. The kitchen worked well for preparing a meal after worship, and there was enough seating space for eating. There was office space, educational space, and an adequate parking lot. Although the structure had not been designed for a congregation, it converted beautifully to the purpose.

It would be a grave mistake to disregard the personal trauma Katrina brought to everyone in the area, including members of the Korean UMC, and the disturbance that change of any sort, even for the better, brings to a group. Considering only the physical surroundings provides a very limited standpoint. Nevertheless, the financial assistance the Katrina event brought forth enabled this group to quickly obtain an excellent, permanent space of its own only one block away from where they wanted to be. It was the members' willingness to prioritize the needs of the group over their own, as well as the commitment of Korean Americans elsewhere to help them, that contributed to this.

Other Entities

Children's Home

It was not a congregation *per se*, but the Methodist Children's Home in New Orleans was an important ministry offered by the UMC. Pre-Katrina, the Louisiana conference had two children's homes, one in the small north Louisiana town of Ruston and the other in New Orleans. The New Orleans location on Washington Avenue was founded near the end of World War I to care for unmarried, pregnant women. As society changed, the Methodist Home Hospital transitioned to a facility for orphaned and later abused or delinquent children and youth.

The neighborhood around the Children's Home in New Orleans became very dangerous in the late twentieth century, with many murders and shootings near the building. The possibility of moving was raised; some

UMC leaders approved while others felt it would be an abandonment of the city's residents.

When Katrina approached, children in residence were evacuated to the Ruston home. When it became clear that they could not return, arrangements were made to care for them there. Ruston is approximately five hours away which complicated many aspects of the work.

The New Orleans home never reopened. In 2008, its replacement was opened in Mandeville, north of Lake Pontchartrain. That is considered a temporary home while land is being sought, also on the North Shore, for a facility that will be called The Methodist Children's Home of Greater New Orleans.[19]

Some United Methodists believe the home's decision to leave the city, working a hardship on the families who would visit or participate in counseling, was a mistake. They see it as a lack of commitment to the recovery of the city. Other United Methodists think that moving the home to the North Shore was an excellent step, because the children are removed from the urban pressures that may have played into their and their families' problems. There are still shootings and dangers in the former home's neighborhood, so they are probably safer in the new residence. Whether the work will be more or less effective remains to be seen.

United Methodist Women

There are entities besides congregations impacted by the flood. The United Methodist Women's organization (UMW), accomplishes much justice work in the United States and across the world. According to June Sanchez, a member at Hartzell in the Lower Ninth Ward and a former district president, "UMW never did stop" as a result of Katrina. When they held the first district-wide meeting after the storm, she was there. "They were surprised to see me," she admitted, "because everything was still in disarray. But we found strength in each other and in UMW."[20]

The UMW organization is completely outside the structure of the United Methodist annual conferences, and thus does not fit into this particular project.[21] Nevertheless, the women's work is a redemptive part of the UMC's identity.

---

19. In 2010, a new facility opened in southwest Louisiana which is an addition to the network, not the replacement for the New Orleans home.

20. June Sanchez, interview by the author, March 18, 2009, New Orleans, LA.

21. Blue, "Women of the United Methodist Church." This material was also published in 2009 under the title, "Spiritual Mothers and Midwives," on the Newcomb College Center for Research on Women website as part of a collection of White Papers; however, that set of documents is no longer hosted there.

7

Four Congregations Partner in Ministry

What is the most wicked problem? In Tremé, people are saying, "Don't let our culture die." But in Central City, people are saying, "Stop the killing." You don't ask them to come to a workshop, give them a folder, and send them home.
— Pat Evans[1]

This chapter examines the work of four individual congregations that have become interlocked in new ministry undertakings since the storm. They have worked together in creative ways to meet the needs of the people of New Orleans. These partnerings were not as thoroughly improbable as the First Grace merger, but it is true that the cooperative work, configured as it is today, would have been unlikely to happen before the storm.

Brief profiles of each of the congregations are followed by a consideration of some of their cooperative ministries. These include the free clinic called Luke's House; a ministry with individuals who are homeless called Open Table; the Crescent City Café; and the award-winning Apex Youth Center.

All address problems that seem to be unfixable. Even in normal circumstances, those who believe God is calling them to be in ministry with their communities can be overwhelmed by the number and severity of the problems the communities face. Surely almost everyone has thought at some time or another, "What can one person do?" A single congregation faced with problems of its own may doubt that it is able to make any real difference in society.

Katrina changed this perspective. Amid such massive devastation, it was obvious that every single person's small contribution toward the

---

1. Pat Evans, interview by the author, February 13, 2009, Metairie, LA.

recovery work would have to be joined with the small contributions of hundreds of thousands of others if there was to be any real progress. This clear necessity for combining efforts led to a willingness to cooperate with others that was simply not present before the storm. Decisions about how it would be possible to do that were based in part on the kinds of damages these congregations' facilities had sustained and how they needed to use their available spaces as a result.

Four Cooperating Congregations

Three UMC churches—Rayne Memorial, Parker Memorial, and Mt. Zion—began partnering in significant ways soon after the storm, and later People's UMC and People's Community Center became part of the interconnected ministries. Going from Parker to Rayne to Mt. Zion is a drive of just 3.1 miles. Another 1.1 miles brings you to People's.

Another way of saying it is that a journey from Parker to People's takes you from one world to another. Parker sits on Nashville Avenue in a posh section of Uptown; Rayne occupies some of the most expensive real estate in New Orleans on St. Charles Avenue; Mt. Zion is on Louisiana Avenue near Claiborne Avenue in a more deteriorated neighborhood; and People's is on Simon Bolivar at Jackson Ave. in what is perhaps the poorest and what is certainly the most dangerous section of town, Central City. With the exception of Rayne and Parker, these churches had little or no cooperative ministry before the storm.

Of the four, two (Mt. Zion and People's) are primarily African-American congregations and two (Rayne and Parker) are primarily Anglo. At one time, the Rayne and Parker congregations probably had much in common, but over the decades, Rayne has retained its strength while Parker's numbers diminished dramatically. Mt. Zion was long considered by many (though some would argue) to have the city's "premier" African-American UMC congregation, while the location of People's in the troubled Central City area made for a quite different context.

Rayne and Parker were established as Methodist Episcopal Church, South (MECS) congregations, while Mt. Zion and People's began as churches affiliated with the Methodist Episcopal Church (MEC). As explained in Chapter 2, these were two separate denominations between 1845 and 1939. Even after the 1939 merger, African-American congregations were segregated in the Central Jurisdiction; occasional cooperation between women's organizations was the only encounter most Methodists ever had across jurisdictions. By 1972, when the segregated Louisiana conferences were united, there was a long established pattern of non-involvement.

In short, in 2005, there was little overlap among the four churches. Their assets differed in amount and kind, and they faced different problems. The risks involved in simply walking into the building for night meetings or on Sunday mornings were unalike, and the kinds of worship members encountered inside varied dramatically, as well.

Rayne Memorial

The strongest of these churches, both before and immediately after the storm, was Rayne Memorial UMC. Its building stands at 3900 St. Charles Avenue. Built in 1875, the church is on the streetcar line and therefore easily reached via public transportation.

Rayne Memorial UMC is blessed with an exceptionally gifted senior pastor, Carol "Callie" Winn Crawford, who has served there for twelve years. The primarily Anglo congregation has an average of about 400 in worship each week. There are around 1,200 members on the rolls, a good number of whom are still in the Katrina diaspora. Because Rayne is on the high ground along St. Charles, it did not flood, and neither did its wonderful parsonage, which is located just behind the church. For these reasons, Crawford was able to return to the city early on.

Crawford's preaching ability is superb, and she is deeply committed to caring for her parishioners. Her father is a native of New Orleans, and she has a strong sense of connection to the city. Her passion for helping New Orleanians and the city recover was unsurpassed. She endured months on end of the "Katrina cough" that afflicted many of those who came back early, and she resisted all attempts to get her to take some time off.

This last remark reflects not just admiration but also an acknowledgement of a problem among all the clergy appointed in the city. The only way to get any break from the stress was to leave town, and although several pastors in north Louisiana volunteered to come south to give pastors there a few weeks off, none of the south Louisiana pastors would take advantage of the offer. The bishop used the term "co-dependent," *not* specifically for Crawford, but for every pastor who served in the city after the storm. Even in Oklahoma, I felt driven to be doing something worthwhile, not just most of the time, but every waking moment.

Crawford's stress was compounded by the fact that its high ground and lack of flooding did not save Rayne's church building from serious damage. Wind blew the steeple off the roof and onto the front yard and circle driveway, causing so much destruction that they could not use the sanctuary for worship for several years.

Rayne had traditionally kept a light burning in its steeple and understood that light to be part of its identity. When the steeple was rededicated in August 2008, Crawford did the children's sermon, using the old children's rhyme that is accompanied by finger motions: "Here is the church, here is the steeple, open the doors, and here are the people." She made the point that while the steeple had been under repair, Rayne members had learned not only the truth of the adage that "the church is the people," but also the Rayne-specific lesson that "the light is the people."

The segment of the liturgy specific to the rededication included the lines: "In remembrance of all those who have labored long before us, with deep gratitude for all who love and serve this church, with bright hope for tomorrow and great joy on this day, we dedicate ourselves anew to be the people of 'the Church of the Lighted Steeple.' Ring the bell! Shine the light! Share the Joy! Go and tell the good news!"[2] Then the bell rang for the first time since 2005.

One of the clergy staff members at Rayne who played an important part in the implementation of some of the joint projects, William Thiele, was also appointed as pastor at Parker Memorial UMC.

Parker Memorial

Parker Memorial UMC is located Uptown, at 1130 Nashville Avenue, and it has traditionally had an Anglo congregation. It is usually thought to be named after a bishop of the MECS, but historian Walter Vernon records that it was named after a local preacher, James D. Parker, who started several Sunday schools during the Civil War.[3] Parker is one of the churches that grew out of Sunday schools, which makes sense given its twenty-first century emphasis on an educated laity.

Like many mainline congregations, it declined in membership over the years. The small group that remained tried several creative approaches, including the establishment in the late 1990s of the Parker Institute, which offered educational opportunities, primarily for laypeople. A number of more conservative individuals left at that time, leaving a particularly progressive core group of members.

---

2. Bulletin for worship at Rayne Memorial United Methodist Church, August 24, 2008, in possession of the author.

3. Vernon, *Becoming One People*, 76, 117.

Eight years ago, William Thiele (pronounced Teel-ee) was appointed as the pastor at Parker and also as an associate minister at Rayne. Thiele holds a PhD in counseling. His dissertation compares the contemplative spirituality of the Christian mystics and that of Alcoholics Anonymous. His book, *Monks in the World: Seeking God in a Frantic Culture*, was published in 2014. Due to his leadership and that of a former pastor, Craig Gilliam, Parker has attracted individuals interested in a more contemplative type of worship.

Together, Parker and Rayne developed the School for Contemplative Living, with Thiele as its director. Calling itself a "monastery without walls," it works not just in the area of spirituality but also in service, fostering a "radical engagement" with the city of New Orleans.[4] Thiele and the congregation are deeply involved in the Open Table and Luke's House ministries, described below.

Mt. Zion

Mt. Zion UMC is located on Louisiana Avenue near Claiborne Avenue. Some of the areas around it were economically depressed even before Katrina. Then the flooding did substantial damage to the church and to the neighborhood. The decision of Mt. Zion's pastor not to return to the city meant that it was left rudderless immediately after the storm and then went forward without the continuation of pastoral leadership from which Rayne and some other congregations benefited.

Several pastors have been assigned to Mt. Zion since Katrina. Simon Chigumira was working with Mt. Zion right after Katrina, and the late Connie Thomas was its pastor when Luke's House opened. Sonya Lars has been appointed there for the past three years. Carver Davenport, director of the Dillard University choir, oversees the music and excellent performance of gospel music is a feature of the worship services.

For days after the floodwalls broke, the Louisiana Conference did not know the whereabouts of most of the pastors who had been displaced. Because my husband, who is a retired pastor, and I lived in Oklahoma where I teach at a seminary, we had electricity. Furthermore, he had been coordinating and sending the "grapevine" messages (notices about births, deaths, illnesses, and so forth) to the pastors of the New Orleans District for several years, so he had email addresses for most of them. Jim spent days after landfall sending emails, making phone calls, and compiling a list of current

---

4. Thiele, *Monks in the World*; More information on the School for Contemplative Living is available at http://www.thescl.net/.

contact information for everyone he could find. People also contacted us with offers of places available for pastors and their families to stay until they could return to their homes, and we served as a clearinghouse of sorts for that information.

A UMC clergy couple living in Tulsa each served a church that had a parsonage. One of those parsonages was quite large, and they volunteered it for a displaced family to use. I thought it would be a particularly good match for Victor McCullough, the pastor from Mt. Zion, because he and his wife Nancy have four children, and they were staying with family members in Arkansas. The situation worked well for them; their daughter was welcomed into college at Oklahoma City University, and the other three children entered school.

As it turned out, Victor had encountered the bishop of the Oklahoma Area in an airport during the crisis, and the bishop first offered him a temporary appointment and later arranged to take him into clergy membership in the Oklahoma conference. Victor was not a native of Louisiana, and after a time of discernment, decided to remain in Oklahoma. Nancy entered Phillips Theological Seminary and earned her MDiv degree, and she, too, is now an ordained elder in the Oklahoma conference.

Mt. Zion was founded in the 1870s as a mission of the "northern church," the MEC. The current structure at 2700 Louisiana Avenue was built in the mid-twentieth century. Even before the storm, its sanctuary had serious foundation trouble, and the flood exacerbated those and caused other structural problems. While the fellowship hall and education building were put back in use relatively soon, the extensive repairs to the sanctuary did not even begin for several years. The joyful rededication of the restored sanctuary was held on November 12, 2010.

In the meantime, a hundred or so congregants worshiped in the fellowship hall each Sunday morning. Each Tuesday evening, the very same room was used for a medical clinic called Luke's House and a ministry with people who were homeless called Open Table. Luke's House and Open Table opened in December 2007 as a result of cooperation among the people of Mt. Zion, Rayne, and Parker UMC. The commitment to let their limited space be used for these purposes is an important comment on the character of Mt. Zion's congregation, and it was instrumental in making several important ministries possible.

People's UMC and People's Community Center

People's UMC is located on Simon Bolivar Avenue near Jackson Avenue, in the area called Central City. It is the most dangerous part of New Orleans; in a city with a tragically high murder rate overall, Central City's murder rate is the highest.

The online Historical Register of the Louisiana conference reports that in 1922, when People's MEC was established, sixty-five members made up the new African American congregation. People's Community Center, located next door, was affiliated with the church. However, when the local Community Chest (a forerunner of United Way) organized in 1925, church-affiliated centers had to be legally separated from those churches, because the Community Chest did not fund work sponsored by single congregations.

People's Community Center "carried on a daily nursery, a free employment service, a kindergarten, a free children's clinic, a welfare bureau with case work, a Boy Scout troop, and an adult education and recreation program."[5] These were quite typical activities at missions run by Methodist churchwomen's organizations during the Social Gospel Era.[6]

Before the storm, the community center space was being used for a child development center. When the Head Start program was developed by the federal government, the center rented space to it, helping children both through the instruction and by enabling their parents to seek and keep employment.

After the storm, People's became one of several stations for the Louisiana Conference Disaster Response, Inc. Volunteers were housed in the community center space. The center had earlier acquired a small residence immediately next door, and that building was used for offices for the station staff. When the disaster response agency disbanded, the conference gave the property back to the People's UMC congregation. Head Start staffers expressed a desire to return to the space.

On March 23, 2009, the center's board met for the first time since the storm under the leadership of its chair, Rev. Marva Mitchell, who had once been director of the child development program. June Sanchez of Hartzell UMC in the Lower Ninth Ward represented the Ruth Carter Auxiliary, a group of women from around the city which provided significant financial assistance to the child development program.

---

5. Vernon, *Becoming One People*, 203.
6. Blue, *St. Mark's and the Social Gospel*.

The superintendent of the New Orleans District at that time, Ramonalynn Bethley, met with the group as a representative of the Louisiana conference. She made it very clear that the bishop and cabinet were hopeful that the space could be used for a more overtly Christian endeavor than Head Start, since that program's federal funding meant that religious instruction was not supposed to be part of the curriculum. On that day, it seemed unlikely to me, but in fact, the center building is now the home of Apex Youth Center, described below, and the former residence is now used by Luke's House, both ministries developed after Katrina.

Cooperative Ministries

Luke's House: A Clinic for Healing and Hope

Luke's House is one of the more creative partnerships that emerged after the storm. It is a cooperative project of Rayne and Mt. Zion UMCs, with participation by Parker and later on by People's. The project brings individual volunteers from congregations throughout the Greater New Orleans area.

Health-care services were devastated by Katrina's aftermath. Louisiana had a statewide system of charity hospitals, the flagship being the huge facility on Tulane Avenue in New Orleans referred to as "Big Charity." In 2005, it was located in a structure built in 1939 that was definitely showing its age. On the other hand, it had one of the most respected Level 1 trauma units in the nation. In a decision that was and remains extremely controversial, the state did not reopen Big Charity. A huge new medical complex is under construction in Mid-City instead. Since 2005, the thousands of patients who received care at Charity Hospital despite being unable to pay for the services have been underserved or unserved entirely. Luke's House was envisioned as a means of filling a small part of the gap that Charity's closure left. It provides free medical care given by volunteer nurses and by medical students from LSU.

Because the clinic was originally housed in the same room Mt. Zion was using for worship, the entire set-up had to be collapsible. The first director, Jiselle Bock, was then a Tulane medical student who had public-health experience in the Soviet Union. She constructed four exam rooms from sheets donated by a hotel, $100 worth of PVC pipe and fittings, and folding massage tables. She sewed the sheets into fabric walls, and she developed a way to fit the pipes that held up those fabric walls for each exam area so that they could be assembled and disassembled each week and stored in a closet until the next service day.[7] Volunteers, including students from Tulane's Wesley Foundation, set up the partitions and triage area every Tuesday afternoon and took them down again after the clinic ended that evening. Seeing the clinic in operation and then seeing every smidgen of the equipment stored in the one utility closet was an amazing experience.

Sue Berry, MD, a lay member at Rayne, is a pediatrician who teaches at LSU Health Sciences Center. When she first heard about the plan for a clinic sponsored by Rayne and Mt. Zion, Berry was not convinced that it was a project that they could accomplish. She was well acquainted with the difficulties they would encounter and knew how much work it would be. She also knew that 30 percent of the city's doctors were not coming back. She explained all this to Crawford and the interested laypeople, but they decided to go ahead with the project anyway. For their general director, they hired Bock, who held a master's in public health, and got the whole program planned. All they lacked were doctors to volunteer. So, despite her initial misgivings, when the clinic opened, Berry agreed to be its medical director.[8]

Berry sent out an email asking for volunteer doctors. One individual, Betty Lo-Blais, who directed LSU's residency program, responded enthusiastically, and in just a few weeks, she had a year's worth of volunteers signed up. Berry says that they drew a "huge group of volunteers from both churches." Nurses from other congregations also regularly volunteer.

Ruby Glenn, a retired RN who is a member at Metairie UMC, was recruited by another member of her church, nurse practitioner Dorien Mahoney. Glenn says she found the clinic a meaningful contribution to the community: "I'm pretty impressed with the range of things they can treat." Many of the patients have issues like blood-pressure problems, diabetes, boils, and backaches. The nurses give many flu shots. Although the clinic is in a very different setting from the Jefferson Parish hospital where she had worked, "I just say a little prayer and go on down." She eventually became a member of the clinic's board of directors.[9]

A pharmacist does a check-out for each patient, using a very thorough questionnaire. They make referrals to other clinics or agencies that can be of help to people with limited means. The goal is to keep the patient from having to return regularly, so the volunteers spend a lot of time providing information for patients. The *Times-Picayune* quoted a then second-year resident who said, "Here, I feel like I've done more than simply treat them

---

7. Stewart, "Prayers for Medical Help."

8. Susan Berry, MD, MPH, Professor of Clinical Pediatrics, LSU Health Sciences Center and former Medical Director, Luke's House, telephone conversation with the author, May 11, 2009.

9. Ruby Glenn, RN, telephone interview with the author, May 11, 2009.

and write a prescription. I'm able to educate them." A patient with diabetes told a reporter, "They have helped me help myself."[10]

A member of Mt. Zion, Erica Washington, has been affiliated with Luke's House since its inception, and she has served as the chair of its board of directors since 2012. Washington is a public health epidemiologist. She was honored by the White House in 2013 as a "Champion of Change" for her work as the State of Louisiana's Healthcare-Associated Infections (HAI) coordinator.[11] Washington says that the provision of clinic services has other positive effects, as well. They find themselves helping young people make a transition to employment. Obtaining a license to operate the bicycle-powered pedicabs now offering transportation on New Orleans streets requires passing a physical examination. Many other kinds of employment also require medical clearance. Yet many of the young people, usually twenty-five to thirty-five years old, who want this kind of job have been unemployed and thus have no medical coverage. Being able to get a free examination at Luke's House lets them make a significant change in their lives.

In March 2012, what the New Orleans *Times-Picayune* called the "suitcase clinic" moved to the People's Community Center campus. The newspaper reported that more than 1,800 patients had been treated since it began operating in 2007.[12] Luke's House had finally found a location where they could leave their equipment in place all the time.

In the summer of 2013, Luke's House added an additional night of service on the first Thursday of the month and has now added another on third Thursdays. The Thursday clinics are geared especially toward Spanish speakers, so there are translators on hand both of those evenings. Washington says that the outreach to Spanish-speaking individuals came about in part because the Latin American Medical Student Association at Tulane (LAMSA) reached out to Luke's House when a clinic in Mid-City that was serving the Latino/a population closed. LAMSA operates a mobile clinic and they had made referrals to the other clinic; they now make those referrals to Luke's House. While the Tuesday clinics close at 8 pm, the Thursday clinics remain open till 9 pm so that people who are employed can have time to get there after they get off work.[13]

Making health care available is an authentically Wesleyan practice. John Wesley had a holistic view of salvation, seeing it as healing for the sin-sick soul. He was concerned not just with spiritual but also with physical

---

10. Stewart, "Prayers for Medical Help."
11. Washington, "Prioritizing Patient Safety."
12. Stewart, "Luke's House 'Suitcase Clinic.'"
13. Erica Washington, telephone interview with the author, March 10, 2014.

healing, and wrote a book, *The Primitive Physick or An Easy and Natural Method of Curing Most Diseases*, which compiled common remedies for physical complaints. Along with establishing schools for children who would otherwise not have received an education, he was responsible for the establishment of free medical clinics that served the poor.

The provision of free health care by Methodists also has historical precedent in New Orleans. The women of the MECS who established St. Mark's Community Center on North Rampart Street provided free medical care until World War II. The clinic was a dramatic move toward better race relations, because it was open to both blacks and whites on a first-come, first-served basis without separate waiting or treatment rooms. The women received many complaints about providing "non-spiritual" services, but they believed that bringing life abundant was their calling, and that life abundant involved more than just spiritual health and growth.[14]

Luke's House, too, provides healing for more than physical ills. Since Katrina, the number of medical professionals in the city has declined, but the decline in the number of trained counselors, psychotherapists, psychologists, and psychiatrists has been even more dramatic. Some professionals may have chosen to move their practices to other locations because they were daunted by the severity of emotional pain that was inevitable in a city full of people who had lost loved ones, friends, and all of their possessions. However, the plunge in the number of psychiatric beds in the city is directly related to the devastating dismantling of state support for psychiatric services under Gov. Bobby Jindal. Crawford says, "Understand that there is almost nothing in the city in the way of mental health services, and there are very few beds in the hospitals. [The state] has cut these services off at the knees. This does not bode well for the long-term."[15] As Rebecca Snedeker has written, "It's no exaggeration to say that people are dying because of these changes."[16]

It's no secret that New Orleans, particularly the city proper, has always had a well-deserved reputation for offering welcome to those who would not easily fit in elsewhere. A Facebook meme that's popular among New Orleanians proclaims, "We don't hide crazy here. We parade it down the street." Rebecca Solnit puts it far more elegantly: "Maybe the clearest way to

---

14. Blue, *St. Mark's and the Social Gospel*. During the war, so many medical personnel were drafted that the women who ran St. Mark's were unable to staff the clinic, and they began using the clinic space for day care to assist the many women who entered the work force then.

15. Carol Winn Crawford, email to the author, October 9, 2013.

16. Snedeker, "Holding It Together, Falling Apart," 145.

say it is that this is a city of volatility, rapture, rawness, and visits to the edge, sometimes with a return ticket, sometimes not . . ."[17]

Yet the barely fettered creative expression of individualism is only one face of life of New Orleans, and it is the enormous psychic trauma and disruption in the lives of thousands who previously led more ordinary lives that has been at crisis stage since Katrina. In 2008, the Krewe of Petronius distributed a krewe favor at its Bal Masque that consisted of a strand of beads with a large medallion that resembled a postcard; it bore the words, "Postcards from the Edge of Extinction." New Orleans continued to feel that way for a very long time.

Licensed professional counselor Rebecca Stilling has been back in the city since November 2005. Caregivers themselves were "the wounded treating the wounded, especially for the first couple of years," she said. She and others she knew had completely full caseloads then. Even though more therapists eventually began returning or moving into the area, most professionals had little motivation to accept Medicaid or limited insurance, because there were more people who needed their services than could be accommodated. For a time, Red Cross provided financial assistance for therapy, but those funds were long gone when I spoke with Stilling in 2009. Stilling also says that she and her colleagues believe behaviors that are sometimes stress-related, like domestic and sexual violence, had increased because families are living with more stress, with fewer financial resources, and often in more crowded conditions.

Anthropologist and First Grace UMC member Martha Ward remarked to me after the evacuation for Hurricane Gustav in 2008 that "the thing with 'post-traumatic stress disorder' is that it isn't 'post.'"[18] Every storm warning can bring back the despair that Katrina wrought. Stilling echoes Ward's assertion that post-traumatic stress disorder has become chronic stress disorder. As hurricane season was only fifteen days away at the time of her interview with me in 2009, Stilling had within the past two weeks turned down six referrals.[19] Thus, at the same time that availability has decreased, the need for professional counseling has increased.

Crawford says that from the time Luke's House opened, those who came for medical services "were always asked if they would like to see a pastor, and many times we met individually in quiet corner to listen and to

---

17. Solnit, "Juju and Cuckoo," 142.

18. Martha Ward, interview by the author, March 20, 2009, New Orleans, LA.

19. Rebecca Stilling, LSCW, LMFT, Diplomate in Clinical Social Work, interview by the author, May 15, 2009, New Orleans, LA.

pray."[20] This kind of presence would be important in any similar ministry, but since Katrina it has been a particularly valuable service. At the new Luke's House location, a pastor is "usually on hand," but space limitations mean that they are unable "to have counseling for more than one person at a time, and the huge demand comes from our mental health patients," Crawford says. On the positive side, they are now able to offer psychiatric counseling provided by a volunteer. Dr. Bob Lancaster, whom Crawford terms "a well-known retired psychiatrist in the city and a member of Rayne," donates his time. "He is still licensed and insured and is still able to write prescriptions. He sees more patients than any other doctor at our clinic and usually has a full schedule each evening we are open." Clinic personnel would like to find another psychiatrist who would volunteer, particularly a child psychologist who could also be of service to Apex, the youth ministry described below.[21]

Washington explained that "Our growing mental health program is trying to fill the gap where health care is being cut," but it is not simply the doctor's services that are not readily available. The clinic works with two prescription assistance programs, so they usually write prescriptions that can be filled with generic drugs. However, some psychiatric medications are not available in generic form. "We cover those costs," she said. Volunteers now organize an annual event called "Brass Bash" that provides some of the funds the clinic needs.

The Methodist Health System Foundation has made grants to help health-care recovery in the wake of the storm, and Luke's House has benefitted at times from those. "The Methodist health system has always had a presence in New Orleans," Washington noted. "It's smaller in scale now, but we're working really hard."

The Open Table

Before the storm, Rayne UMC had an active ministry with individuals who were homeless. They served sandwiches, cookies, and cold drinks "to 75–100 persons experiencing homelessness each week," pastor Carol Winn Crawford said. They also gave out vouchers for the shelter run by the Salvation Army; it cost $8 a night then to stay at that shelter.[22] After the distribution of food and vouchers, they held a chapel service for any people who chose to stay for it; usually between twelve and twenty-five people attended.

20. Carol Winn Crawford, email to the author, October 9, 2013.
21. Ibid.
22. The price at the Salvation Army shelter is $10 per night at the time of this writing.

The church employed a seminary graduate part-time to serve as chaplain to homeless people.

The damage to the front of the church described above completely disrupted the ministry. Rayne was able to reopen its highly regarded Early Childhood Program fairly quickly, and since young children are dropped off and picked up at the back of the church, it was not possible to move the work with homeless individuals to that side of the building.

Furthermore, right after the storm, Rayne began housing work teams in the building. The presence of volunteers from all around the country has, as Crawford said, "saved the city." Nevertheless, she struggled with how to renew the church's ministry with homeless people, who had vastly increased in number, in light of the diminished resources in the church building.[23]

As noted above, Rayne was an instrumental part of the establishment of Luke's House, which was first housed at Mt. Zion UMC. When the clinic opened, Rayne reinstituted the hospitality ministry at the clinic site. For several hours before the clinic opened each Tuesday, volunteers would dispense snacks, toiletries, hygiene items, and books and magazines. Bibles and devotional materials are available. A small building out back holds used clothing. The volunteers also make many referrals to other agencies for various kinds of help.

When Luke's House moved to a permanent location next to People's Community Center, the Open Table ministry continued to be conducted at Mt. Zion. The locations are just a little over a mile apart. Using freed-up space at Mt. Zion, the Open Table "has evolved," Crawford said. "We expanded services to include a hot meal for 75 to 100 homeless people." Rayne members cook twice a month, and other churches, including Mt. Zion, Munholland UMC, and St. Andrew's Episcopal Church, provide other meals. Participants in the School for Contemplative Living at Parker Memorial serve the meals. William Thiele gathers those in attendance in a circle for a blessing before they eat. Guests also, Crawford said, receive friendship. Pastoral counseling is available if they request it.

In his book *Monks in the World*, Thiele writes that while the volunteers are gathered in the circle,

> They are praying that the Great Love might dissolve each person's suffering today. They are hoping to serve *from* the Presence within, not from some misguided desire to fix people's problems. As they are learning from this time spent with the poor, poverty is always more complex and deep-seated than our

---

23. Carol Winn Crawford, interview by the author, August 12, 2008, New Orleans, LA.

futile efforts to change it. The volunteers hope to be *in* the One that transcends the circumstances of poverty, who is *in* the poor already.

As an example, he tells about an instance when "Murray, a man in need of shelter," said that it would have been better if a volunteer who had prayed aloud had not used the term "homeless" in his prayer. "Murray said calling people homeless boxes them in. He explained, 'Everyone here is in transition. They are on their way to finding a place to live.'" The comment led to a name change in the ministry, which had originally been called "Homeless Hospitality."[24]

Crescent City Café

Rayne's Sunday bulletins feature many small, attractive notices designed rather like ads about the various ministries in which the church is engaged. One is for the Crescent City Café, a ministry in which Rayne is a partner with St. Charles Avenue Presbyterian Church, and for which they serve as host. The project has two purposes. The first is to feed hungry people in a way that offers dignity along with the food. The second is to create "opportunities for young adults to serve our community, build relationships with our patrons and connect with one another." Twice a month, the group gathers to prepare and serve breakfasts, using linens and real dishes. At a recent event, guests could choose either shrimp and cheese grits, with ricotta and gorgonzola cheeses, French bread and peaches; or cinnamon and sugar biscuits, eggs, bacon and orange slices. They usually serve eighty to one hundred people, whom they term "guests." They have served over seven thousand meals since they began the project in 2009.[25]

Crawford said the project was founded "by one of our young adult members, Georgia McBride, and a young adult friend of hers, Kim Thompson. Many of our young adults at Rayne are regular volunteers." She said it is "one of the best organized outfits I have ever seen, with a volunteer waiting list most weeks!" Church partners such as St. Charles Avenue Presbyterian Church and other funding agencies chip in. Rayne holds regular fundraisers and also supports Open Table with space and supplies.[26] Currently, the leaders are trying to create a separate non-profit that will keep a café open all the time to both paying and non-paying customers.

---

24. Thiele, *Monks in the World*, 70–71.
25. Crescent City Café, email to the author, February 2, 2014.
26. Carol Winn Crawford, email to the author, October 9, 2013.

Apex Youth Center

Another innovative ministry which, like Luke's House, is now located at People's Community Center has ties to several of the congregations discussed in this chapter. People's is located in the area of New Orleans called Central City, the most dangerous part of the city. In a city with a tragically high murder rate overall, Central City's murder rate is the highest.

Pat Evans, who died in 2013, was an influential activist in New Orleans whose career involved several kinds of work.[27] She ran political campaigns, including former US Senator Mary Landrieu's first successful statewide race. Evans was formerly director of a state agency that focused on women's services. She helped establish a nonprofit sector in Latvia after the collapse of the USSR. After Katrina, she was affiliated with the University of New Orleans (UNO) as director of the International Project for Nonprofit Organizations. She worked with graduate students who were studying various kinds of public administration and nonprofit endeavors.

While Evans lived in Tremé, a historic primarily African-American neighborhood next to the French Quarter, she worked to improve neighborhoods around New Orleans. She recognized clearly how needs and how the levels of difficulty in meeting those needs differ from one area of the city to another. Some things are the same for all residents, of course. "Everyone needs a house, a school, a job," she says. But the most "wicked problems"—those that are most severe and most resistant to solutions—vary. "In Tremé, people are saying, 'Don't let our culture die.' But in Central City, people are saying, 'Stop the killing.' In that circumstance, you don't ask people to come to a workshop, give them a folder, and send them home," she said.[28]

Apex Youth Center is a ministry that offers space and community to the youth of Central City. "Apex" is an acronym for "Always Pursuing Excellence." The center has won national recognition for its work; a number of their awards are mentioned on Apex's website. Lisa Fitzpatrick, the director of Apex and until 2014 the pastor of the Center's worshiping community, was named a "CNN Hero" in 2013. She was designated as a "Harvey's Hero" and appeared on Steve Harvey's show in Chicago. One honor was a $50,000 grant awarded by the 5-Hour Energy company. Handing her the check, the company representative asked, "Do you need this right now?" Fitzpatrick responded, "We ran out of snacks on Thursday." In a video the company produced, an interviewer asked Fitzpatrick's husband, Danny, "Tell me

---

27. Pope, "Pat Evans."
28. Pat Evans, interview by the author, February 13, 2009, Metairie, LA.

about her passion for the children." He responded, "Her passion is keeping kids alive, because that is the issue here."[29]

Fitzpatrick grew up in Oklahoma, and she had a personal encounter with gang violence in Oklahoma City when she was grazed by a bullet while sitting in a car outside a convenience store. It turned out to have been part of a gang initiation, and she remembers the faces of the twelve-year-old boys who tried to kill her. Police told her later that "the children were told they had to kill someone that night or someone in their family would suffer violent consequences."[30] She spent most of her adult life in Los Angeles. Her career as a health-care executive brought her to north Louisiana in 2000, then to Lafayette, and then to New Orleans in 2006. It was in 2009 that Donato, a child she knew and the cousin of her daughter's best friend, was murdered. "I realized I couldn't stand on the wrong side of the yellow tape anymore," she said.[31]

During a worship service when she was sixteen, Fitzpatrick experienced a call to ministry, but when she went down the aisle, she was ushered to the back of the sanctuary and informed "that they only meant for the boys to come down." Decades later, she was attending a United Methodist church in Lafayette and began talking with pastor Ann Sutton, who helped her discern that her call was still valid.

Fitzpatrick became associate pastor at People's UMC, where Eunice Chigumira is senior pastor. Chigumira conducted the regular worship service in the church's sanctuary, and Fitzpatrick led her worshiping community's service at 9:30 Sunday mornings in the community room. There's a platform that served as a worship center. The young people gathered at 9 o'clock for breakfast, and "there are kids waiting at the gate." For music, they mainly used videos, although, she said, laughing, "I do a pretty mean rap." The laughter is not to indicate that what she's saying is a joke—it isn't—but simply to recognize the incongruity of the situation of a white woman rapping for a group of black teens.

Fitzpatrick doesn't buy it when people insist they "don't see color." She says, "We do see color. Race matters." Yet she learned from her paternal great-grandmother, a Native woman who was married to a white man, to see beyond race, too. "She always talked about 'the evil white man' and the terrible things white people had done. But she loved her husband very much, and I was beloved by her, too."

---

29. Stewart, "Always Pursuing Excellence."
30. Clarke, "Teaching Nonviolence."
31. Lisa Fitzpatrick, interview by the author, October 10, 2013, New Orleans, LA.

Apex really began in an informal way when teenagers began to find Lisa and Danny's house in Broadmoor a comfortable place to be. Kids would gather there, near the place where Broadmoor touches the tip of Central City. "I'm a 'sit on the front porch' and a 'wake up to random kids on the porch' kind of gal," Fitzpatrick says.

In June 2011, she was in a meeting with Callie Crawford, senior pastor at Rayne UMC, to talk about establishing a new worshiping community for young people. While she was there, she got calls from Brandon, one of the young people, and the fourth time, she thought she should answer. Brandon asked, "This church we've been talking about, when it will start?" She told him she was in a meeting about it right then and that maybe it would start in the spring. She asked what he thought, and he answered, "What about tonight?"

She recalled that Crawford told her, "'Go, I'll arrange it.' She called the district superintendent while I was on the way home, and she had made me a supply pastor before I got to my house." When Fitzpatrick got home, "there were nine kids in the yard, ranging from sixteen to nineteen," and they had worship that evening. She asked whether they wanted to meet the next Sunday, because it was Father's Day and she didn't want to interrupt their plans. One boy spoke for the group: "All our fathers are dead or in jail."

Before long, she recalled, some of their parents began to say, "What about us?" They became what is called a "mission worshiping community" under the auspices of Rayne UMC. "The people at Rayne were wonderful," Fitzpatrick says. They had as many as sixteen young people attending worship on what she terms the "Pews of Chaos," and Rayne was never anything but welcoming.

Although things were going well at Rayne, people thought the teens might be "more comfortable worshiping with folks who looked more like them," and they moved to First Street Peck Wesley, an African American congregation with a black senior pastor. However, they were not received as well there, perhaps, Fitzpatrick thinks, because of socioeconomic differences. In her experience, socioeconomic standing matters even more than color in New Orleans.

Eventually, they moved to the People's Community Center building and Fitzpatrick was appointed as an associate pastor at People's UMC. They conduct daily activities in the center space and also had worship there on Sunday mornings. At People's, they again found warmth and hospitality. "People at People's have been warm and welcoming. Plus it's closer to where we started, and the kids don't have to go so far into the neighborhood," Fitzpatrick said.

Her community baptized forty-three people, and took in ninety-six members. At first, because they were not precisely a church, those members were "in holding" under Rayne, then under the district, and next under People's UMC. It is an impressive testament to the depths of the need Fitzpatrick is meeting.

Her entrance criteria to determine who can come to the center is: "They found the door and left their weapons outside. And I will give them a second chance to leave the weapon. That scares a lot of people." Fitzpatrick got the criteria from Father Greg Boyle, who runs Homeboy Industries in California. She makes his book, *Tattoos on the Heart*, required reading for her staff. Subtitled *The Power of Boundless Compassion*, it is a discussion of Boyle's work in the heart of gang territory in Los Angeles. His primary strategy is offering acceptance to young people, which he sees as a reflection of the immense acceptance that God offers to all humans.[32]

At the moment, there is only one paid employee at Apex; the program director is a woman who has a master's degree in public health. Other participants are volunteers. Fitzpatrick's family is also deeply involved. Her husband, Danny, whom the teens call "Mr. D," is an active and willing participant in the work. Her daughter volunteered while she was in college, and the other two children, aged ten and eleven, "are here all the time."

She lectures a few times a year at Tulane. Undergraduate students from Tulane and Loyola complete service learning projects at Apex, and students in graduate social work programs provide help. Two researchers at Tulane University, David Seal and Peter Scharf, have a grant to study Apex for eighteen months. Fitzpatrick says that they were intrigued because "anecdotally" there are fewer murders where she's working. Seal, who is also director of research for the Mayor's Strategic Command to Reduce Murders, said their major aim is "to examine the relationship between community programs that focus on reducing the rate of gun violence, murder and other major offenses among youth, with a particular focus on the impact of Apex programming on reducing violent crime risks."[33] "They are trying to quantify what Scharf calls 'this love stuff,'" Fitzpatrick says. "He keeps asking me, 'But what do you *do*?' I tell him, 'I open the door.'"[34] As she told a CNN reporter, "When I ask them why they hang out with (me) every Friday night, they say, 'Because you're the first person who ever let us in the door.' That is an indictment on our society."[35]

32. Boyle, *Tattoos on the Heart*.
33. David W. Seal, PhD, email to the author, November 2, 2013.
34. Lisa Fitzpatrick, interview by the author, October 10, 2013, New Orleans, LA.
35. Clarke, "Teaching Nonviolence."

The building they now use has room for a library, a computer room, a homework room, indoor recreational space, and outdoor space for basketball and other activities. They also have some musical instruments the young people can use.[36] Fitzpatrick pointed to a pool table and other games, and noted that the room around us was arranged to foster small groups of two to ten. "We use contextual learning and building relationships, even with perceived enemies."[37] She told CNN, "Our motto is 'Reconciliation, never retaliation,' and that's a hard lesson in an eye-for-an-eye world." The staff is constantly asking, "How can we address this differently? What could we do to de-escalate this situation instead of escalate the situation?" Then, she said, "The young people come up with the answers."[38]

Apex also operates on the idea that "If you feed them, they will come. We go through lots of pizza and red beans." But primarily, she said, she's just there and lets the young people be there as well. A young woman on the video explains, "No matter where you come from, no matter what you did, it's like she give you a clean slate. She never holds anything against you." Another young woman says, "She's amazing." A teenage boy told the interviewer, "I can actually say she's an angel. If it wasn't for her, I wouldn't know where these kids would be."[39]

I suggested that what she was talking about bore similarities to the work of a midwife or doula who "holds the space" while a mother gives birth. The mother is doing the hard work of birthing, but it is often the midwife's calm and knowledgeable presence that allows the mom to labor successfully. Fitzpatrick's face lit up, and she exclaimed, "My public health job was being a doula!" She founded a parenting center in Los Angeles that dramatically reduced the rate of infant mortality/morbidity. She wrote a computer program and input risk factors so as to maximize assistance to clients. "Computers are my hobby," she said, but it is clear that she uses them for more than just entertainment.

Fitzpatrick is grateful for funding and other kinds of assistance, but she's also just a little bemused by the attention. "People call it innovative programming, but I tell them it's not so innovative; someone tried it about two thousand years ago." As Jesus recommended to a rich young man, the Fitzpatricks divested themselves of their assets. They sold their house and most of their possessions in order to begin the ministry. In 2013, Fitzpatrick told me that she was on the "pay to preach" program. "Women always laugh

---

36. Stewart, "Always Pursuing Excellence."
37. Lisa Fitzpatrick, interview by the author, October 10, 2013, New Orleans, LA.
38. Clarke, "Teaching Nonviolence."
39. Stewart, "Always Pursuing Excellence."

when I say that, but men say 'What's that?' and look confused. I sometimes say this or that is 'above my pay grade, because my pay grade is zero.'"[40]

Local contributions decreased after the large awards from national entities were publicized; donors may have thought Apex had the resources it needed. It did not, and the ministry was on the verge of having to close. As a solution, in 2014, the conference appointed Fitzpatrick to a different position, a two-point charge composed of St. Paul's UMC in Harahan (a suburb in Jefferson Parish) and Hartzell UMC in the Lower Ninth Ward (see Chapter 8). She continues to volunteer as Executive Director at Apex.

On the days when she can be at the center, Fitzpatrick always walks around the block. This might not mean much in many places, but her walking in Central City makes a statement. "One kid told me, 'I'm not afraid of the police, but I'm a little afraid of you.'" She has earned the respect of the young people in the neighborhood by her willingness to be physically there with them, and by offering them "this love thing." Perhaps in time the funding will come for her to be there full-time again.

---

40. Lisa Fitzpatrick, interview by the author, October 10, 2013, New Orleans, LA.

8

"Holler Back If You Can Hear Me"

It was not the time to run scared.
—Hadley Edwards[1]

This chapter recounts the stories of some representative congregations across the city. Their neighborhood contexts have played a determinative role in these churches' recovery. Bethany UMC is in Pontchartrain Park, a suburb near the lake. Hartzell is in the Lower Ninth Ward, a troubled area which has still not recovered from the flood. St. Mark's UMC is in the French Quarter, on North Rampart Street. First Street Peck Wesley UMC is located in Central City, the most dangerous section of town, and Williams Ross UMC is in the Black Pearl District of Uptown.

Bethany UMC

Bethany UMC is in Pontchartrain Park, one of the first suburbs developed for middle-class African American families after World War II. Situated to the east of the city's older sections, it abuts the Industrial Canal and flooded badly after Katrina.

I have a photo of a student who took my first "Church's Response to Katrina" class in March 2006. Chad Perceful is over six feet tall, and his reach is seven feet, ten inches. In the photo, he is standing outside Bethany UMC, stretching up to touch the high water line on the building, but he is not able to reach it. The fact that Bethany UMC is still operating today after being inundated by eight feet of floodwaters is a remarkable testament to the gifts of committed leadership, a determined congregation, and the power of Methodist connectionalism.

---

1. Hadley Edwards, interview by the author and students, January 14, 2007.

The founders of Bethany met in a private home when they first gathered in 1957. Then Dillard, a historically black college affiliated with The Methodist Church and the United Church of Christ denomination, offered them a meeting space. The church moved into its current location at 4533 Mendez in 1958. Across the street, there is a golf course in the park from which the subdivision takes its name, and Southern University, a historically black, state-owned institution, is nearby. Bethany is now served by Anice Moses, who worked with Thomas UMC in Kenner during the Mission Zone years, and by Marva Mitchell, a retired pastor who serves one-quarter time and who formerly oversaw the child development program at People's Community Center before the storm.

At the time of Katrina, Bethany's senior pastor was Hadley Edwards, who later served as District Superintendent in the New Orleans District. Bethany had 850 members, around 500 of whom could be considered active.

Getting in touch and staying in touch with members was an especially important dimension of recovery. Edwards recalls,

> On the second or third day after the storm I heard in my spirit saying send an email to your members. I had my laptop. I never leave home without my laptop, and [post-Katrina] Bethany was an electronic church before it was a physical church, because I got in touch.

He knew that when his members went to a library or somewhere with internet access in order to contact their insurance companies, they would no doubt check their email. "'Holler back if you can hear me'—that was the name of the email. And I started getting hits back."

He said, "Every morning, I sent a daily devotional, sitting in Dallas in a friend's apartment. It went to all the members for whom I had addresses." He let them know where he was and gave them his cell phone number. Then he told them, "Print the daily devotional, and if you see members in different places, give them a copy. It has my contact information, so if you can give it to them, they can get back." He saw results. "That went like hot cakes; I mean, it spread!"

Edwards still has the notebook at home where he recorded the information "as [he] received emails of where they were and how they were."

Today, Bethany's website offers opportunities to connect with the church through Facebook and Twitter, and it also has a QR code on the main page. In 2007, Edwards advised my students, "Get email, have a laptop, and take it everywhere you go." Now, all students at our seminary are required to have an active email account. In 2005, however, there were many displaced pastors who either didn't have email or who didn't have access to the internet where they were staying. Even now, there are still a surprising number of churches in Louisiana without a website. Many small churches cannot afford to hire someone to do web design and maintenance. Many churches and parsonages in rural locations still have slow and unreliable Internet connections. And while an urban location like New Orleans would seem to guarantee good access, getting electricity back up after Katrina was an unbelievably lengthy process. Ten years on, there are still lots of buildings that have no electricity, because in order to do repair work, you have to have get a building permit; in order to get a building permit, you have to have electricity at the site; in order to get electricity at the site, you have to have repaired it enough to be safe; in order to do those repairs, you need power tools, which require electricity. Catch-22, it seems, is not only for the military.

In his article, "Water in Sacred Places: Rebuilding New Orleans Black Churches as Sites of Community Empowerment," scholar Donald DeVore examined the recovery of Bethany. He recounted some of the strategies Edwards used to create a virtual congregation before people were able to return. DeVore pointed to the necessity for a church to be intimately connected to the recovery of the community around it. Black membership churches have traditionally served as a center for far more than a neighborhood's spiritual life. They have "functioned not merely as houses of worship, but as school buildings, lecture halls, meeting houses, and entertainment center."[2]

But how can a building serve in these ways when it is uninhabitable? Edwards' house did not flood, and he quickly determined that it would need to be the locus of the Bethany community until the church was repaired. He recalled,

> We couldn't do anything that mimicked worship, because we had business interruption insurance, and we had to draw the money. So we had Bible study, and I cooked and fed them every Tuesday. These persons were either living in trailers or they were living in hotels. Since my house didn't get ruined, I told them to bring their dirty clothes and washing powder and wash their clothes, and they did. We started at 6:30 or so, and there were many nights that folks were going back to their dwellings at 12 o'clock.[3]

Despite the good condition of his house, getting Edwards assigned back to New Orleans following his evacuation to Dallas was no simple matter. The conference initially made arrangements for him to be put on staff at

2. DeVore, "Water in Sacred Places."
3. Hadley Edwards, interview by the author, July 16, 2013, Metairie, LA.

a Houston church. When his District Superintendent, Freddie Henderson, called to inform him, Edwards said he didn't want to go to Houston.

> I said, "Why would you pick me up and send me to a large steeple church in Houston when I have a home that I can live in and there is nothing wrong with it?" And I said, "On top of that, Rev. Henderson, who is going to take care of rebuilding Bethany?"
>
> Then he gives me the speech about this being an itineracy system and when the bishop and the cabinet say you are going to be relocated, you are relocated. He says, "Someone will be calling you. Is this the right number?" I said, "That is the right number." But I got on that number with Jesus, and I prayed, "You know I don't want to leave here, and I don't want to go to Houston. I will work to put this back together." I had written to the bishop when I was in Dallas, just days afterwards. I said, "I am coming back to New Orleans, and I am going to help to rebuild the church in New Orleans. I will be as strong and dedicated as I always was, if not stronger." At the time, I didn't know how I was going to get paid, because I didn't think about all that stuff, because I had not been in that position.

The bishop, however, had to think about such things. But in the end, Edwards's commitment and desire to remain at Bethany won out, and they did not send him to Houston. Instead, they named Bethany one of the station churches that were considered strong enough to stand alone outside a mission zone. The bishop told me later:

> I could clearly recall the night I went there to meet with their leadership and ask the now infamous question, "Are you willing to be more than you were?" We then gave the station churches a set of benchmarks to meet and talked of expectations and their role as the symbols of willingness to work beyond their former efforts in order to lead the recovery.[4]

Bethany's efforts were extraordinary, indeed. When the conference treasurer, Carl Rhoads sent him a check for living expenses, Edwards didn't know what to do with it. Edwards told Rhoads, "But Bethany is going to pay me, when people get back," to which Rhoads responded, "You need to live until Bethany can pay you." That was an important moment for the church, Edwards explained.

---

4. William Hutchinson, email to the author, December 20, 2013.

We were doing well at that time, and Bethany had a reputation. We knew that we were a larger church, and we knew that we didn't want a handout; that was a big piece of who we were. So I never will forget that in early December, when my officers got back together, I went to Baton Rouge and put in Carl's hand a check for every dollar that the conference had sent for my salary, because Bethany had paid me. We knew that there were people who were suffering more than we were, and the way that people were blessing us and helping us, we needed to let that go back to them. Carl Rhoads was just amazed.

As people heard about what was happening at Bethany, they wanted to help. One employee of a company from which Bethany had bought pencils, ribbons, and book markers prior to Katrina called to find out how they fared. Edwards explained:

> I was telling her the story of the place. She and her husband started to send in a check once a month to feed the people. I would do spaghetti, I would do red beans and rice, and feed as many as could come. Everybody that was there was told to invite somebody; I said: "I don't care who it is, you bring somebody along with you, and we can all eat together and have Bible study together." Some went on back to their own church once it got up and going. Some who came joined the church and are still members of the church.

In mid-October 2005, Edwards was working in the churchyard trying to prepare it for an outdoor gathering to celebrate Bethany's forty-eighth anniversary. While he was in Texas during the evacuation, St. Luke's Community UMC in Dallas had promised to rent a tent and chairs for that service. That required clearing the grounds of the storm-related debris so that there would be room to pitch the tent. At the end of one such day, Edwards received a phone call from the associate pastor at a California church, who asked, "How can we help you? What do you need?" He replied, "Oh, I need yellow ribbons. If you have got a Sunday school class that can make me yellow ribbons, yellow bows, I want to tie them on the live oak trees." His intention was that "Everything that would stand still from Gentilly Boulevard all the way back to Bethany, I was going to have a yellow ribbon around it."

The pastor told him, "'Okay, we can do that. Now what else do you need?' I said, 'That is an awful a lot to ask for.' He said, 'Reverend, this is a nice church, a large church, and we want to help with something, a big project.'"

At that point, Edwards made what I consider to be one of the most brilliant decisions made during the recovery process. Told that the choice of how to spend the money was completely up to him, he picked landscaping. "There were some that wondered if I was crazy," Edwards admitted. But he picked landscaping "because everything was horrible. Every tree, every shrub, everything on that place was dead. Only three palm trees survived Katrina." So, as Edwards put it, "one thing led to another," and the upshot was the gift from First UMC in Santa Monica and Culver City UMC of a $42,000 landscaping job that included laying five to seven inches of soil on top of the ground to prevent contamination and installing a new irrigation system.[5]

I might not appreciate the level of inspiration the decision reflected if I had not driven for miles through the completely browned out city to arrive at Bethany's green and beautifully landscaped grounds. The members of a class I taught in New Orleans at the beginning of 2015 could not grasp his rationale, and with the green of a golf course in sight and normal-looking yards all around, it must have been impossible for them to imagine the conditions in 2006 and 2007. Those of us who don't have to imagine because we can remember it are those who can understand on a cellular level what a symbol of hope and renewed life the colorful Bethany grounds were for their neighbors.

> People in that neighborhood needed to know this church is coming back. They needed to know this was not something that was just for Bethany, but it was for the Pontchartrain Park community. I got a note a few days ago that said, "I don't think I ever told you that my husband and I made a decision to come back to New Orleans because of Bethany church and seeing what you have done up there on that corner." We became the oasis in the middle of a desert. It was the cleanest, most beautiful spot in all that devastation.

By March 2006, enough people had returned so that Edwards could no longer host them in his house, but construction was going on in the church. "There is a contractor who literally built that building around us because we had no money to rent a space, and there was no space to rent," he recalled. They would worship in a corner of the sanctuary, moving around the room from week to week as the contractor moved equipment around. One Sunday, they worshiped

---

5. Hadley Edwards, interview by the author, July 16, 2013, Metairie, LA.

> with one of those little mini bulldozers right in the room. We had insurance, you know, but we didn't have enough. That church in almost fifty years had never had water in it. It just was unheard of. So the contractor went to work rebuilding that sanctuary knowing that I did not have his money. We started that process, and there never was a payment date that we could not write a check to pay him. That was God and this people called United Methodists.

Edwards knew that it was crucial for the recovery to keep his members connected to the church.

> I wrote my members, I said, "We are the United Methodist Church, and whether we have a building or not, your tithes and offerings have got to still come in. We need you doing what you know is right to do. Send your tithes and offerings." And they did just that.

During worship each week, someone read a list of the contributions that had been mailed in.

> That was people's participation in our worship; they joined our numbers, and even if you were not there on the seat, you were counted as one of those who were with us.

When people from out of town came on mission trips to help Bethany recover, Edwards said he made it a "requirement" that local members who were not working should be at the church.

> If you can't hoe and lay sod, maybe you can pull a cart with cold drinks in it. If you have a job, come by in the morning and bring us a case of water, bring us a case of soda. That is how I made sure the church members stayed connected and stayed a part of the work that was going on that place. It was not just a handout.

In this way, he said, Bethany members worked side by side with those who came to the city.

> The people had to give a part of themselves, because we were getting so much. The Scripture says, "To whom much is given, from them much is required." My passion was just in it.

Bethany members also spent time delivering water and fruit to people who had returned to the neighborhood to live in FEMA trailers and work on their houses. Edwards told my students, "We've gone door to door—or I should say, trailer to trailer." Because African Americans tend to have a high incidence of hypertension, they also took instruments with them to take blood pressure readings.[6]

However, infrastructure issues were not the only obstacle that Bethany had to overcome. When my students in a 2007 class came to Bethany and visited with Edwards, he told them repeatedly that he had to ignore the UMC *Book of Discipline* in order to get the recovery accomplished. In 2013, I asked him, "What's your opinion about that statement, now that it's you who's sitting in the DS chair?"

After some laughter and a bit of body language that displayed his awareness of the irony, he responded,

> The *Book of Discipline* called for going before the district Board of Church Location and Building and making sure that everything was correct [before construction began]. Well, in this case, we had to look beyond what the page of the *Book of Discipline* said, because the need for having a church back was most important, and at that time, the district board was not even functioning. So we had to go forth with the job at hand to have a church on the premises so there could be worship and a continued body called Bethany United Methodist Church. The *Discipline* had nothing I could use to help me, because the church had not encountered such devastation. And there was no rule book, there was no guide to follow, no script to follow. So I built the script as I went along and asked the Lord for guidance.[7]

Looking back at the conference's overall performance, Edwards acknowledged, "There are a few things that I think we could have done differently." Specifically, he thought it was "a great opportunity for us to really exercise the authority that the United Methodist Church has." They knew that it would be necessary to have between 100 and 125 people in worship every Sunday to meet the financial needs of a church.

> [It would have been] a wonderful time for us to lead congregations into believing that merging with another church is probably one of the strongest things and best things that can happen for their overall ministry. That could have really benefited the church and community.

He acknowledged that

> some people would feel differently, because nobody wants to give up their space. But that would have been an open door for

---

6. Hadley Edwards, interview by the author and students, January 14, 2007.
7. Hadley Edwards, interview by the author, July 16, 2013, Metairie, LA.

us to think differently. If the church had been proactive and just made a decision that this church and this church and this church are going to become one church . . .

He did not complete the thought, and instead went on,

> . . . But we did the best we could do under the circumstances we had, and Bishop Hutchinson led us through that. He led us through that in tears sometimes, he led us through that by taking off the clerical garb and walking through the muck and the mud, putting his hands in the debris. He didn't have his beautiful crozier with him, but his crozier was leading the way, he was leading the way the best that he could, and his connections across this United Methodist connection were very important.

He thought it was at least in part "an emotional decision. What do you say to people who have lost their home and then you come along and take away their church?" They were unable to see far enough down the road "to know that some of their homes were not going to come back as quickly as rebuilding a church. Today, there are Bethany members who are still not back here."

Edwards was inspired to change Bethany's logo after the storm.

> We were broken, and United Methodist people around the world helped to put us back together. When Bethany came back as a church, that church was not only Bethany, that church was all these other United Methodists and others who helped us. We replaced the "t" in our name with the cross and flame.

The cross and flame is the official United Methodist logo, and the two strokes of the cross visually represent the two strokes of the letter.

> I saw the connection at work like I had never seen it at work before. I saw the connection not only in the money, but in the people who came, the people who, if they didn't come, they sent or they sponsored somebody else to come.

The circumstances gave new meaning to John Wesley's proclamation that "the world is my parish," he said. He continued,

> There is nothing that anyone can do to lead me from the United Methodist church, because I believe in the product, and I have been a witness to what this church can do. I grew up poor. My mother worked as a cook.

He told my students in 2007 that when he was a child, "for Christmas, we got socks and undies and jammies." In 2013, he said,

> We didn't have any money to go to school, and this church schooled me, educated me for the work in this church. I went to Methodist colleges and seminary; I know what this church can do. It has shown me all of my life the power and the beauty of the connection of this church.[8]

The ministry at Bethany UMC today has gone forward in new ways. For instance, when the New Orleans Superdome was selected to host Super Bowl XLVII in February 2013, persons concerned with human trafficking saw a strong likelihood that the event would be accompanied by an increase in that crime. Bethany took "a leadership role in New Orleans" to reduce trafficking surrounding the game and beyond. In early January 2013, Bethany's Human Trafficking and Domestic Violence Committee co-sponsored a conference with the congregation's United Methodist Women's (UMW) unit and the UMC's General Board of Church and Society (GBCS). Titled "Our Sisters' and Brothers' Keepers," the event was intended to raise awareness about what one speaker termed "modern day slavery." Bethany received a Peace with Justice grant from the church's General Board of Church and Society that spring to aid its continuing work on the issue with its partner, Eden House, a recently opened shelter for survivors of trafficking.[9]

Hartzell UMC in the Lower Ninth Ward

Hartzell is the only UMC church in the Lower Ninth Ward, a part of New Orleans that received a great deal of media attention after the storm because of its poverty, the extent of its devastation, and the extreme delay before officials let residents back into the area even for a quick "look and leave" visit. Although the Lower Ninth had a high percentage of African American residents who lived in poverty prior to Katrina, it also had one of the higher percentages of home ownership in the country. But when the floodwall broke, the water came through with such a rush that houses were literally thrown off their foundations, carried for blocks, and broken apart. "My mama's house, we never did find it," Hartzell member June Sanchez told my students.[10]

---

8. Ibid.
9. Backstrom, "Church Ministries."
10. Blue, "'Yes, We are Everywhere.'"

To understand the recovery story of Hartzell UMC, it is necessary to understand the troubled history of the Lower Ninth Ward. The Great Mississippi Flood of 1927 is a landmark event in United States history. It provides the fodder for books, both fiction and nonfiction, for songs like Randy Newman's "Louisiana 1927," for truth and for lies, and for myth—truth so profound that it can be conveyed only in the form of a story. Many believe that the story of dynamiting the levees in the Lower Ninth Ward in 1927 so that the more affluent sections of the city would be saved is "just a myth," but it is historically accurate—it happened.

Others believe that the dynamiting was repeated during Hurricane Betsy in 1965 and during Hurricane Katrina in 2005. In Spike Lee's documentary, *When the Levees Broke*, Marc Morial, the former mayor of New Orleans and now president of the National Urban League, said that it had never been investigated whether levees were dynamited during Betsy and that it could not be stated that they had or they hadn't.[11]

A scholar who recently worked on the history of the flood in the Lower Ninth Ward that occurred after Betsy considered the origin of the belief that city government had arranged for the levee on the Industrial Canal to be bombed in order to save other sections of the city. He concluded that there is no evidence that the levee was bombed, but there is evidence that the city made decisions which made the flooding in Lower Nine worse than it would have been had they not closed floodgates to keep floodwaters contained there. He also makes plain that actions of the city's government and elite before, during, and after the flood make the people's belief that the levee was bombed a reasonable interpretation of events, not the "crazy" claim that a previous historian had labeled it.[12]

The levees and floodwalls were not dynamited during Katrina, but the underlying truth—that affluent people are often willing to see others suffer in order to preserve their own wealth—is undeniable. Therefore, it does not seem as unlikely as it might that I have heard people state publicly that it is very "strange"—as in, does anyone *really* think it was a coincidence?—that just one barge was left in the Industrial Canal when all the rest were secured. That barge broke free, and its banging into the floodwall that protected Lower Nine from the Industrial Canal was a contributing factor in its breaking. Past history and past experience created a climate where the suggestion that it was left there deliberately does not indicate that the speaker could be labeled a "conspiracy nut."

---

11. Lee and Pollard, *When the Levees Broke*.
12. Horowitz, "Hurricane Betsy," 913–16.

Noting that the belief that explosives were used to direct the water "is sometimes regarded as being on par with the belief that the US government introduced the AIDS epidemic into African American communities," Penner and Ferdinand nevertheless understand that people "with a history of feeling deceived" will "tend to find the assertions of people they trust more credible than those of outsiders, even if they are from respected institutions." Further, they assert, "The belief that whites tried to kill blacks by blowing up the levees contributed to the decision on the part of some not to return to the home of their ancestors. This, in turn, inadvertently assisted those who have unabashedly sized upon Katrina as an opportunity to remake New Orleans as a smaller, less black city."[13]

Juliette Landphair's article, "The Forgotten People of New Orleans: Community, Vulnerability, and the Lower Ninth Ward," manages to convey a great deal about the situation through its title alone.[14] She provides some of the statistical realities that made recovery more difficult in Lower Nine than in some other sections of the city. However, as many obstacles as their pre-storm lives placed on the residents, the unwarranted foot dragging by officials exacerbated the problems they faced in several important ways. I strongly recommend Spike Lee's documentary, *When the Levees Broke*, as a vivid introduction to the issues involved. It is not easy to watch and definitely not appropriate for children, but through extensive use of personal interviews, it provides the kind of insight that typical scholarly work cannot.[15]

Actor Brad Pitt brought additional attention to the lack of recovery in the Lower Ninth Ward in 2007, when he established the Make It Right Foundation to help build homes there. The Make It Right website notes that the foundation placed some 150 pink-draped temporary structures around the neighborhood closest to the Industrial Canal to symbolize the environmentally friendly structures that they would erect. That kickoff event, called the Pink Project, was covered by media nationwide. Pitt and his wife, actor Angelina Jolie, have a home in the French Quarter, and Pitt reportedly loves being in the city. He bikes from the Quarter out to the area where construction is underway. The new homes are designed to be largely solar powered, and they look quite different from the homes that filled the area before the storm. However, most of the area is still unrecovered. Large portions have simply returned to native vegetation, and for a stranger driving through, it would be hard to imagine that anyone ever lived in certain portions of the ward.

13. Penner and Ferdinand, *Overcoming Katrina*, 223–24.
14. Landphair, "'Forgotten People of New Orleans.'"
15. Lee and Pollard, *When the Levees Broke*.

The decision about whether a United Methodist church would reopen in New Orleans was to be based in large part on how many of its members and how much of the neighborhood could return, but it is fair to say that Hartzell would no longer exist if that were the only criteria used. Most of the area around it is still vacant land where devastated buildings were bulldozed. Whole blocks have been completely reclaimed by vegetation, so that except for the fact that streets exist, it would appear that the area had never been the site of a neighborhood. The building was repaired and reopened strictly because of the commitment of Martha Orphe and others that the church would not abandon the Lower Ninth Ward. Renovations at Hartzell were halted more than once because thieves stole building materials. Copper, used in plumbing and other aspects of construction, is particularly valuable, and such burglaries occurred throughout the city.

Hartzell was placed in Mission Zone 6 with Cornerstone UMC, a larger congregation in New Orleans East, and with Covenant UMC, a merged church which had two buildings and before the storm held worship in two locations, Arabi and Chalmette. The pastoral team of James Haynes, Barbara Murray, Jeff Connor, and Rebecca Connor served this zone. The next Hartzell pastor, Elenora Mackey Cushenberry, served a two-point charge that yoked Hartzell with Phillips Memorial, where she pastored when it was a part of Mission Zone 2.[16] Phillips is in the section of the city called Gert Town, home also to Xavier University, a historically black Catholic university. Cushenberry notes that while Gert Town was "listed as one of the poorest communities in the United States, even prior to Katrina, there are a few signs that economic development is taking place." She notes that Gert Town and the Lower Ninth Ward share a number of characteristics.

As 2013 drew to a close, Cushenberry said

> [Hartzell] was struggling—struggling in the sense of it's a small membership church. We are struggling financially, just like the economy. As far as worship is concerned, the spirit of the church is good. Through the evangelism efforts, we have canvassed the Lower Ninth Ward. People are coming back gradually. Three or four blocks down from the church, some new homes are being built. If we can hold on and weather the storm, then I believe we'll make it.

The congregation is in a process of discernment, she says. They are holding a series of meetings after worship service on Sunday to discuss "where we are and where we see God calling us to be as a church." They had

---

16. Elenora Mackey Cushenberry, telephone interview with the author, December 11, 2013.

plans to meet with their representative to the City Council to discover what the city's plans are for the economically deprived Lower Ninth Ward. "It's definitely been a struggle since Katrina for that community, for that area, and the church is a part of that struggle."

She points toward signs of progress that are encouraging the people. The area's fire station is being rebuilt. The MLK Jr. Elementary School, located about a half-mile from Hartzell, at the corner of Caffin and Claiborne, has been refurbished and reopened. And at last, the Andrew P. Sanchez Sr. Multi-Service Center, located across the street from the school, is being reconstructed. Andrew Sanchez Sr. was a member of Hartzell and a leader in activist organizations during the Civil Rights movement. His son, Andrew, Jr., was King Zulu at Mardi Gras in 2015, a clear sign of his own prominence in the community.

June Sanchez, Andrew's wife, led the Women for Progressive Action, Lower Ninth Ward, an organization formed in the 1970s. Like several other prominent black leaders in New Orleans Methodism, June Sanchez graduated from the Methodist-run Gilbert Academy, a short-lived college-prep school for black youth in New Orleans. She went on to earn a degree from Dillard University and then a master's degree in early childhood education from Harvard. Pre-Katrina, Hartzell housed an exceptionally fine child-development center for several decades. June's sister, Gloria White, who has died since the storm, ran the center for many years. My article, "Yes, We Are Everywhere," in *Methodist History* discusses the work at Hartzell in much more detail.[17]

On the negative side, Hurricane Isaac damaged the church again when it struck the city in August 2012. "Thank God it wasn't as bad, but part of the church still had to be gutted, and we had to pull up the carpet in the sanctuary," Cushenberry says. Many New Orleanians have found subsequent storms extremely distressing. Cushenberry said the scriptural promises like those in Romans 5 about suffering, endurance, and hope, and those in Isaiah 40 that those who wait on the Lord will find their strength renewed and not faint, have helped them persevere. "If we can continue to struggle with the community, if we can hold on, we will begin to reap fruit," she said.

In June 2014, Cushenberry was appointed to a church in Shreveport. Lisa Fitzpatrick, whose work at Apex Youth Center is discussed in Chapter 7, was appointed to serve a two-point charge consisting of Hartzell and St. Paul's UMC, a predominantly white congregation in Harahan, a suburb on the other side of New Orleans, in Jefferson Parish. The location of Apex in

---

17. Blue, "'Yes, We are Everywhere.'"

the building that was People's Community Center should serve as a connection between Fitzpatrick and the congregation.

June Sanchez and other women from Hartzell were also long-time members of the Ruth Carter Auxiliary that supported the People's Community Center, located on Simon Bolivar in Central City, where Apex Youth Center is now housed. After Katrina, the Hartzell church building was used for a number of years for housing long-term volunteers, including college students who spent their summers mucking and gutting homes.

On a temporary basis, Hartzell is now renting some of its space to Total Community Action, and that organization has placed two agencies, the Lower Ninth Neighborhood Council and the Florida Desire Council, there until their previous settings, the Andrew P. Sanchez, Sr. Multi-Service Center Complex (named for June Sanchez's husband) and the Desire Community Center, reopen. The agencies provide funds for weatherization of houses and utilities for the needy, and they distribute food commodities on a quarterly basis.

Hartzell UMC thus seems to reflect what Melissa Harris-Perry notes in her study of cultural influences on black political behavior, that the church

> is the oldest indigenous black institution, and it is historically and currently significant in developing African American political culture and encouraging African American political participation. . . . Their sacred and spiritual functions, not their political ones, are the primary purpose of their existence. However, the historic and contemporary centrality of the black church has extended into social, political, and economic realms.[18]

St. Mark's UMC and North Rampart Community Center

St. Mark's UMC has an especially interesting post-Katrina story. My book *St. Mark's and the Social Gospel: Methodist Women and Civil Rights in New Orleans, 1895–1965* chronicles the work that female activists in the MEC, South did throughout the first half of the twentieth century. St. Mark's Community Center began as a settlement house, comparable to Hull House in Chicago founded by Nobel laureate Jane Addams, except that St. Mark's and other Methodist settlements throughout the country remained affiliated with their denomination rather than claiming a nonsectarian identity.[19] It

---

18. Harris-Lacewell, *Barbershops, Bibles, and BET*, Kindle locations 435–38.
19. Blue, *St. Mark's and the Social Gospel*.

was a classic Social Gospel ministry developed at the turn of the twentieth century to address problems created by the industrial revolution and increasing urbanization. Thousands of immigrants came to the city, and serving them and their children was just part of a wide variety of programs operated by deaconesses and local laywomen.

The St. Mark's congregation has always occupied space used primarily for the Center in a building owned by the Methodist women's organization. However, after the storm, the center had to be reorganized and renamed; the North Rampart Community Center was rededicated in October 2007. The congregation continues to be St. Mark's UMC.

Other cities have medians that separate traffic moving in opposite directions on boulevards. In New Orleans those medians are called "neutral grounds."[20] The neutral ground in the middle of North Rampart Street marks the border between the French Quarter and the Tremé neighborhood. St. Mark's is on the French Quarter side, at the corner of Gov. Nicholls Street. The congregation consists primarily of French Quarter residents and a mix of New Orleans citizens whose homes are on the streets. The community center has served residents in the Quarter, Tremé, the Faubourg Marigny, and other sections of the city.

Early settlements are usually located on higher ground, and the French Quarter is the oldest section of New Orleans. It is a part of the 20 percent of the city that did not flood, but a bit of water did come into the first floor of the community center, which interrupted their use of the space for a time. Further, most former participants in center programming were absent for some time, in part because no schools were functioning in the city.

Peg Culligan, a pre-storm board member who lives in the French Quarter, began seeing to the community center's swimming pool immediately after Katrina. She was there when a group of Broadway artists came to New Orleans and worked with local young people to stage a production of *Once on This Island*, a musical whose theme was a hurricane. They used the facilities of the community center, built in 1923 with a stage at the end of its gymnasium. The entire enterprise was captured on film for a documentary, *After the Storm*.[21]

Anita Dinwiddie had been appointed as pastor at St. Mark's in the summer of 2005. After Katrina, she was made part of the pastoral team for the mission zone that included St. Mark's, but she worked most closely with the St. Mark's congregation. When the congregation began to gather for

---

20. Legend says the name arose because the middle of the wide thoroughfare, Canal Street, served as the border between the American and European sectors of the city.

21. *After the Storm*, directed by Hilla Medalia.

worship again, they made a commitment to be in ministry with the individuals who live on the streets. Every Sunday, volunteers serve a hot meal after worship to anyone who wants to eat. Unlike many other ministries in the city, St. Mark's does not require those who eat to attend worship ahead of time. They hand out tickets after worship for the sole purpose of making sure that everyone gets a first serving before anyone gets seconds, and there is no distinction made between those who attended worship and those who did not. Therefore, it is quite significant that a large number of street residents choose to attend worship there each Sunday.

The congregation has long been known for its openness to LGBTQ people. In 1973, an arson-caused fire in a French Quarter gay bar, the Upstairs Lounge, killed thirty-two people. Among them were the pastor and many members of the Metropolitan Community Church, a denomination to which many LGBTQ persons belong. Churches in New Orleans refused to hold funerals or memorial services for the dead, because it was assumed that anyone in a gay bar was homosexual. St. Mark's volunteered to hold a memorial service. It is considered a pivotal moment in the history of gay life in New Orleans, because the crowd in attendance had the opportunity to leave through a side door and avoid the press gathered outside on North Rampart Street. Instead, they left through the front door, making the statement that they refused to hide their identities.[22] The congregation still holds a service commemorating the event every single year.

The "Disorganized Religion" program began July 2012. It "is an open space for critical and thoughtful questions about religion, faith, spirituality, and life. When a question is posed, there is the potential for a very stimulating discussion. There is no expectation that 'answers' will result." Sometimes there are guests, such as a local rabbi who has been to the group a few times.

The most significant thing about the congregation though, is the opportunity it affords to attend worship with a truly diverse group of God's children every Sunday morning. Rev. Anita Dinwiddie's gifted leadership has provided a safe and nurturing space for all those who attend.

Ross Williams UMC

Ross UMC was a small African American congregation located in Jefferson Parish near the place where Causeway Boulevard ends at the Mississippi River levee. It was proposed that they merge with Thomas UMC, another African-American congregation in Jefferson Parish. However, the members refused to worship at Thomas.

22. The story of the event is told in my book—Blue, *St. Mark's and the Social Gospel*.

They eventually wound up joining with Williams UMC, a small church that had been established for African Americans after the Civil War by northern missionaries from the MEC. Their building is located in the Black Pearl District of Uptown New Orleans.

The merged church, Ross Williams UMC, is part of a two-point charge served by Martha Orphe. She is also appointed to First Street Peck Wesley UMC, described below.

First Street Peck Wesley UMC

First Street UMC was built at the corner of First Street and Dryades Street in Central City, arguably the most troubled and dangerous section of New Orleans. Post-Katrina, the congregation merged with Peck UMC, located 1.6 miles away on Washington Avenue, and Wesley UMC, slightly over a half mile from the First Street church.

Lance Eden, pastor at First Street in 2005, was a young man not long out of seminary. He responded to the situation with enormous dedication to the congregation and the neighborhood. His work received a good bit of national press; he was featured in stories in the *ColorsNW Magazine* in 2005, the *Washington Post* in 2006, and in PBS's *Religion and Ethics Newsweekly* in 2007, and he was mentioned in Edward Wimberly's revised edition of his book, *African American Pastoral Care*.[23] He also helped organize a non-profit entity, United Saints, which operated from church property and housed and outfitted volunteer teams who came in to repair houses. It was not affiliated with the Louisiana conference's disaster agency which housed volunteers in several other locations around town.

In April 2007, Peck and Wesley churches had a joint charge conference with First Street UMC, and voted that the three churches should merge. An article about the merger from a June issue of the conference newsletter was also posted on the Louisiana conference's website's "Historical Register" page for all three churches. The article noted that parishioners from Peck and Wesley had been worshiping at First Street since 2005, because their own churches had suffered so much damage following the hurricane. Eden was quoted as saying,

> Hurricane Katrina's devastation and the breaking of the levees caused much sadness and despair in the city of New Orleans and the United Methodist community. But out of this sadness,

---

23. Ishisaka, "After the Storm"; Lawton, "Finding New Meaning"; Lawton, "Lance Eden Extended Interview"; Wimberly, *African American Pastoral Care*.

three congregations have come together in love and Christian fellowship to form a new church out of the ruins.

In 2008, I interviewed Carolyn Bowers, who was the district-wide president of the United Methodist Women's organization (UMW). Bowers's church membership before the storm was at First Street UMC. Regarding the merger and her membership in First Street Peck Wesley she said, "We are one church now. We are staying together."[24]

Eden was still working through the process toward ordination in the UMC at the time of Katrina. He was to be ordained at the Louisiana conference's annual gathering in 2009. Instead, at the clergy session where he would have been voted on, a representative of the Board of Ordained Ministry announced that Eden had been discontinued from the process. He had appealed, she said, and he would remain in his appointment at First Street Peck Wesley until the appeal process had been completed.

As it turned out, after the appeal, Eden's discontinuance stood. The bishop appointed Martha Orphe to First Street Peck Wesley. Orphe had been the director of the Mission Zone program and after its discontinuance served as director of multicultural ministries, working from the conference office in Baton Rouge. She moved mid-year into the First Street Peck Wesley parsonage and began her ministry there.

It would have been a difficult appointment no matter what, as the congregation was conflicted over Eden's departure. But Eden started the non-denominational Blessings Beyond International Church just a couple of blocks away. There are parishioners who attend both churches, expressing loyalty to Eden as well as loyalty to the church and congregation which they have belonged to for years and where they expect their funerals to be held.

Because the discontinuance was a personnel issue, no one on the Board of Ordained Ministry or in the conference office has spoken to me about it. That is, of course, the appropriate course for them to take, but it means that their side of the story remains untold. However, Eden himself talked to me about the matter in summer 2013, telling me that the charges against him were the result of a betrayal by a young man whom he had tried to help, in part by letting him stay in an apartment attached to Eden's parsonage. He said this person became angry at him and brought complaints that were not truthful. Eden said that the issue was intertwined with his own openness to gay and lesbian persons and the UMC's resistance to equal treatment for LGBTQ people. The Facebook page for Eden's new church says, "We are a Nondenominational Christian Church who serves the local community and

---

24. Carolyn Bowers, interview by the author, October 18, 2008, New Orleans, LA.

the world" and then adds, in italics, "believing in unconditional acceptance of all people."

At First Street Peck Wesley, the work of United Saints has been carried forward. In fall 2013, a Peace with Justice grant went to the church for its "Let Peace Prevail" project. On Saturdays, volunteers provide meals and Bible study, "along with classes in conflict resolution, digital photography and music," with occasional field trips. The overall goal is "inspiring children—especially those living in the highest crime district in New Orleans—with a 'respect for life, a respect for learning, and aspirations for a quality of life free of drugs, violence and other risky behaviors.'"[25]

---

25. Backstrom, "Church Ministries."

9

What's God Got to Do with It?

To be is to have an effect.
— Marjorie Suchocki

Collateral Circulation and the Stroke Called Katrina

In this book's Introduction, I talked about parallels between the recovery of the city and the recovery that some patients are able to make after suffering a stroke. A stroke is one of the most feared catastrophic medical emergencies because it can almost instantaneously destroy the aspects of a person's intellectual and emotional capabilities that define them as an individual.

However, even then, healing may occur. When it does, it happens over time. Although normal circulation and thus normal communication within the brain is blocked, the human body has the capacity to develop collateral circulation, to build new pathways for blood to flow and nourish the cells that allow messages to travel throughout the brain and the body. This healing tends to be slow, and it can seem erratic. Though "erratic" might also appear to be a good word to describe recovery in New Orleans, it is not sufficient. There are deep-seated socioeconomic reasons that determined which neighborhoods have failed to thrive.

There are other ways in which using this analogy for the city's recovery falls short, as all analogies do. Still, the capacity for self-healing through collateral circulation, for the development of new connections, seems to me to be the most apt metaphor for the better aspects of how the city has healed and certainly for the better aspects of how the UMC has put itself back together again as churches have learned to communicate and cooperate in unprecedented ways. It is in keeping with the best of United Methodist theology and with what the UMC sees as its defining characteristic—connectionalism.

The preceding chapters have described the development of collateral circulation within and among the United Methodist congregations and the construction of new avenues of communication and collaboration and cooperation. Yet even successful healing of this kind does not make the stroke patient physically identical at the cellular level to the person who existed before the incident. Nor is she precisely the same in emotional and intellectual ways. Some things are lost forever, while others are unexpectedly gained.

How *Does* God Act in the World?

Among other changes, tragedy dramatically alters the survivors' spiritual lives. It would be lovely to write that tragedy brings survivors closer to God, but it isn't necessarily so. It depends in part on how they have been taught to understand what God had to do with the tragedy and with the recovery. In Christian theology, it is the doctrine of providence that considers this question.

This is a matter of crucial importance to the people of New Orleans. For many New Orleanians, it was natural to conclude that religion was part of the problem rather than part of the solution. While the city was still underwater, while dead bodies still floated in the streets, while desperate people were still trying to hack their ways out of attics, some well-known individuals who claimed to speak for God blamed the disaster on the wickedness of the victims. Televangelists seem to be guaranteed media coverage for anything outrageous they say, and the more inflammatory, the better. After 9/11, we heard the verdict from Moral Majority leader Jerry Falwell that "abortionists, feminists, gays and lesbians, the ACLU, and the People for the American Way" were to blame. After the Katrina flood, the reputation of New Orleans's French Quarter as a place where sex of any kind was freely available led to the immediate assertion by well-known conservative Christians that God's anger had been justifiably roused and then displayed in the storm. With these statements, they quite literally added insult to injury, shaming those who had undergone grievous loss. (Furthermore, since the French Quarter is one of the few places that did *not* flood, it would appear that God has bad aim.)

In one of the first volumes of essays on religion and Katrina, *The Sky Is Crying*, several contributors addressed this blame-casting. Valerie Bridgeman Davis wrote,

> If the storms are the deity's punishment, we will have to explain why the people dying and caught in the maelstrom of pain are mostly all poor, mostly of color, and mostly very young and very

old. Do we really believe that the God who claims to defend widows and orphans, and who stands with the poor, would "punish" New Orleans by causing their deaths?[1]

Indeed, Katrina does force us to ask: How does God act in the world? Does God stand with the poor? Blaming victims for rousing God's wrath is not the only way of wrongly talking about God's role in things, though, and not the most insidious. It is easy for most of us to see the damaging effects of deeming the flood a punishment. However, the flip side—giving thanks because "God spared me" from the trouble a neighbor experienced—is not as easy to identify as harmful. As with, "There, but for the grace of God, go I," the intention of the speaker is presumably good. The words indicate humility, a recognition that one is not totally self-made and that God's good gifts have enhanced life. On the surface, this seems admirable. But while "God spared me" is not as obviously malignant as declaring others were punished because they were wicked, the teaching it conveys about providence has a distinctly malevolent side.

Sister Mary Daniel, OP, then director of the Dominican Conference Center, told my students that she was incensed when people told her the Dominican sisters were "blessed" because their facility did not flood. Located on the river side of St. Charles Avenue near Broadway, the former site of Dominican College was safe from the floodwaters "because our founders were smart enough to buy land on the high ground, back when it was affordable," she said. When people referred to them as blessed, she would demand, "Are you saying God cares about us and doesn't care about poor people in the Lower Ninth Ward?"[2] Her challenge is appropriate.

Among Christians, beliefs about God's activity in the world vary widely. At one end of a continuum are some who view God as a puppeteer who "pulls the strings" to arrange every single event in the lives of believers. The opposite end is occupied by those who believe God to be like a clockmaker who built and set the world in motion but then stepped back and now does nothing more than observe to see what will happen.

Charles M. Wood, author of *The Question of Providence*, taught those of us in his systematic theology class that there is a serious discrepancy in logic underneath believing that everything that happens is God's will. If I believe I am capable of acting outside God's will—sinning—and that anything I do wrong is my fault for *not* doing God's will, then it makes no sense for me to simultaneously believe that everything that happens to me

---

1. Davis, "Retribution as First Response," 10.

2. Sister Mary Daniel, OP, interview by the author and students, March 17, 2006, New Orleans, LA.

is God's will. As I tell my classes, if I hit a student in the front row and hurt him, I'm going against God's will. They agree. Then I point out that if I am the student in the front row who's been hit, I might think, "If God 'allowed' that to happen to me, then it must have been God's will." The discrepancy becomes clear.

Misidentifying Prosperity as God's Favor

In our culture, it is somehow perceived as particularly pious and holy to believe that God is directing everything that happens. In fact, as one of my husband's seminary professors pointed out, to do so would mean that we have to blame God for doing things for which we would put a human in jail.

The idea that God punishes sinners with events like Katrina has been around at least as long as Protestants have. A 1538 Lutheran catechism taught that if a person does not obey God, "God will scorn such a one in his deepest anguish and not hear him; he will punish him severely with many diseases, to wit: fever, swellings, pestilence, inflation, war, fire and hailstones, sores and boils, and altogether so much terror, misery, suffering, curses, confusions, and frustrations that he must fall into despair."[3]

Both Lutherans and Calvinists built belief systems on predestination, the idea that even before we are born, God has already decided whether we will be "saved" or "doomed" when we die. It is natural to wonder what one's eternal fate will be. Having to simply wonder, with no action that can affect the decision, can cause great anxiety around the question, "How can I know whether I am saved?" Not surprisingly, a technique for coping with this anxiety developed. People began to think that if a person would be saved in the afterlife, then God would probably bless them in this life, too. Correspondingly, if a person were not among God's elect, things would not be going so well for him or her here. This gave rise to the idea that those who were healthy and wealthy in this life enjoyed these benefits because God had selected them for salvation.

The Church of England created by Henry VIII was originally quite congruent with Catholicism, but under his son, Edward VI, its theology began to demonstrate some Calvinist influences. Members of the church's Puritan sect were convinced the Church of England did not go far enough toward Calvinism. When they came to North America, the Puritans brought the understanding that prosperity was a sign of God's eternal favor with them. It became a common way of looking at things in the United States.

---

3. Catechism of Caspar of Aquila, Superintendent in Saxony, cited in Miles, *Word Made Flesh*, 253.

The idea that the rich and powerful are that way due to God's blessings is still too prevalent today.

As Wood put it, the Christian doctrine of providence "at least in its traditional formulations"—the version that is "commonly taught and embedded in the lives of believers"—tends to "encourage passivity and resignation in those who are relatively powerless and to intensify their sense of guilt and worthlessness." It simultaneously fosters "a sense of well-being and self-satisfaction among the relatively powerful—not exactly the effect one would naturally associate with the teachings of Jesus as represented by the Gospels."[4] It is also worth noting that Methodism's founder, John Wesley, spent much time insisting that Calvinist theology was wrong and supporting his own Armenian understandings.

Creation is Not Finished

Wood thinks that one of the big problems with the common Christian view of things is that in it, "providence has been severed from creation." Separating creation out as an event that was finished long ago truncates our understanding of how God is acting in the here and now. As he put it,

> If there is any proper sense in which creation is "finished," . . . there is a very important sense in which it is not finished; its finishing, like its beginning, is ongoing.

Viewing creation as finished saps the creative energy from our own engagement in God's activity. If, as Christianity has often taught, "Our duty under God's providence is to adjust to the way things are, to accept the order of things, and to receive with all humility and gratitude what God sends us," then we bear responsibility only for being properly passive. Conversely,

> To recapture the unity of creation and providence . . . might aid in the liberation of the doctrine of providence from its long captivity to "the way things are." It might give the doctrine a better chance than it has ordinarily had to serve the ends of God rather than those of earthly sovereigns of one sort or another.

The impacts would spread far beyond the one question of providence, he asserts.

> Finally, to view creation and providence, and, for that matter, new creation, *together* as one ongoing work, one eternal act of God being realized through time and space, might not only

---

4. Wood, *Question of Providence*, 78.

renew the doctrine of providence but also provide new perspective on every other aspect of the Christian witness.[5]

Indeed, a bedrock of childish theology is altered by thinking of creation as unfinished. The first line of the narrative of how things came to be the way they are, "God created the world and then . . .," becomes something quite different. Granted, no human is God, and a moment when someone forgets that is a moment when evil takes hold. Nevertheless, we humans are in a real sense co-creators *with* God, co-creating something that is still in progress and whose shape and character depend in part on what we do.

Though Wood is not a process theologian *per se*, there are parallels between some of his thought and some of the work of process theologians like Marjorie Suchocki. Creation's ongoing nature is one of the most striking of these. Suchocki thinks the term "process-relational theology" is more apt than "process theology." Its practitioners work to integrate the "thoroughly interdependent universe into how we live and express our faith." This is because we are "convinced that everything is dynamically interconnected; that everything matters; that everything has an effect."[6]

She talks about the way classical philosophy influenced Christianity.

> There have been various relational ways of talking about the world since "way back when," but most philosophers talked as if the ideal thing should be something solid that doesn't depend on anything beyond itself. To be in relation was considered a lesser value than total self-sufficiency.[7]

She is referring to a pattern of white male European thought that insisted a "disinterested" love is superior to a intensely personal one where both are affected by the relationship; therefore, since God is superior to humanity, God's love must be distant and disinterested. Thus, the transcendent God took precedence over the incarnate God. However, "In the twentieth century we began to see that the ability to relate to another wasn't just a happenstance of the way things are, but it is the core of the way things are. To exist is to be in relation."[8]

What does it mean that God chooses to be in creative relationship with us rather than to be a puppeteer? Another way of naming at least a part of this struggle to understand is to ask the questions: Does God coerce people

---

5. Ibid., 72.
6. Suchocki, "What *is* Process Theology?" 3.
7. Ibid., 6.
8. Ibid.

into doing God's will, or does God choose to affect things through call and persuasion? In other words, does God act coercively or persuasively?

Throughout much of Christian history, the common assumption has been that things are as they are because that is how God intends them—because that is how God made them to be. As understandings of society and how it is composed and how it changes have evolved, it now seems more likely that things are *not* as they are supposed to be, because we humans have not done what God would have us do; furthermore, God calls each of us to make life on Earth more nearly like what God intends it to become.

To say "God calls us" is to opt for the "persuasive" adjective, since human freedom gives us the very real option of saying no to God's call. The freedom to "be whatever we want to be" is limited by the context into which we are born and by many other factors. But we have a great deal of say over who and what we become. Corporately, too, we have this freedom. As Suchocki put it,

> Finally, the world determines what it does with God's possibilities in every moment.... The world enters into something like a creative dance with God, emerging anew in every moment, as it takes its past in God's future into its becoming self.

For the world, for the church, and for individuals, "to be is to have an effect. Each individual influences what other individuals may become."[9]

It would be an anachronism to say that John Wesley was a process theologian, as process theology *per se* would not be developed till long after he died in 1791. However, it is no coincidence that two United Methodist theologians chose the same terms when they titled their systematic studies of Wesleyan thought; Randy Maddox chose *Responsible Grace*, and John Cobb used *Grace and Responsibility*. Both emphasize that humans must be an integral part of God's activity in the world.[10] John Wesley was not a "works righteousness" theologian, and he did not believe that good works were necessary for salvation. The story in Luke 23 of the man on the cross who was promised by Jesus that he would see him in paradise settled that question for Wesley. However, Wesley was absolutely sure that those of us who have the opportunity to do good works after we accept God's grace have a profound responsibility to do them. He saw that his own actions—including how he spent his money—affected the lives of others for good or for ill.

---

9. Ibid., 8–9, 18.
10. Maddox, *Responsible Grace*; Cobb, *Grace and Responsibility*.

Who Does the Church Think It Is?

Roman Catholics believe that people can accept or reject God, but for the Catholic hierarchy, the meaning of "being in right relationship with God" is identical to "being in right relationship with the Roman Catholic Church." Since the Roman Catholic hierarchy holds the power to excommunicate defiant lay members, and since Roman Catholics are taught that to be excommunicated is to lose eternal salvation, the power differential between clergy and faithful laypeople is almost absolute. Roman Catholic official teaching gave the archbishop in New Orleans much more than the power to eject troublesome parishioners from their buildings and send them to jail; it gave him the power to eject them from good standing in the church which, according to their teaching, would also eject them from an eternity with God.

As an Arminian theologian, Wesley was convinced that salvation is available to every human who chooses to accept it and that every human has the freedom and ability to accept or to reject God's grace. United Methodists do not believe that any individual can deny salvation to any other person. While bishops have great professional authority over clergy, they do not have and do not perceive themselves to have the ability to change a layperson or a clergyperson's standing before God by means of altering a relationship with the church (or in any other way).

Thus, the methodology of the Roman Catholics and the United Methodists (which occasioned such different responses on the part of parishioners) seems to me to be linked to the basic theology of the two churches with regard to salvation itself. It has to do with their understandings of what it is to be the church and of what kind of power the church does and should hold. Wesley himself had no doubt that a person's relationship with the Deity was just that—a personal relationship, which the church might enhance but certainly could not sever.

Wesley also believed that each person had freedom to do or not do what God would have them do at every moment of their lives. Because of our ability to say "yes" or "no" to God at every moment, God's activity in the world is inextricably linked with our own activity. It is both God's call on our lives and our responses to that call that determine what life is like, not just for us, but also for others. Furthermore, it is both our good and our sinful actions that have consequences, some of which last for generations. In Chapter 3, I noted that one can talk about "that bitch Katrina," or one can say "the levees broke," a phrase laden with possibility that people had simply been mistaken in thinking they were high enough. But when we face the facts that "contractors deliberately chose to make more money by not sinking floodwalls to the specified depths" and "for reasons yet to be determined, the Corps of Engineers did not see that the work was done correctly," we are talking about sin. So, did sin cause the catastrophe? Yes, but not the kind of sin the televangelists meant.

Thinking back to the images of the people left in the city after Katrina, I do not see them as God-forsaken. I see them as government-forsaken. Yes, there have been centuries of sin in the city, but I refer not so much to consensual sex as to sex trafficking that makes money for some and exploits others. I refer to slavery, Jim Crow segregation, and institutional racism and classism. The poverty-stricken individuals at the Convention Center and Superdome have been the victims, not the perpetrators, of these sins.

Beginning to deal with that reality moves us into a different category of public theology and public speech than those to which we are accustomed. Condemning drunkenness and sexual activity on Bourbon Street is easy. Speaking out against and trying to stop corporate and governmental graft, greed, and corruption is hard. It is difficult to know how to begin and how to acquire support among other Christians. It is hard to imagine encountering the anger of fellow church members who might be offended.

Frankly, it is easier to say that whatever happens, God intended, and that we should simply submit to it. I do not mean that submitting to everything that happens is easy—it most decidedly is not. What I do mean is that it can be easier to believe that we *should* simply submit than to believe that what I do makes a difference in how things will turn out not just for me and for those I love, but also for total strangers and unborn generations. Profound interconnectedness means that my life impacts all other lives, whether I want it to, and whether I am aware of it or not.

Jeong is More Powerful Than Love

In recent decades, a number of Korean and Korean-American theologians have worked with the concept of *han*, a way of understanding the long term consequences of what we do. *Han* is a negative force related to ongoing suffering as a consequence of sin, including sin which others have committed. In New Orleans, one might use the concept of *han* to help construct an explanation for the race-based poverty that left poor residents in the city after the levees broke. Within New Orleans United Methodism, one might talk about *han* in considering how centuries of institutionalized and individual racism left so many small, segregated congregations, some black and some white, struggling to survive before the storm.

In *Heart of the Cross*, Korean-American theologian Wonhee Anne Joh recognizes the reality and power of *han*. She cites the work of Andrew

Sung Park, who noted that along with the experience of terrible pain, *han* is "dominated by feelings of abandonment and helplessness."[11] Thinking of the indelible images of both the living and the dead abandoned in New Orleans and imagining the helpless anger of those who were "rescued" only to then be left on an interstate bridge for days without shade, food, or water can make me sick to my stomach ten years later.

To ignore *han* when doing theology about New Orleans would be inexcusable. However, Wonhee Anne Joh also harnesses a different concept for theological reflection: *jeong*. In conversation, she describes *jeong* as the substance which makes grains of rice stick together. In writing, she expands:

> *Jeong* saturates daily living and all forms of relationships. As a concept, *jeong* encompasses but is not limited to notions of compassion, affection, solidarity, relationship, vulnerability, and forgiveness. The word for *jeong*, when written using Chinese characters, is composed primarily of words for heart, vulnerability, and something "arising."[12]

In the West, we like to think of love as the most powerful emotion. Our Scriptures tell us that "love is as strong as death," and in Christian theology, love is profoundly important.[13] But Joh says, "Many Koreans have a common understanding of *jeong* as even more powerful, lasting, and transformative than love."[14]

Jeong has to do with the complex nature of all relationships. In conversation, Joh notes that *jeong* is not limited to human interaction. She gives an example of a favorite pen that no longer writes, saying that even though it doesn't work anymore, she can't throw it away, because she has *jeong* with it. In writing, she says, "*Jeong* forms attachments that are difficult to sever."[15]

One way of looking at what *jeong* has to do with this project would be to say that people might be unable to leave their previous churches with which they had *jeong*, even if those churches were not "working" any more. Another way, though, would be to say that United Methodists had *jeong* enough to stick together even when their understandings of church had to be drastically altered.

---

11. Park, *Wounded Heart of God*, 15, cited in Joh, *Heart of the Cross*, 21.
12. Joh, *Heart of the Cross*, xiii.
13. Song of Solomon 8:6c.
14. Joh, *Heart of the Cross*, xiii–xiv
15. Ibid., 34.

Having *Jeong* with a Place

I don't want to leave town. I don't care where it is or what they have there, I am not interested in it. —Hadley Edwards[16]

Connections with other humans are not the only kind of relationships with which theologians work. Theology of place is a relatively new topic for religious scholars, but it is quite applicable to a post-Katrina study. Anne Daniell is one of the scholars who has worked in this area. Her dissertation, entitled, "Incarnating Theology in an Estuary-Carnival Place: New Orleans in the Pontchartrain Basin," explored some aspects of the city's unique setting and culture. She completed it in October 2005, just after Katrina's landfall. At that time, she would not have known that her husband, Shawn Anglim, who was appointed in Baton Rouge, would be sent to New Orleans the next June as part of the Mission Zone program and become the founding pastor of First Grace UMC.

Anglim's repeated assertion in worship at First Grace that New Orleans is "the Holy City" is deeply linked to Daniell's intensive exploration of what an ethics of place involves. She points to the philosophical insight

> that life, and so ethics, can never be entirely *dis*interested. Though these ideas have sometimes been viewed as contradictory, in the sense that *either* one can be self-concerned *or* one can be other-concerned, a relational ontology provides a way to view them as complementary. To care about another person, place, ecosystem, the greater world, or even God is to care about those event-entities that are part of us and are always in the process of shaping us, and so this is a way of also caring for ourselves.[17]

Theological stances affect actions. "To truly care about a place means to act based on the knowledge that our ethical practices fan out into the many sets of relations that constitute place." They should also motivate us to assess things that are not as they should be and to strive for transformation of them. An "ethics of place," Daniell said, "calls us to critically appreciate, care for, and work to transform the places to which we belong, knowing that in doing so we also are nourishing and cultivating our own lives."[18]

---

16. Hadley Edwards, interview by the author and students, January 14, 2007, New Orleans, LA.

17. Ontology refers to the study of the nature of being or existence. Daniell, "Incarnating Theology," 202. Emphasis hers.

18. Ibid., 203.

Joerg Rieger made the same point as he considered models of ministry with "the Poor, the Underrepresented, and the Ignored." He wrote,

> We need to understand that our neighbors are not just recipients of charity, but that they are part of who we are and that loving them "as ourselves" implies loving them "as being part of ourselves."[19]

As Anne Joh put it,

> Living by *jeong* we know that often the life of the self is inextricably connected with the well-being of the other and vice versa. We are, in effect, locked into life with the other. We are permeable selves . . .[20]

There Were Other Boats

Bishop Bill Hutchinson's thoughts were along the same line as these theologians' when he talked about the church's work after Katrina. He referred to the story in Mark 4:35–41 in which Jesus is on a boat with some of the disciples. He falls asleep, and a storm so strong that the disciples think they will die begins to blow. They wake Jesus, who speaks to the storm and stills the winds and waters, bringing peace and calm. The bishop pointed out that there were other boats with them on the sea. The author of Mark wrote, "And there were also with him other little ships."[21] What happened in Jesus' boat affected the people in all the other boats, Hutchinson said.

He felt that the church's presence in the post-storm city also affected more than the church itself.

> You can't rely on what you've always known. It's like being in a war-torn country—there's no infrastructure. This is the point at which the church must remain sane and solid. What we do as the church is critical to the stability of the whole world.[22]

Hutchinson tried to model his leadership on that of Jesus. He said that Jesus' ministry was accomplished in close relationship with the disciples, and their actions and their understanding (or lack thereof) influenced how he did his work. Hutchinson's primary theological observation about the

---

19. Rieger, "Contemporary Issues," 197.
20. Joh, *Heart of the Cross*, 64.
21. Mark 4:36b (KJV).
22. William Hutchinson, interview by the author, June 21, 2007, Fayetteville, AR.

Katrina event is that it has been "a great unfolding of faith." He spoke of his increasing awareness that God's grace is constantly outpoured and absolutely sufficient for the day—even the days after Katrina.[23]

For tens of thousands of people, Katrina wiped out, at least for a while, the feeling of despondence connected with the common sentiment, "I'm only one person—what can I really do?" In an urban scene of utter destruction, it was obvious that recovery was going to take the efforts of many thousands of people and that no one working alone or with a small group could possibly do what would be required to turn the situation around. Gary Harbaugh's tiny but immensely helpful volume, *Act of God, Active God*, can help individuals who want to be of service in a time of disaster, particularly his reminder: "It is faithful to do the best you can, even if it is not enough. By definition, a disaster is overwhelming, and so no matter what any individual human can do to help, it can never be enough."[24] The enormous extent of Katrina's damage made it clear that working together was the only way to accomplish any significant recovery.

Hutchinson said, "It reinforced our need for community. We learned again that no person is an island."[25] Standing in solidarity with others is another way of thinking about this kind of relationship. "Solidarity is a great idea, but what does it look like in practice?" author Jordan Flaherty asked. His answer was that it is not congruent with an idea that "we can go down there and do something *for* those people." Nor is it an assumption that while we have something to offer them, they have nothing of value to give in return.[26] Hutchinson had the spiritual maturity to say early on, "No one has a grasp of this whole thing. I realized immediately that I didn't have the answer. I knew that the more heads we were able to have at the table, the more chance we would have to get it right." The recognition that others have gifts and wisdom to offer to the process is an important theological insight that underlay the conference's attempts to have decision making come from the bottom up.

> It was important not to say to the people, "We're going to close your church." It would have been easy to do. It would still be easy.... But we've chosen to give the work back to the people. The hope was that people would see that they needed to band

---

23. William Hutchinson, interview by the author and students, March 17, 2006, Baton Rouge, LA.

24. Harbaugh, *Act of God, Active God*, 61.

25. William Hutchinson, interview by the author, January 12, 2007, Baton Rouge, LA.

26. Flaherty, *Floodlines*, 107.

together to work and to be a critical mass. Unfortunately, every small group—even two people—wanted their faith community restored.

This was not a surprising reaction to the situation, of course. "They're traumatized. They know their job is to reach out with the Gospel, but they are so traumatized that they don't know if they can," he said in 2007. By 2009, he could look back on having "had to help people work through what we can do and what they can be." [27]

Two centuries of Methodist connectionalism seem to me to be one manifestation of *jeong*. This does not mean that the church cannot be broken apart—we have formally broken into pieces on more than one occasion—but an event like Katrina brings our "stickiness" to the forefront of our lives.

Katharine Rhodes Henderson, author of *God's Troublemakers: How Women of Faith Are Changing the World*, noted,

> Educational psychologists would say that what we are doing is negotiating a critical shift in consciousness. We are learning the radically interconnected and interdependent nature of our world. We are learning that we cannot merely give this concept lip-service. We actually need to trust and practice it as if our lives depend on it. Because they do.[28]

"We've been on a journey together," Louisiana conference provost Don Cottrill said. "It's been a strong affirmation for connectionalism. We had to find a systemic way of assisting." He noted that the challenge was for the church to be both pastoral and prophetic at the same time.

> Early on, questions about race and justice were raised. It was too early then; there was too much pain. Now, we're asking how the UMC can be involved in bringing this to the table in a helpful way. How can we learn from that and bring what we learn to the future?[29]

---

27. William Hutchinson, interview by the author and students, January 12, 2007, Baton Rouge, LA; William Hutchinson, interview by the author, April 17, 2009, Baton Rouge, LA.

28. Henderson, *God's Troublemakers*, 87.

29. Don Cottrill, interview by the author, June 21, 2007, New Orleans, LA.

Diversity—A Hybrid City, A Less Hybrid Church

Along with *jeong*, Anne Joh's work is also concerned with hybridity. A hybrid plant is produced by cross-pollinating, and the people who create these hybrid plants hope to make a new one that combines the best qualities of both plants.[30] Culture, particularly in the so-called "melting pot" of the United States, is also a hybrid product, and when the idea is transferred from horticulture to human life in neighborhoods and cities, there is less consensus on whether hybridity makes things better or worse. Other philosophers and theologians, including Christopher Baker, whose work is cited in Chapter 10, have explored the impacts of cultural hybridity on Christian thought and practice.

Reflection on this topic can offer substantive contributions to a church still struggling to create its post-Katrina identity. Although "hybridity" is not a word in common usage in New Orleans churches, hybridity is something that the city experiences as profoundly as any city in the United States, and its churches do, as well. While it is a complex topic, for New Orleanians who are familiar with the term "Creole," it is hardly a new concept. The word "Creole" carries many different meanings, depending on one's upbringing. Scholars still debate its origin and definition; Joseph Logsdon and Arnold Hirsch edited a volume that deals with some of the richness of the term.[31] Some people insist it applies only to the first generation born in the city to European parents, but this is far too limited to express what the word conveys today. Outsiders sometimes think that "Creole" is synonymous with "Cajun," but this is not even close to accurate. Though it is by no means limited to this, Creole identity has much more to do with the social construct we call racial identity. Language, foodways, and many others aspects of culture also play their parts.

Playwright Tennessee Williams is said to have maintained, "America has only three cities: New York, San Francisco, and New Orleans. Everywhere else is Cleveland." Lafcadio Hearn agreed: "It is better to live here in sackcloth and ashes than to own the whole state of Ohio."[32] Countless writers have taken a stab at describing how and why New Orleans is unique. The reality of hybridity seems to me an integral part of the explanation.

---

30. Similarly, grafting one kind of tree onto another can, with care, result in a tree that is capable of producing more than one kind of fruit.

31. Logsdon and Hirsch, *Creole New Orleans*.

32. Starr, *Inventing New Orleans*.

One major takeaway from an exploration of hybridity is that the identity of every individual is much more complex than had been previously realized. I see New Orleans as providing a place where almost anyone can not only feel, "I can be myself," but can also believe, "I can safely be my selves." I am not referring to a phenomenon like dissociative disorder or multiple personality disorder. I am referring to the fact that even a well-integrated person still has various "sides" to her or his personality. Baker pointed to the "boho" or bohemian character of certain cities that draws creative people who are able to express themselves in a wide variety of ways. New Orleans had this quality before the storm, and since 2005, it has drawn even more talented and interesting people who want to be part of the re-creation of this beloved and endlessly varied city.

The church in New Orleans needs to come to a stronger appreciation of its hybrid identity. This is complicated by the fact that for decades, church growth specialists taught that homogeneity is a requirement for building large and healthy congregations. Going forward, it will be increasingly important to abandon that belief. Katharine Rhodes Henderson interviewed women who are engaged in successful non-traditional (or "entrepreneurial") ministries that are meeting the needs of marginalized people in their cities. She found that these leaders had some things in common. One of them, she wrote, is that "Instead of managing diversity as a necessary evil, they trust and cultivate inclusiveness as a means of strengthening their organizations."[33]

The disparities that exist around race and ethnicity, in society, in the larger church, and in the UMC, are so obvious that it seems pointless to try to document them here in a way that would convince someone who has never noticed them. It is much less obvious how much prejudice exists as a result of socio-economic standing. We have seen examples already. Think of former District Superintendent Ralph Ford explaining to my students that churchgoers in New Orleans sometimes told him that they did not want to reach out to those in need, because "They are not our people." Think of Lisa Fitzpatrick stating her belief that the African American youth of Apex were not welcomed in a particular African American congregation because of "socio-economic differences."

Over 100,000 people in the city live in dire financial circumstances. Data from the 2008–2012 census revealed that almost 30 percent (28.8) of the inhabitants of New Orleans lived below the poverty line; in other words, 102,770 New Orleanians could not afford even the essentials of life.[34] John

---

33. Henderson, *God's Troublemakers*, 44.

34. Bloch, Ericson and Giratikanon, "Mapping Poverty in America." *The New York Times* used 2008–2012 census data, with $23,283 as the poverty line for a family of four, and $11,945 for a single person younger than sixty-five.

Wesley thought and wrote a great deal about how the circumstances of poor people affect the spiritual lives of people who are not poor. In his sermon called "The Use of Money," he urged Christians to "gain all you can, save all you can, and give all you can."[35] The terms "gain," "save," "give," and "all you can" need clarification; fortunately, he provided it. No Christian should practice a livelihood which harmed others, but everyone should earn enough to provide necessities for themselves and their families. Christians should have sufficient (but not overly fancy or expensive) food and decent (neither overly adorned nor ragged) clothing, and they should provide shelter for their families.

Past these essentials, though, he was convinced that owning more than one needed was to take away essentials from others. When he said, "Give all you can," he did not mean, "Drop your change in the bucket after you shop." As Randy Maddox has noted, "while Adam Smith held that surplus accumulation was the foundation of economic well-being, Wesley viewed it as mortal sin!"[36]

John's mother, Susanna, had profound theological influence on him. Her husband frequently owed more than he could pay, and she was left to raise the children on her own while he was in debtor's prison. This influenced prayers she composed. In "Sincere Devotion," she wrote that if she could ask for anything in the world, "I would humbly choose and beg that I might be placed in such a station where I might have daily bread with moderate care."[37] In "The Way to the Father," she prayed that God might "vouchsafe to give me food to eat and raiment to put on, without debt; without this extreme distress . . ."[38] John was shaped by the same experiences, and always insisted that Methodists with means not only help those in need, but also recognize their humanity. He was insistent that they should spend time each week with people who were poorer than they were, despite a long list of excuses the affluent developed to try to convince him they shouldn't. He knew that personal contact formed a bond that helped Christians follow Jesus. Wesley saw it as his, and our, task to forge connections across boundaries, not just in theory, but also in our own lived experiences, and not just in our hearts and minds, but also in our actions, including those that have to do with our possessions and resources.

The determination to build relationships—to create *jeong*—with people who do *not* have nearly everything in common with us, who do not

---

35. Wesley, "Use of Money."
36. Maddox, *Responsible Grace*, 244–45.
37. McMullen, *Prayers and Meditations*, 57.
38. Ibid., 69.

meet the homogeneity standard that old-fashioned church growth advice recommended is not just following the teaching of Jesus, it is also a decidedly Wesleyan theological practice.

The Midwife as an Agent of Birth and Change

I tell my students that the primary job of the pastor is to stay sane in the pastorate. They laugh, but I'm completely serious. Having a clear picture of what Christian leadership looks like is a crucial part of that process. Many metaphors have been proposed for how clergypeople should think about being in relationship with church members.

Ramonalynn "RL" Bethley was the District Superintendent who replaced Martha Orphe and Ralph Ford when the Mission Zone program came to an end. Her background and leadership philosophy are profiled in Chapter 4. Admiring the work of Benjamin and Rosamund Zander, Bethley tends to ask what any individual can contribute to the work at hand, and to provide opportunities for them to make those contributions.[39] "Listening and building relationships is 98 percent of my job," she told me.[40] It can be difficult for any leader to learn that she does not always need to be "doing" something in the common sense of the word.

Bethley told me she thought she tended to mother the congregations in the New Orleans district during her tenure there. There are aspects of mothering in what she does, but not in the pejorative meaning sometimes attached to "mothering" when the topic is women's leadership—doing things for others that they could do for themselves or taking responsibility for things for which others should be responsible. Rather, Bethley mothered in the sense of preparing one's children to stand on their own.

Overall, I think it is more helpful to think of "midwife" rather than "parent" as the model for ministry, and probably a more accurate description of what Bethley accomplished in New Orleans. The parent is obligated to do everything for a small child. A midwife does not and cannot do the work for the mother who is in labor; she can only help the laboring woman to recognize the resources she already has and make them sufficient for the moment. Though the midwife (or doula) does not give birth herself, her wisdom and presence allow the mother to labor successfully.

Bethley was a good midwife who helped congregations give birth to something new. In her work in the district, she was able to maintain the

---

39. Zander and Zander, *Art of Possibility*.

40. Ramonalynn Bethley, interviews by the author, March 18, 2009 and June 20, 2009, New Orleans, LA.

beneficial level of self-differentiation that it is so difficult for a parent to maintain. She was willing for people to use their own gifts and assets, to make their own contributions to the work that God was doing in the city. She was a helpful presence with them as they did so.

Anthropologist Dr. Martha Ward, a member of First Grace UMC, talked about the role of women after the storm and also the role of people in priestly or pastoral roles. She spoke of the shamanic practice of "holding the space," a term also used for the work of a midwife during a mother's labor. Holding space during birth may be "a set of practical actions. It is caring embodied in compassion and vigilance." In other situations, the one who holds space is "a competent presence, someone willing to witness, to take it in and tell it back."[41] Katharine Rhodes Henderson uses the term "holding environment," a phrase she borrowed from the work of a child psychologist. She defined it as a "hospitable space created to provide physical and psychological safety mixed with appropriate challenge and structure so as to best sponsor wholeness and healing."[42]

Lisa Fitzpatrick, director of the Apex Youth Center, whose work with tweens and teens in Central City was discussed in Chapter 7, worked for years in Los Angeles as a doula. She founded a parenting center there that dramatically reduced the rate of infant mortality/morbidity. Researchers at Tulane are fascinated with the success of her work at Apex and keep asking her, "But what is it that you *do*?" She usually responds, "I open the door." This opening of the door is precisely the work to which I am referring.[43]

As noted above, Bishop Hutchinson could look back in 2009 on having "had to help people work through what we can do and what they can be." When I told him once that his leadership style was quite congruent with feminist thought on collaborative leadership, he responded, "I've always led this way. It frustrated some of my congregations terribly." [44] Martha Orphe told me in 2013 that there are still some United Methodists in the city who use the language, "the conference made us" when they consider the steps their congregations took.[45] After ten years of watching this process, I can say with assurance that this view is held by a small minority, and the view reflected in the section below is far more prevalent. The midwifery that honored the work of the people was based on a healthy view of the Spirit's activity as manifested in the lives of the laity and clergy in New Orleans, and it was overall a successful strategy.

41. Martha Ward, interview by the author, December 5, 2008, New Orleans, LA.
42. Henderson, *God's Troublemakers*, 29.
43. Lisa Fitzpatrick, interview by the author, October 10, 2013, New Orleans, LA.
44. William Hutchinson, interview by the author, April 17, 2009, Baton Rouge, LA; William Hutchinson, interview by the author, June 21, 2007, Fayetteville, AR.
45. Martha Orphe, telephone interview by the author, November 13, 2013.

Decommissioning Brooks

On January 3, 2009, a group of people who had belonged to Brooks UMC gathered outside the building at 4000 Buchanan to decommission the structure. The conference had a buyer for the property who wanted immediate possession. As a result, the church's decommissioning was planned and executed so quickly that neither the bishop nor the district superintendent could attend. By that time, its congregation had completed a merger with another African American congregation, Shaw Temple UMC. Now, the pastor of Brooks-Shaw Temple, Eunice Chigumira, stood under an umbrella and preached the last sermon at Brooks.

Going inside for the service was not an option because the church had never been mucked and gutted after Katrina, and untreated mold made even a short stay inside too dangerous to risk. It was not a particularly cold day, but there was a drizzle that required the pastor to deliver part of her sermon from under an umbrella. Eunice and her husband, Simon, both natives of Zimbabwe and graduates of the seminary at Emory University, had come to the city after Katrina to be part of the Mission Zone program. She spoke to the small gathering in a kind and helpful way. She talked of missing Africa but of having found a good life and a productive ministry in the United States. The parallel with the laypeople who had found, or more aptly, created a new church home was clear.

The decommissioning of Brooks UMC afforded me an important lens on the entire UMC process, because the people themselves performed most of the liturgy, simply speaking from their hearts. There were many tears, but every person used phrases about the necessity to move forward and celebrated their having become a genuine part of the newly merged Brooks-Shaw Temple congregation.[46] Both their language and their attitudes clearly indicated that their genuine acceptance of the merger with Shaw was a function of their having had an opportunity to decide for themselves what was best for them and to answer God's call to create a future for their church.

---

46. The one exception was a man who said that women should not hold authority in church, so he was attending a UMC congregation with a male pastor. Though he objected to the bishop's having appointed a woman as pastor of Brooks-Shaw Temple, he did not say anything against the merger itself.

10

It's Time

*The lethal mess that followed Katrina was . . . a
man-made disaster . . . and entirely preventable.
Entirely preventable . . . and yet it
wasn't being prevented.*
— Jed Horne[1]

This book has addressed things the United Methodist Church did after the flood, especially the things the church did well. These include a genuine effort to use collaborative leadership and to let decisions come from a longer and more inclusive process than from the easier, more hierarchical approach it could have taken. It did not do everything perfectly; that would have been impossible even in good circumstances. Good intentions did not manage to eradicate institutional racism and sexism, but the results within the church itself were much more aligned with justice than they could have been.

The most important thing the UMC did not do well was an omission rather than a commission. Specifically, the church did not speak with a prophetic voice for justice in areas where a prophetic voice was needed. Ten years out, it is time to rectify that omission.

Doing Public Theology

To do public theology is to provide theological support for the pursuit of the common good. Note that this is not the same as supporting whatever the government wants to do or whatever the majority of citizens happens to be for, nor the same as uncritically supporting the norms of society in

---

1. Horne, *Breach of Faith*, 410.

any given place or time and the maintenance of the status quo. It begins with serious reflection on what "the common good" might be. Some people maintain there is no such thing as a common good, because what is good for the dominant segment of a society cannot also be good for the segments that are marginalized. Nevertheless, if theologians truly understand that a "good" society would be one where "the least of these" are equally valued and cared for and accept that achieving common good might require more change than is comfortable, I think it can be helpful terminology. Struggling with questions about the common good, as over against assuming that the answer is obvious, is in itself a productive enterprise. Developing the best answers possible and working toward making those answers a reality is the heart of public theology.

In my view, the practice of public theology has been far too absent in post-Katrina New Orleans, and not only in the United Methodist segment of the church. This does not mean that no church leaders noticed and talked about the issues. It does mean that the church did not have, take, or make the time and resources to contribute to the public discourse as effectively as it should have.

In some ways, this is not surprising. Just as catastrophic illness in a family shuts out almost all thoughts of other aspects of life, especially in the early phase, so the cell-by-cell focus on its own recovery and on helping thousands of south Louisiana families return to their homes made it difficult for church leaders in Louisiana to see the bigger picture and to speak helpfully about it. Though this book has not focused on disaster response, I must state again that the UMC used its resources to help people who desperately needed help, addressing both immediate and long-term needs. It would be a mistake to dismiss the worth of mercy ministries, and the UMC definitely excelled there, especially in case management. This emphasis on assisting people to return to their homes was by no means wrong.

However, the UMC did not excel in justice ministry. Some years ago, I co-authored a book of case studies for theological students. I can imagine developing a case about a person who must choose in a given moment whether to provide one meal for someone who is hungry or to leave in order to preside at a meeting of an organization addressing food justice. The ethics involved would make for an interesting exercise. But the post-Katrina UMC did not have the luxury of pondering an academic assignment. It was a real-life situation, where the decisions that church leaders made would impact real people, for good or for ill.

Another contributor to the conference's failure to turn the focus outward was the fact that other storms have struck Louisiana since Katrina and Rita. A newsletter that described UMC efforts to help survivors of 2013's

Hurricane Sandy in the Northeast carried an article on the same page asking for more response teams to come to Louisiana because "Louisiana still needs assistance in recovery from Isaac" which made landfall in August 2012. The article specifically mentioned needs in LaPlace and Maurepas.[2]

An acknowledgement of the church's failure to get a category of work accomplished does not equal an assertion that leaders' personal theologies do not portray God as longing for real justice. There was such a massive drawing of focus to seemingly more urgent needs that some issues simply got lost in the chaos. In fact, if I am to be honest, I have to admit that it took me a good five months of constant presence in the New Orleans of 2008 to begin to see the extent of this gap—this large and significant gap—in the church's activity.

Along with the many United Methodist meetings and other church events that I attended during my 2008–9 sabbatical, I went to scores of conferences, panel discussions, and meetings held by a variety of non-church-related groups, including universities and nonprofits. An audience member at a conference on rebuilding assisted me in—or more accurately, prodded me into—recognizing this gap. As we sat in a third-floor lecture room at the US Mint, she posed a question to three of us who were making presentations on religion-related topics: "Why is the church so absent from the larger discussion about rebuilding the city?"

What I might have answered in the moment is lost to me now. But I knew immediately that I had no evidence to counter her charge that the church—and like her, I mean the larger church, all sizes and flavors—was missing from the action in vital ways. At first, that seemed counterintuitive, because the church was visible in a way that it usually wasn't. The thousands of church vans making their way through the streets made a positive impression on residents who hadn't thought about the church in years. Wearing t-shirts emblazoned with the logos of the religious organizations under whose auspices they came to muck and gut houses, tens of thousands of volunteers filled city restaurants and stores and were often willing to listen to the stories of servers and clerks who needed to process their own losses even while they worked. I have often heard volunteers say that people asked them, "Why did you come all the way down here to help us?" It was astonishing to local folks that so many church people would travel here at their own expense to work for no pay, and that so many of them returned again and again to do so.

As I thought back over all the non-church meetings I had already attended and observed carefully at all the rest of the non-church events that I

---

2. "United Methodists Rally"; "Louisiana Still Needs Assistance."

would attend throughout the rest of my sabbatical and in the ensuing years, I learned to my dismay that the questioner at the Mint was right on target. At meetings, at conferences, at policy-making tables where decisions about the future of the city were being made, no one from the church was there, and furthermore, no one seemed to notice that absence. No one expected the church to be at the table—not even the church.

Being "absent from the table" is a loaded metaphor for Christians, because a lot of our theological rhetoric centers on the question, "Who is at the table?" This usually means the table for Eucharist (also called Holy Communion or the Lord's Supper). The debate centers on whether all of humanity should be welcome to participate in the ritual as it is practiced in a particular group. But while churches have been busy attending to our own tables, and in the case of the UMC, arguing about who can and cannot preside at our tables, we failed to notice that we have been absent at tables where significant decisions are made in the city.

Why was the church not included?

The first reason for the church's absence was the lack of invitations. In New Orleans, hardly any group is knocking on the doors of the church asking for representatives to their conferences and meetings. "We were never invited to sit at governmental tables by [Mayor] Ray Nagin or by the state," Bishop Hutchinson recalled.[3] Though the church provided enormous help to the governments—$40 to $50 million of in-kind service—he said, "The church is the last place they would have turned" for policy advice.

It seems to me that the behavior of the Roman Catholic Church, discussed in Chapter 4, may be one of the causes; it is impossible to quantify how much damage the archdiocese did to its own reputation post-Katrina. The occupations of St. Henry and Our Lady of Good Counsel and the arrest of parishioners made news around the world. The failed attempt to close St. Augustine, a historic and predominantly African-American congregation in Tremé, was particularly ill-advised. Their approach left non-Catholics and many of the faithful disenchanted. There has been such a serious loss of trust that it does not seem surprising that in a predominantly Catholic city, no one thought of the church as an entity that would speak for the oppressed or bring a needed voice for justice to the public sphere. As emphasized earlier, Catholic Charities and many Roman Catholic individuals worked for justice for marginalized people; I refer here strictly to the actions of the archdiocesan hierarchy. Other Christian denominations, including

---

3. William Hutchinson, interview by the author, April 17, 2009, Baton Rouge, LA.

the United Methodist Church, have by no means been blameless, but their mistakes did not go viral the way the Catholics' did.

The second reason was a lack of awareness on the part of churches that they should have been at the tables and a resultant lack of energy put into trying to get there. It seems best if I confine my assessment to the UMC and let readers decide for themselves whether the same is true for their own denominations. The UMC has been absent in large part because United Methodists in Louisiana failed to imagine ourselves in that role, and we have not done the work that would enable us to be represented.

Missing Connections, the report of a research project conducted by Auburn Seminary in 1999, documented "the invisibility of religious leaders in the public arena."[4] Auburn's president, Katharine Rhodes Henderson, was troubled by the findings. Pondering some of the significant justice work that she has been able to accomplish, she noted that it has often meant "inviting myself to tables where religious leaders normally do not get invited."[5] Learning to get invited, learning to invite ourselves, and learning to speak effectively once we obtain a place should be the task for the next decade and beyond.

A Time to Speak: Moving from Mercy to Justice Ministry

When many Methodists, especially Methodist laywomen, were doing courageous and successful work in New Orleans (and throughout the country) during the Social Gospel movement of the early twentieth century, there were Methodists who objected strenuously to their provision of free health care for both black and white people, after-school athletic activities and clubs for young people, and education for kindergarteners and for adult immigrants who needed to learn English, homemaking skills, or job skills. This strong resistance came from those who believed the church should confine itself solely to "spiritual" matters.[6] Today, the women's work would be viewed as "mercy ministries" as over against "justice ministries." Participation in mercy ministries is no longer challenged very often; now it is usually justice ministries which are controversial.

To clarify, an example of post-Katrina mercy ministry was helping people first to muck and gut their flooded homes and then to rebuild them. Justice ministry would have involved questioning the often voiced assertion

4. Henderson, *God's Troublemakers*, 9–10, 216.
5. Ibid., 231.
6. Blue, *St. Mark's and the Social Gospel*.

that the city needed a "smaller footprint" and that people from certain neighborhoods (primarily black and poor) should not be encouraged to return. Another example of mercy ministry is providing free doctor visits, as Luke's House does. Justice ministry would have involved questioning why "Big Charity," the flagship of the state's charity hospital system, was not reopened after Katrina and advocating for some comparable system of health care for poor people. In 2009, LeKisha Reed, who was then associate pastor at First Grace, commented to me that the church had had no input into decisions about the destruction of a large portion of a Mid-City neighborhood quite near the church for the construction of the huge hospital complex that will replace Big Charity. Some people maintain that a new, cleaner, and more efficient hospital will make things better for those who need free care. Others insist that the new facility will never be as dedicated to providing for "the least of these" as Big Charity was and that ten years was too long to wait for it. Since the new hospital did not open until late 2015, the evidence needed to decide will not be available for quite some time to come. My point, and Reed's, is that the profound ethical implications of these decisions made them an area where the church might have been expected to participate in the discussion.

At this point, it is not that productive to consider areas where the church might have spoken but did not in the first decade after the storm. What is important is to consider the areas where the church can focus its voice and its moral authority in the immediate and middle-term future. I believe the two most pressing places where the church should speak both to ourselves and to the larger public are: (1) in the realms of recognizing and honoring the intrinsic worth of *all* people; and (2) on the problems of coastal erosion and climate change. Both issues shaped the Katrina event, both are shaping the city right now and will shape it in the future, and both are areas where the church's voice could be a determining factor if Christians are willing to take the risks involved in speaking out.

Race, Class, and The Hybrid Church

One mega-issue after Katrina with which the church has not adequately dealt is how race and class impacted the storm's devastation and has impacted the recovery from it. Cheryl Kirk-Duggan's edited volume, *The Sky Is Crying: Race, Class and Natural Disaster*, appeared slightly over a year after landfall. Scholars who contributed saw the inequities that left so many poor individuals stranded during the levee breaks as a function of racism, and they saw the failure of government, especially that of the George W. Bush administration, to respond appropriately as a function of racism, as well.[7] The ways the issue of race is still impacting the city are intertwined with gender and class. The large percentage of the population living in poverty before the storm and the gentrification of various parts of town after it have had a great deal to do with determining who has been able to return and who has not.

The host of *Speaking of Faith*, Krista Tippett, wrote that

> [Katrina] temporarily broke the self-protective dam many of us had erected between the blight of poverty in the United States and the semi-controlled havens of our own lives. Terrible images came into our living rooms of one hundred thousand New Orleanians, mostly African American, who were too poor to evacuate the city and were then left to fester in subhuman conditions.

She commented on FEMA director Michael Brown's having said, "We're seeing people we didn't know existed." It was, she said,

> [an] awakening that echoed across our nation. How can it be, communicators asked, in the richest country in the world, that so many residents of the core of New Orleans were invisible even to authorities. And how did the rest of us become isolated from their despair?[8]

At a conference at Xavier University on the use of social media and alternative media in justice work, professor Robin Vander pointed out how easy it is to forget that it is real people who are affected by social problems. "How do we begin to reorient ourselves? How do we get in touch with the intimate aspects of these issues?" she asked.[9]

This is a place where John Wesley's insistence that Methodists have frequent, personal contact with people in need fits beautifully into the Katrina story.[10] For instance, the actions of the people in Gretna who used guns to turn away other people trying to walk out of the flooded city could not have happened had the residents in Gretna truly known the New Orleanians trying to escape and had therefore seen them as human beings, but they did not. Forging *jeong*, building connections among people quite unlike one

---

7. Kirk-Duggan, *Sky Is Crying*.

8. Tippett, *Speaking of Faith*, 197.

9. Robin Vander, panel at the "Beyond Jena" conference, Xavier University, New Orleans, LA. January 31, 2009.

10. Maddox, "Visit the Poor," 77–79.

another goes a long distance toward preventing the invisibility that Tippett observed and the violence that invisibility fosters.

Because injustice is systemic and thoroughly embedded in institutionalized structures, it can never be "fixed" overnight. There is always pushback from people who benefit from having economic, political, legal, and even social and religious structures remain as they are. Yet when racism (and sexism and classism) remain entrenched, it results in loss on many levels. For instance, several talented leaders who worked in the city after Katrina are no longer part of the Louisiana conference and in some cases, of the UMC, and a disproportionate number of them are younger people of color. Many young African American clergy are discovering that they have to leave Louisiana if they hope to advance in their careers, because there are so few African American congregations that are able to afford seasoned clergy. Further, appointments of African American clergy as senior pastors of large white congregations are still so rare that "handful" is too large a term to describe them.

LeKisha Reed, a gifted young African American woman who served in New Orleans after the storm and who was in the process of ordination in Louisiana, chose to move to Indiana instead. She was ordained there in 2010. Before she left, she was offered an appointment at a black membership church in another part of the state, but the District Superintendent asked if she would consent to being called "junior minister" rather than "associate minister," because she was young and older ministers might be offended. There is no such thing as a "junior minister" in the UMC, and she wisely did not agree to pioneer it.[11] In her new conference, Reed served as associate director for mission and advocacy, and she has more recently accepted a position with the General Board of Global Ministries in New York City as the Executive Secretary for Networks and Constituencies, working with community organizers and rural and urban networks. Reed is just one of a number of African Americans who faced barriers in Louisiana.[12] Until the UMC achieves its stated goal of open itinerancy—a situation where any pastor, regardless of race, ethnicity, or sex, can be appointed to any church — there will not be as much room for professional advancement for young black pastors as for young white ones. I ask my students to find hope in the fact that open itinerancy is the UMC's goal, something not every denomination can say, but progress toward achieving it is disturbingly slow.

---

11. LeKisha Reed, interview by the author, March 30, 2009, New Orleans, LA.

12. Louisiana is by no means the only conference where prejudice on the part of congregations still affects appointments. That is probably the case in most, if not all, conferences, though some have made more progress than others.

The cliché "changing laws does not change hearts" is a cliché precisely because there is some truth contained in it, even when the "laws" consist of a church's *Book of Discipline*. Yet every Christian, clergy or lay, has some capacity to change hearts, and the small steps which accumulate into big change should never be dismissed as unimportant. Suggesting a pulpit or choir exchange between two segregated congregations of different races, or organizing a mission project of any kind at all which involves mixing volunteers from those churches is a deliberate step toward creating the kind of *jeong* that allows the overlooking of cultural mistakes and awkwardness. Achieving equality of all people is a process, a long and immense process, and every effort is valuable, even one that consists merely of doing something wrong and learning from it.

The Church in the Third Space

Anne Joh's use of *jeong* as a theological concept was discussed in the last chapter, along with her work on hybridity. Theologian Christopher Baker's work also follows the philosophy of Homi Bhabha and others who are interested in hybridity, but *The Hybrid Church in the City* is more closely focused on ecclesiology, the study of how churches actually function in their communities and what that might have to do with the way they think about the things of God.

He explained that as "the fusion of two or more identities into a new identity," hybridity becomes the "cultural norm that informs all our identities as individuals and urban dwellers, and the spatial and political realities that shape our daily existence." In other words, hybridity is not just placing people with disparate cultural identities near each other; proximity results in changes in both parties. As those who live in cities shape and change one another's identities, larger entities, those "spatial and political realities that shape our daily existence," evolve as well.[13]

Baker used Third Space theory to reflect on Christian practice in Manchester, England, and other locations in the United Kingdom. Much of Manchester's racial diversity is the result of immigration, and some of that has to do with England's history as a colonizing empire. The legacy of being a colonizer is quite different from the legacy of being colonized. Louisiana was a colony of several different countries, including France and Spain, both of which left visible and audible marks on New Orleans that persist today. Large infusions of immigrants from Haiti during the rebellion of enslaved

---

13. Baker, *Hybrid Church in the City*, 26.

people there (1791–1804) and at various times since have continued to fuel the mix of French colonial and African cultures.

In time, a city like New Orleans becomes itself a hybrid entity. According to Baker, in a hybrid city "diversity and cultural creativity emerge alongside growing extremes of wealth, poverty, and opportunity."[14] In order to talk about how churches might best exist in these environments, Baker developed what he calls "Third Space ecclesiology." He defines it as "ways of being a church that resist binary definitions . . . and instead place the church in that contested Third Space where new patterns, new forms, and new thinking can emerge."

Discussing the creativity that results from the intensive mixing in urban areas, he acknowledges that some see it as problematic, because it can cause conflict. The Third Space "is often a difficult place to be," precisely because it is "a place where we must have the courage to face the Other in a mutual encounter, rather than hurling platitudes or insults from a safe space across the binary divide."[15] It is, however, "a space of renewal, excitement, and new opportunity—to learn, to encounter, but above all, to create new hybrid forms of church."

The most significant feature of this way of being church is "the construction of a local performative theology." In local performative theologies the church "takes the risk of adapting its performance and identity in a critically reflective way that fits in [with] local conditions on the ground." Performative theology, then, is a kind of action. Intended to "transform the locality at a political, economic, social and spiritual level," it requires churches and theologians "to have a strong enough critique" of values and methods, "to communicate this critique effectively (the work of translation)," and to work flexibly and creatively "for pragmatic solutions to intractable problems (the ongoing work of negotiation)."[16]

There have been some concrete examples of how we might live out our mission and vision in the public square. In *An American Awakening*, Episcopal theologian Courtney Cowart tells how the bishop of the Episcopalian diocese of New Orleans, Charles Jenkins, responded to the Katrina event by becoming linked to the residents of Central City and learning to speak with a prophetic voice on their behalf. He participated in a march to City Hall to call for city leadership to address violence. Groups marched from different locations, and Jenkins chose to march with the residents of Central City. He consulted Cowart that morning about what to wear, and she confirmed his

---

14. Ibid., ix.
15. Ibid., 154.
16. Baker, *Hybrid Church in the City*, x, 125–26, 140.

instinct that his ecclesiastical robes were appropriate and in fact necessary to convey the church's presence—"The purpler you can be today the better." The main organizer from Central City who waited at City Hall to greet marchers and guide them to their places told Cowart later,

> Because the bishop's tall and he's a big man, and he was all in purple, he was the one you could see. And you could see him walking with his staff and the flags of the church waving, and you could hear the drum. It was a sea of people—six thousand—who turned their heads to look.

Jenkins emphasized that he was not an organizer, but that it was extremely important for him to be present.

> We didn't need to be a leader that day but to begin to stand publicly for the rights and dignity and the safety of all. That seemed very important.[17]

Jenkins's example is one that UMC ministers could emulate. Jenkins retired in 2010 at the age of fifty-eight.

> He is damaged in that he lives, medicated, with a formal diagnosis of post-traumatic stress disorder. He said the condition is worsening, so much so that after nine years in office he has announced he will retire . . .[18]

Then *Times-Picayune* religion editor Bruce Nolan noted that

> the post-Katrina suffering of poor New Orleanians transformed [Jenkins's] ministry and awakened him to the broad social and economic inequalities of life.

As a result, he rebuilt the diocese in Louisiana "to reflect his own radical conversion to social justice and racial reconciliation." The storm's aftermath also "left him medicated, prone to depression and frequently unable to focus on administration."[19]

Though he retired, his example had lasting impact on the diocese. In January 2014, Episcopalians in New Orleans held a ritual to acknowledge the need for "atonement and reconciliation" with regard to their promise in the post-Katrina city. Orissa Arend wrote,

---

17. Cowart, *American Awakening*, 138–45.
18. Nolan, "Episcopal Bishop Charles Jenkins."
19. Nolan, "Bishop Charles Jenkins Retires."

Our history and our liturgy beg a question: What next? If the spirit really moved the 500 people who attended the service of atonement and reconciliation, what will come of it?

She ended her reflection on the event like this:

We looked within. We made some promises. We asked for cleansing in front of God. We had witnesses. I am hoping that those who might doubt our commitment to the radical transformation that we asked for will stay tuned, will work with us, will hold our feet to the fire, and will ask us, year after year, what we have done and are doing to live our vows.[20]

Unfortunately, intractable or the most wicked problems are often those where the church itself still needs critique. Yet Baker insists,

As a person of faith from within the Christian tradition, I am also clear that this world unfolding before us is still God's world, and the Spirit of God is still challenging the church (and indeed all human society) to be hopeful, to be clear about its place in society, but above all to be creative in the way we open ourselves to engaging with our world.[21]

Developing this creative sort of courage is precisely what the church needs to do in order to address the sorts of gaps identified in this chapter: gaps between our works of mercy and our words about justice; gaps among our various identities that prevent our embracing a hybrid identity; gaps between our public and private theologies; and the gaps between our profession of faithfulness to a Creator God and our failure to care for creation, especially in the face of climate change and coastal erosion. It is time to do constructive work in anticipation of a hopeful future, and not just for New Orleans.

The Reconciling Movement as Performative Theology

Robert Putnam, who wrote the well-known essay, "Bowling Alone: America's Declining Social Capital" about the waning of organizations of all kind, co-authored a volume called *Better Together*. It argues that social capital exists in two forms: "bonding social capital" which occurs among people with many things in common; and "bridging social capital" which can develop

---

20. Arend, "Racism and the Church."
21. Baker, *Hybrid Church in the City*, 154.

between those who have fewer similarities in their lives and contexts. "The problem is that bridging social capital is harder to create than bonding social capital—after all, birds of a feather flock together. So the kind of social capital that is most essential for healthy public life in an increasingly diverse society like ours is precisely the kind that is hardest to build."[22]

As a genuinely cosmopolitan city, New Orleans has traditionally welcomed people who do not belong within traditional heterosexual categories. Being truly open to diversity is not possible without engaging with the LGBTQ community and with changes in the society at large that allow gay and lesbian people to marry while large segments of the church still refuse to perform their weddings.

Counteracting the exclusion that openly gay and lesbian people have experienced from the church is one vital way of bridging the divides of which Baker spoke. For instance, in the 1970s, St. Mark's UMC was the only church that would allow a memorial service for the thirty-two men killed in an arson-caused fire at a gay bar in the French Quarter. It was a formative moment for the gay community who left together from the front door of the church where the press waited rather than take an offered route out the back. When the Roman Catholic Church and many Protestant congregations refused to hold the service, St. Mark's volunteered. A service of remembrance is still held at St. Mark's each year. Their hospitality is well-remembered in the gay community, and it was even commemorated in an art installation at the Contemporary Arts Center in 2008–9.[23]

This is a perfect example of performative theology. I think the growing willingness of many twenty-first century congregations in the city to state publicly that it is not necessary to discriminate against homosexual people in order to be a Christian is in part a result of the outrageous proclamations after the storm that its sexual openness prompted God to "wreak judgment" on the city. Within the UMC, there is an organization called the Reconciling Ministries Network (RMN) which offers United Methodist churches (or smaller entities such as adult Sunday school classes) a way to indicate that they are open to having gay and lesbian members in lay leadership. For years, St. Mark's was the only Reconciling congregation in Louisiana, but since Katrina, that situation has changed.

The debate over the place of LGBTQ people in the church, especially in the ordained ministry, has been a subject of extreme controversy within the UMC for the last few decades. General Conference, a body which meets

---

22. Putnam, "Bowling Alone"; Putnam, *Bowling Alone*; Putnam and Feldstein, *Better Together*, 2–3.

23. Blue, *St. Mark's and the Social Gospel*, 215.

only every four years, is the sole entity which can speak for the UMC and make changes in its "rule book," the *Book of Discipline*. (See the Appendix for more information on UMC terms and governance.) The current *Book of Discipline*, produced in 2012, still forbids the ordination of "self-avowed practicing homosexuals" and forbids holding same-sex weddings in UMC buildings. A number of clergy have been brought up on charges and defrocked in recent years for officiating at same-sex marriages. There will be no opportunity to change these policies until the General Conference in May 2016. Many clergy and laity want the church to end discrimination against gay and lesbian people, but others believe it would be a mistake to do so.

In New Orleans, these questions are part of the church's struggle with engaging in public theology. While the arguments continue, more congregations have made the decision to join St. Mark's in the Reconciling movement and provide a more intentional welcome to LGBTQ individuals. Not everyone agrees, of course; a long-time pastor of a New Orleans congregation brings resolutions to the annual conference gathering almost every year urging the conference to object not just to church but also to secular openness to gay and lesbian people. These have so far been defeated.

In the fall of 2012, both Rayne Memorial UMC and Parker Memorial UMC voted to become Reconciling Congregations. The Parker congregation reported to the RMN,

> We have been openly welcoming LGBTQ friends for a while, but have just had the awakening this year that it is time to make a formal, public proclamation of our welcoming stance. One of our members who leads our spiritual formation classes helped us see that "some of us are supporters from the sideline during civil rights transformations and some of us get on the bus!" Our people decided they are ready to "get on the bus."

Parker's official statement asserts

> that "all means all," including people of all sexual orientations, gender identities, race, ethnicity, age, faith history, economic status, marital status, physical and mental ability, and education. The Parker community works for equal rights for all humans and the natural world. We believe that the diversity of our community makes our faith stronger, our spirituality deeper, and our service more helpful.[24]

---

24. "New Reconciling Congregations—Parker Memorial UMC," Reconciling Ministries Network.

For Carol Winn Crawford and Rayne, becoming a Reconciling Congregation was "a natural culmination" of their history. The decision was the result of "years of practicing radical hospitality without regard to gender identity or sexual orientation, a growing sensitivity to the plight of persons who have been scorned and isolated by the faith community, an ever-increasing love for LGBT individuals, couples, and families who are a precious part of our community, and the desire to make our solidarity with them public." They developed this statement:

> We are a community of faith and love representing, celebrating, and embracing all God's children as persons of sacred worth, regardless of race, gender, ethnicity, national origin, culture, tradition, sexual orientation, gender identity, personal and family history, or station in life. In the full expression of the radically transforming and all-inclusive love of God as revealed through Jesus Christ, all are welcome![25]

Rayne's sanctuary is packed for their worship services. According to its pastor, at least one other congregation in Greater New Orleans is also in the process of moving toward a vote to become part of the Reconciling network; I prefer not to name the church until their vote is taken. In addition, although First Grace UMC has not yet voted to join the Reconciling network officially, they have adopted a strong statement of affirmation which appears in their Sunday bulletins. It reads:

> First Grace is an urban community of faith embracing all of God's children as persons of sacred worth, regardless of station in life, race, ethnicity, sexual orientation, or gender identity. We invite and welcome all persons to join us as disciples who believe in the transforming love of God revealed in Jesus Christ from which nothing can separate us.[26]

Part of the process of its development is recounted in Chapter 5.

Public Theology: What *Can* Make a Difference?

In an article aptly titled, "Boundary Issues," environmental historian Ari Kelman noted that the leaders making decisions about what the city's footprint would look like after recovery—i.e., whether people would be allowed

---

25. "New Reconciling Congregations—Rayne Memorial UMC," Reconciling Ministries Network.

26. Statement of Affirmation adopted by First Grace UMC which now appears in the Sunday bulletin each week.

to resettle in the areas of lowest elevation—seemed "captivated by the notion that it is possible to separate the city from its surroundings, a myth that will not die, no matter how many of New Orleans's residents do."[27]

This idea is very much in keeping with the theological concepts presented in Chapter 9, including the profound interconnectedness discussed in Anne Daniell's theology of place and in the discussion of *jeong* by Anne Joh. Drawing artificial boundaries and borders is always theologically suspect and impoverishes (in many senses) those on both sides. Teaching, preaching, writing, and conversing about Christian responsibility to cultivate an intimate relationship with the environment of south Louisiana and of the Gulf of Mexico could help break down the boundaries that keep us all from seeing reality as it is: we are dependent on God's creation, and we are responsible to and for it.

Combatting Coastal Erosion: "Preventable" Does Not Equal "Prevented"

A couple of years after the storm, addressing the question of whether risk of flooding was hampering reinvestment in the city, Jed Horne wrote,

> There wasn't much you could do to avert an earthquake or Miami-style hurricane, beyond enforcing a building code that would reduce the chances of buildings flying to pieces when it struck. Helplessness engendered a sense of fatalism that simply removed the risk of catastrophe from the investor's calculations.

But helplessness and fatalism can also contaminate situations that are *not* inevitable. In New Orleans, Horne continued,

> Ironically, there was a lot you could do about the flood threat. The lethal mess that followed Katrina was, after all, a man-made disaster, an engineering problem, and, as such, entirely preventable. Entirely preventable ... and yet it wasn't being prevented.[28]

Along with the mix of graft, corruption, and sheer incompetence that kept the floodwalls that failed from being constructed correctly, other issues have played a huge role in increasing the damage that storms in the Gulf of Mexico can inflict. Coastal erosion and the resultant loss of the barrier islands may be chief among them, and there is absolutely no doubt that

---

27. Kelman, "Boundary Issues," 695.
28. Horne, *Breach of Faith*, 410.

human activity is compounding the problem and no doubt that it contributed to the flooding in New Orleans.

As one author put it, "The sinking of the delta is a natural process put on steroids by human activity."[29] There are solutions for the human contribution to coastal erosion on the table, and they have been on the table for decades. They have not been implemented because governments have been unwilling to spend the needed money and because politicians from both parties have been unwilling to assign blame to energy companies for their part in speeding erosion—administering those "steroids."

River Diversion

The people of Louisiana failed to act quickly and decisively enough to stop coastal erosion. The problem has been known since the late 1960s when Dr. Sherwood "Woody" Gagliano, head of the consulting firm Coastal Environments, Inc., recognized and called attention to it.

There has long been a plan to divert some water from the Mississippi River into the Atchafalaya and replenish the sediments needed to keep coastal lands from disappearing. Like all rivers, the Mississippi has changed its course many times over thousands of years. The Atchafalaya River is a relict channel of the Mississippi and has carried its waters many times. The Mississippi drains an enormous swath of the United States, and by the time it reaches the Gulf, it has a correspondingly large load of silt. That silt is deposited in the river's delta, where it builds up land. After the major flooding that occurred in 1927, the Corps of Engineers began the system of levees which now controls flooding, and they built a structure located where the Red River flows into the Mississippi intended to keep the Mississippi in its current channel which flows through Baton Rouge and New Orleans. The river has decided it is time to move back to its Atchafalaya channel, and the pressure it exerts as it tries to do that almost broke the structure in the 1970s, but the Corps was able to repair it and keep the river's main channel artificially routed through New Orleans.

The Atchafalaya Basin which is essentially a huge triangle of lowland in the middle of the southern part of the state is an important wetland area for the nation and the world. Environmentalists say that letting the river go back would damage the wetlands. However, they also know that not letting it go back is inflicting a different kind of damage. The silt load that created the land on that part of the coast is not being replenished, and the land is eroding at a frightening pace. Many of the offshore islands that used to

---

29. Hiles, "Environment," 9.

help protect coastal areas from the brunt of Gulf hurricanes no longer exist. In the meantime, more delta was deposited downriver from New Orleans, but after a certain amount of land creation, the river's mouth reached the continental shelf, and now the silt simply pours off into such deep water that it is not useful in building up the coast.

Letting the river divert itself would have a negative economic impact. However, it is finally beginning to be understood by more people that not letting the river divert itself is also having a negative impact. The proposed partial diversion seems to offer possibilities of helping more than hurting. Because of the environmental and human consequences, the church ought to be participating in the discussion.

Their Profit, Our Loss

Land loss has been exacerbated by the actions of oil companies that have dug countless miles of straight canals through the fragile coastland despite the fact that a straight channel causes rapid erosion. Considering the damage that oil companies have done to the coastland to increase their profits, the tiny amount of work a few companies have done toward repairing it fail to reach even the level of "token effort."

The issues are complicated, and every single facet is far too complex to address adequately in this volume. For an introduction to it that is also a beautiful and captivating read, I recommend *Bayou Farewell*. When I taught my post-Katrina class the first time in March 2006, my choices for the reading list were very limited. One book I selected had been written a few years previously by journalist and environmentalist Mike Tidwell. *Bayou Farewell* chronicled his journey down south Louisiana bayous to the Gulf of Mexico, hitching rides on shrimp boats. His use of the language brought the Cajun culture of south Louisiana alive.

Boat owners showed him how quickly the water was rising and the previously inhabited land was disappearing, and he wrote about the inevitable problems that coastal erosion would bring to the fishing and shrimping industries which have supported Louisianians for generations. He also visited an off-shore oil rig and talked about how the exploitation of the Gulf by oil companies was destroying both the land and the ocean.[30]

In his acclaimed 2010 book, *Floodlines*, Jordan Flaherty says that if the city is truly to recover, the first step has to be "getting out the truth that New Orleans is not 'okay.' Most of the country believes either that New Orleans has been rebuilt, or that, if not, it's because people here are lazy and/or

30. Tidwell, *Bayou Farewell*.

corrupt and wasted the nation's generous assistance." In fact, five years out, "The oft-promised aid, whether from FEMA or various federal and private agencies, has not arrived. We don't need charity; we need the federal and corporate entities responsible for the devastation of New Orleans to be held accountable for supporting its rebuilding."[31]

Flaherty's chastisement of "corporate entities responsible for the devastation" is on target. The massive oil spill caused by BP's Deepwater Horizon well in April 2010 revealed the unwillingness of some elected officials to stand up against the industry. Louisiana's then-junior US Senator, David Vitter, began trying right away to limit the amount of damages that could be imposed against British Petroleum. Three years later, while BP ran ad campaigns to tout how "committed" it is to the region, tar mats weighing tens of thousands of pounds continued to appear along the Gulf Coast. "The weathered oil contains toxic hydrocarbon components than [sic] can remain a threat to fish, wildlife, and human health for fifty years."[32]

Even more egregiously, on March 16, 2015, BP released a statement "claiming the environment of the northern Gulf of Mexico had returned to its 'baseline condition' five years after its Deepwater Horizon disaster pumped more than 200 million gallons of oil into the Gulf off Louisiana's coast." Yet the *very next day*, "the U. S. Coast Guard was supervising the ongoing removal of a large oil tar mat on East Grand Terre Island that has yielded more than 25,000 pounds of oil mixed with sand since late February, BP spokesman Jason Ryan confirmed." BP began work to clean the beach on February 23, 2015, but did not "notify the Coast Guard of the mess until March 13, said Seth Johnson, a spokesman for that agency. Meanwhile, the report continued, "a few miles to the west, two dead adult bottlenose dolphins had washed up on Queen Bess Island, continuing what has been a large die-off of dolphins in Barataria Bay since the oil washed into the critical coastal estuary five years ago." Long-term environmental impacts have yet to be determined.[33]

---

31. Flaherty, *Floodlines*, 2. Late in 2015—ten years out—FEMA finally settled, agreeing to pay $2 billion for infrastructure repairs. The city's streets are still so bad as to defy description and need $9 billion of work.

32. Marshall, "More Massive Tar Balls."

33. Marshall, "Day after Boasting." They serve to exacerbate other impacts that were quickly obvious, including the loss of workers' lives in the initial explosion, and the damage inflicted on the economic lives of people all over Louisiana, including those engaged in the tourism and fishing industries.

Speaking Truth about Climate Change

In early 2014, the *Times-Picayune* could report that "support for restoring coastal wetlands has increased dramatically in Louisiana over the past decade." A December 2013 survey of voters showed that 85 percent of Democrats, 74 percent of Republicans, and 70 percent of Independents agreed that "saving our state's coast is the most important issue of my lifetime." In 2003, less than half (43 percent) had "agreed that restoring coastal wetlands" was "the most import [sic] concern facing Louisiana." The year after Katrina and Rita hit, 66 percent of respondents "said that wetland loss was one of the state's most important issues." By 2014, despite opposition from the fishing industry, 75 percent thought the state should "move forward" with Mississippi River diversions that would "return some of the natural sediment and nutrients to dying wetlands."

Not coincidentally, the survey revealed that respondents' opinions were in part motivated by a fear of rising rates for flood insurance.[34] Furthermore, while some of the hesitancy to speak out against the oil companies' guilt has been related to the large number of church members whose livelihood was dependent on the industry, we have now reached a place where thousands will *lose* their livelihoods within a few years if the situation is not corrected. As more and more data becomes available, it becomes clearer that we humans, we Christians, we United Methodists are compounding our past corporate sin—ignoring coastal erosion—with another corporate sin, ignoring climate change.

"Everybody talks about the weather, but nobody does anything about it" is not something we can say any more. All of us have been doing something about the weather—about the climate, in fact—but it wasn't something we knew we were doing. Unfortunately, it was not a move in the right direction.

A key area in which the church has failed to speak and to act has to do with climate change. While Katrina's destruction of life and property was immense, warming of the oceans and the continuing settlement of coastal areas will result in even more destructive storms in the future. Hurricane Sandy's landfall in New Jersey in October 2013 did not rival Katrina in any category, but it was powerful enough to show that coastal areas all over the United States are vulnerable to the same fate. Typhoon Haiyan which hit the Philippines in November 2013 was deemed by many meteorologists

---

34. Alexander-Bloch, "Support for Wetland Restoration." The study was commissioned by the America's Wetland Foundation.

to be the strongest storm to have made landfall "anywhere in the world in recorded history."[35]

There are only a few scientists who continue to reject mainstream climate science and who do not think global warming is a real phenomenon, yet those few are frequently cited by politicians who do not wish to offend the oil and gas industries. Energy interests fund their campaigns and employ large work forces in their states. It is not a coincidence that the political climate-change-denier-in-chief Jim Inhofe is a senator from oil-driven Oklahoma. Almost all scientists agree that climate change is indeed happening and, more specifically, that human activity contributes to it. More specifically, the rising sea level is gaining attention and consensus; controversy centers only on "how much" and "by when," rather than "if" it will occur.

When he wrote "The Flood Next Time" in early 2014, award-winning environmental journalist Justin Gillis was concerned about sinking land and rising seas, but they were not in the vicinity of New Orleans. He was citing a major study at Rutgers University that showed Battery Park in New York City and most other coastal locations along the eastern shore of the United States "from southern Maine to northern Florida" are at risk. "People considering whether to buy or rebuild at the storm-damaged Jersey Shore, for instance, could be looking at nearly a foot of sea-level rise by the time they would pay off a thirty-year mortgage, according to the Rutgers projections," he wrote.

Some areas are at greater risk than others, and for various reasons the Tidewater area of Virginia is particularly vulnerable to the amounts of sea level rise that are predicted. Gillis writes,

> These numbers are profoundly threatening, and among the American public, the impulse toward denial is still strong. But in towns like Norfolk—where neighborhoods are already flooding repeatedly even in the absence of storms, and where some homes have become unsaleable—people are starting to pay attention.[36]

Mike Tidwell's next book after *Bayou Farewell*, entitled *The Ravaging Tide: Strange Weather, Future Katrinas, and the Coming Death of America's Coastal Cities*, places the Katrina event into its larger context. Tidwell is the director of the Chesapeake Climate Action Network and is acutely aware of the dangers to the eastern seaboard.

35. Mullen, "Super Typhoon Haiyan."
36. Gillis, "Flood Next Time"; Bauers, "Study Finds Sea Levels Rising"; Branson, "New Jersey Shore."

When Sallie McFague published *The Body of God* in 1993, some critics greeted her suggestion that envisioning the world as part of God's body would be helpful with responses that ranged from calling it idolatrous to calling it too warm and fuzzy to be taken seriously. It was neither. A decade later, Kwok Pui-Lan helped to refute critics who see theological reflection on the environment as a "soft topic," in part by asserting when white women talk about "nature," the discussion is different from the lived experience of many women of color in poorer countries. "Instead of seeing nature as 'natural,' we have to talk about distribution of resources, ownership of the land, and the extraction of natural resources for profit."[37]

There is still an immense amount of work for theologians to do in this arena. It does not help that the religious right has not been neutral on this point. For decades, they have disputed the idea that the church should foster the care of creation, maintaining that Jesus' return and the end of the world as we know it will occur before we make the Earth unlivable. Some evangelicals are beginning to depart from this stance and to view responsible use of Earth's resources as part of their call to be Christian. Mainline denominations, including United Methodism, have members all along the gamut of theological understandings, but there are a Wesleyan example and a history of Methodist actions on which to draw.

Thomas Kemper, top executive of the UMC's agency that oversees UMCOR, saw a headline that read, "Churches Shelve Theology for Disaster Relief Efforts." In response, he wrote that United Methodists were by no means setting aside their theology, but instead working from it. He pointed to founder John Wesley's "strong concern for people in jeopardy because of human-caused or natural calamities. Wesley saw some of the results of rapid industrialization as disastrous. He railed against factories' pollution of the air, water and soil, and he started small enterprise programs to rescue at least some women and children from the mills."

Although in Wesley's lifetime, 1703–1791, the understandings of how societies work and how individuals might be able to impact their workings were not nearly so developed as ours today, he was in many ways "a man ahead of his time." His deep involvement with and commitment to the life of the spirit *and* the needs of those who lived in the changing world around him allowed him to speak to issues in new ways and lay the groundwork for a church that would speak prophetically on issues that Wesley could never have imagined. The kind of work that Kemper mentioned led Wesley some distance toward an understanding of corporate sin that is vital to our own work as Christians today.

---

37. McFague, *Body of God*; Kwok, *Postcolonial Imagination*, 223.

Rabbi Jay Michaelson wrote that although individual change is needed,

> personal actions are a tiny drop in a large bucket. We need systemic change and political change, and we're not going to get that by turning inward on ourselves, finding additional ways to be personally and pointlessly pious. Climate change is a collective sin, and it requires collective repentance . . . and a departisanization of moral good and evil.[38]

This seems to me to be at the heart of things. We need to engage in analysis in a more thoughtful theological vein, and to be astute enough to make that analysis heard.

The Power of Ritual

In the fall of 2007, Oklahoma passed a law which made it a crime to help an undocumented immigrant in any way. Taking an undocumented person to a doctor's office or hospital became an act for which a person can be arrested and jailed. It is a draconian piece of legislation, and many faith communities tried to prevent its passage and openly opposed it when it took effect.

That month, I was absolutely devastated by a death in my immediate family. When I returned to Tulsa after the funeral, I learned that there would be a public protest of the new law in front of city hall. Clergy were asked to wear their robes and stoles and be part of a procession up to the platform, where representatives of several faiths and Christian denominations were going to speak. I wanted to go, but I was physically exhausted and emotionally vulnerable. Finally, I decided that since I would not have to say anything at all, I could go with my husband who is also clergy, put on my vestments, and just stand with the group.

The event was intended to show that many churches opposed the law, and it had been designed to provide a good visual for television news cameras. Yet in the coverage that night, there was not a single shot of all the vested clergy arrayed across the platform. The story was aired as though some Latino/a individuals had gathered to protest, with no mention whatsoever of the fact that a large group of clergy, most of them from the dominant racial group, had stood in solidarity with them and provided most of the speakers. The only indication of clergy presence was a one-to-two-second shot of the procession of robed people walking into the protest. I happened to be one of the few people shown in that shot.

---

38. Michaelson, "Climate Change is a Sin."

It was a hard evening for me. Several times I had to stand near the back of the platform in order to pull myself back together. I was glad I had gone, but seeing the press coverage, I felt that the slanting by reporters had robbed the effort of most of its significance. Then, months later, one of my students who was planning to pursue a PhD told me she had also decided to pursue ordination in her denomination. "You did that," she said. "When I saw you on the news at that demonstration, I thought, 'That's what I want. I want the authority and the respect that ordination gives you when you speak. I want to be able to walk in wearing a stole.'"

It is precisely the authority that much of society bestows on the church that makes the church responsible for voicing the situation of the disenfranchised. Even its silence speaks. Silence speaks whether we intend for it to or not.

The church has a way of countering our past silence which is an immensely powerful medium. It is the medium of religious liturgy and ritual. Those who study worship or ritual understand the concept of performative utterances. Put succinctly, these occur when something happens because certain words are said and would not have happened without the words. When we *say*, "I apologize," then we have apologized. There are many examples in Christian ritual. If I pour water on you during a service, I have simply gotten you wet. If I say as I am placing water on your head, "I baptize you," then something far more than transferring water or resultant wetness has occurred. It is the saying of the words that matters. Weddings offer several opportunities to consider this phenomenon, such as the moment when the officiant says, "I now pronounce you husband and wife." Though not every Christian ritual carries that particular kind of power, they all carry power of one kind of another. At best, a ritual is a transformative encounter with God; at worst, it reinforces the conviction that Christianity is irrelevant to the larger community.

Regarding the responsibility the church held to help end apartheid in South Africa, Walter Wink wrote, "Waving holy water and a crucifix over Buchenwald would scarcely have stopped the Nazi genocide of Jews, but think about it—what if the church in Germany *had* staged ritual acts of protest outside those gates?"[39]

Wink's inquiry about Buchenwald—what if the church in Germany *had* staged ritual acts of protest outside those gates?—is something that the church in Louisiana (and places much farther afield) should consider. What if the church were to stage ritual acts of protest along the Gulf Coast to build support for protecting the area from continued coastal erosion?

---

39. Wink, *Unmasking the Powers*, 64–65, cited in Driver, *Magic of Ritual*, 183.

The economic dependence of the region on the oil and gas industry makes the prospect daunting. It would be naïve to think that the huge contributions that members of Congress and the Senate receive from the oil and gas industry have no effect on legislators' unwillingness to deal with climate change. This problem was exacerbated by the *Citizens United v. Federal Election Commission* decision handed down in January 2010. The granting of human status to corporations seems to me to be a theological issue and indeed, a theological problem. The need to overturn *Citizens United* cries out to me for performative theology and transformative ritual.

"Caring with Creation Should Not Be Cutting-Edge Ministry"

The *New York Times* recently profiled Tyler Sit, founder of Simple Church in Grafton, Massachusetts, as part of "a small cadre of Methodist ministers" planting churches "with an environmentalist Gospel." For these pastors,

> environmentalism is about more than pollution and global warming; it's about connections between consumption patterns and inequality. The earth is God's creation, they say, so waste is a sin. They try to eat local, and they pay attention to how environmental problems disproportionally affect poor people and minorities.[40]

Other United Methodists are also leading in engagement with issues of environmental care. Pat Hoerth and her sister, Ann Denney, are co-directors of the Turtle Rock Farm and Center for Sustainability, Spirituality, and Healing, and Hoerth teaches spirituality courses at Phillips Theological Seminary.[41] Turtle Rock is out on the prairie in north-central Oklahoma, and the directors work with students from Oklahoma universities.

A United Methodist deaconess commissioned "for a life-time of ministry in love, justice and service," Hoerth noted in a presentation at Phillips Seminary that as a deaconess, she is "sent out to do cutting-edge ministry—the work the main church isn't ready to do; in this case, ecospirituality and environmental justice. Cutting edge? That is crazy to me. Caring with creation should not be cutting-edge ministry."

A well-trained and gifted spiritual director, Hoerth is a wise and calm presence. Thus it was particularly attention-grabbing when she issued a clarion call to pastors, exhorting them to help change people's perspective

---

40. Oppenheimer, "Young Methodists Plant Churches."
41. Turtle Rock Farm's website is at http://www.turtlerockfarmretreat.com.

about the place of humans "in God's great web of life" on earth. "*We need clergy to step up to this work. It is time for it to become mainstream.*"[42] She urged clergy to preach often about climate change "and our responsibility to make changes that will ensure a healthy planet, a healthy home in which all can thrive." Clergy need support and encouragement from the laity if they are to lead in ways that make people and institutions rethink values and change behavior.

As a resource, Hoerth recommends the work of theologians who are also scientists, or "geologians," the term preferred by ecotheologian Thomas Berry.[43] They critique the privileging of human interest over the interests of the rest of the creation (even though in the long run, abusing creation will not benefit humanity).

Using non-human metaphors for God could help Christians value God's creation, Hoerth says. Although it is probably easier than preaching about climate change, she thinks it might be "even more transformative" if pastors would simply "*start using language in worship that will help parishioners begin to experience a different perspective.*" She suggests a way to make that happen: "What if, in addressing God as you open prayers, or lead calls to worship, or pray Eucharistic prayers, you use images/metaphors from the natural world, from creation, to address God—instead of human characteristics?"[44]

The opening of such a pastoral prayer might sound something like this:

> O most gracious God, you are like the day's first breeze, moving gently, before we even notice. You are like the rain after a drought, reminding us what we need for life. O most steadfast God, you are like Earth, a beautiful home on which we live and breathe and have our being."

Another of Hoerth's examples took images from both sea and land:

> O God, like the giant humpback whale, breeching from the vast expanse of ocean, you bring awe and wonder. Like the tiny hummingbird, its wings whirring, squeaking as it zips past, hovering in mid-air to collect nectar from a blossom: you bring joy. Like the intricate, beautiful, complex planet that is our home, you sustain us.

---

42. Hoerth, "Changing the Climate," 9 (emphasis hers).

43. Berry was honored by Loyola University in New Orleans with an honorary doctorate in 1994.

44. Ibid., emphasis hers.

A prayer of confession might go:

> O God, we hear you in the thunderous, haunting crackle of a dying glacier. We confess that we are abusing your creation. As giant chunks of ancient ice fall into the sea, as polar bears and others lose their habitat, as waters rise and dangerous gases enter the atmosphere, we must admit that our thoughtlessness, our desire for luxury and comfort, for more than is sufficient, has contributed to such destruction. We hear the thunderous cries. May they penetrate our hearts and minds. May we once again turn to you for answers, for courage and conviction so that your creation, our planet home, may recover its health.[45]

This kind of ritual and liturgy can make a difference. Ritual is powerful. Christians believe ritual does something. The goal of all Christian ritual is, or should be, to be transformative.[46] Transforming the church's relationship with the human and non-human world around it is not too big a goal for the people of God.

Readiness for Change

In the summer of 2013, the new bishop who had come to Louisiana in September 2012, Cynthia Fierro Harvey, preached at a bilingual service at First Grace UMC. She lifted up the new set of five core values the conference had recently adopted under her leadership; they are published on the "Mission, Vision, and Core Values" page of the Louisiana Conference website. The first two values are integrity and accountability.

The third, "unrelenting love for all people," means placing "the needs and interests of people before the needs and interests of the institution. We will prioritize transformative relationships over sustaining buildings and budgets." The fifth, "holding nothing sacred but the mission," means being open "to the creative movement of God's spirit, not institutional priorities." Both specifically move maintaining the institution out of first place. This seems to reflect learning from the post-Katrina experience.

About the fourth value, "courage and risk," the conference says, "We believe that new times call for new actions. We are willing to trust ourselves and each other, and risk acting in new and courageous ways in order to transform a dying institution into a vibrant movement of faith and action."

---

45. Ibid.

46. Tom Driver offers an extended and excellent discussion of this topic. Driver, *Magic of Ritual*.

For decades, mainline Protestantism has been in decline, but for an annual conference to term itself "a dying institution" in a published document, even if it be in the context of language about transforming that reality, is uncommon.

As one way of demonstrating adaptability, the conference decided to create a Planting Zone in New Orleans. The idea was to sponsor non-traditional types of ministries. A large pool of money voted by the annual conference would fund the endeavor. The Congregational Development professional on the conference staff would oversee the project.

At least one attempt was judged quickly not to have worked. In 2014, the tiny remaining congregation at Carrollton UMC agreed to have their structure used for a new church. It is located near the intersection of Carrollton and St. Charles Avenues, a trendy area with many new residents and deep connections to Tulane and Loyola Universities. Two pastors were appointed there to an entity which was named, perhaps not imaginatively enough, "New Church on South Carrollton." The Facebook page for the new church focused on Sunday morning worship and a weeknight evening bible study which essentially replicated previous programming. In 2015, both pastors were reappointed elsewhere, and the name reverted to the previous one. The new pastor, an attorney, is bivocational and appointed to Carrollton only part-time. The conference also made a change in the Congregational Development appointment, and the task is now handled by a District Superintendent who splits his time between the two jobs.

Appointed to the Seventh Ward

Another project implemented as part of the Planting Zone seems to hold more promise. For ten years after the storm, the UMC had no active presence whatsoever in the Seventh Ward, the largest ward in New Orleans.[47] All the UMC congregations located there were merged with churches outside the area and/or decommissioned. The UMC still owns the Trinity of Gentilly UMC building which is situated on Filmore Avenue near its intersection with Elysian Fields Avenue, but it is being rented to the Presbyterian Church USA for their Project Homecoming offices. It was previously rented to Mennonites who were in the city to complete construction projects.

---

47. "Ward" is political terminology, and the Lower Ninth Ward is only one of the areas of New Orleans commonly referred to using the term. There are plenty of neighborhood names in use, as well, but the Seventh Ward is clearly understood by New Orleanians.

For the 2015–16 conference year (July 1 to June 30), Hadley Edwards has been appointed to the Seventh Ward. This is an unusual and possibly unprecedented appointment for this conference. Edwards is moving to this position after three years as superintendent of the New Orleans District. Previously he was the pastor who revitalized Bethany UMC immediately after the storm, a process discussed in depth in Chapter 8.

This new ministry is called "The Spirit Church: A Ministry of the United Methodist Church." Bishop Harvey sent a conference-wide email which a description of the project.

> What we as people of faith know is that even with no building, with no cross and flame—the symbol of Methodism—the Spirit continues to stir and prepares the field for yet another harvest. After this period of "lying fallow," the Seventh Ward will become "an intentional mission focus" for the Louisiana conference.

She made clear that Edwards "is not being appointed to a church or a church building but to the Ward itself. Working with a team of dreamers and discerners, Rev. Edwards will listen to the leading of the Spirit for what might be once again."[48]

This is a positive sign of recommitment to the city. As demonstrated in his work at Bethany, Edwards is an effective pastor full of energy and passion, and it will be important to watch how this particular endeavor develops.

What Are We Talking About?

The Presbyterian Church USA's peacekeeping agency sponsors a conference every year, and I attended in 1992. Participants learn about world events, and leaders make clear that local people need information because these events ought to be mentioned in local churches on Sunday morning. The "prayers of the people" should not be confined only to the illnesses and concerns of people they know. I had previously not noticed that this insularity is what we usually demonstrate in public prayer. If a massive event like the 2011 tsunami in Japan occurs, it may be mentioned. Otherwise, the focus is almost always on the local congregation itself. Although creating community in the sense of caring for one another is an important part of being the church, that cannot be all there is to it.

In 2009, I sat in on a class for future priests at Notre Dame seminary in New Orleans where Sister Jane Remson, OCarm, was a guest speaker. She

48. Cynthia Harvey, email to the author, March 3, 2015.

heads the international Carmelite NGO, a non-governmental organization which cooperates with the United Nations (UN). She was there to remind future priests that problems across the world, not just those close to home, should receive consideration in Sunday morning worship. She talked about the Millennium Goals, a list of work that the UN set for the first decade-and-a-half of the twenty-first century.[49] Although the document is very much in keeping with the Social Principles of the UMC which I teach on a regular basis, I had never heard of the Millennium Goals before she spoke that day.

The UMC's General Board of Church and Society (GBCS) maintains an office across from the Capitol in Washington, DC and advocates for legislation congruent with the Social Principles.[50] GBCS has an office in New York, too, where staffers work with the UN. Both offices will arrange week-long seminars for adults or youth from local congregations, providing education on the issues of the congregation's choice, and in Washington, arranging for attendees to meet with their elected representatives. Travel and housing costs are borne by the local church, but there is no charge for the planning and instructional time of the staff members.[51]

Since 1963, the United Methodist Women's organization (UMW) has owned the twelve-story office building across from the UN complex. Several other denominations also house their agencies that work with that international body there. UMW offers space for gatherings of women from around the world, and information on many issues can be obtained on the UMW website.[52]

Disseminating such information at the local level encourages and enables Christians to put their own situations into a larger context. It reminds us to try to grasp the true interconnectedness of all created beings that was discussed in the last chapter. It gives us the capacity to feel *jeong* with those who are not just like us; "I have heard of your troubles, and I have prayed for you" is surely a beginning of its creation. As Katharine Henderson wrote, "Churches and synagogues and mosques need to send and support the message that public issues . . . are intimately and inextricably related to the faith. They should build in time for their leaders to do public issue homework and to preach about it from the pulpit." She thinks, "No one should graduate

---

49. Carmelite NGO, "We the Peoples: A Call to Action for the UN Millennium Declaration: Goals and Targets"; Carmelite NGO, "UN Issues Focused on by the Carmelite NGO."

50. Some explanation of the Social Principles is included in this book's Appendix.

51. The General Board of Church and Society's webpage is at www.umc-gbcs.org. The Social Principles of the UMC can be found there, along with information on educational services the GBCS provides.

52. United Methodist Women's website: www.unitedmethodistwomen.org.

from seminary or rabbinical school—or, I would suggest, become a lay leader in a local congregation—without having developed some understanding of their identity as a public leader and a beginning passion for and competency in at least one public issue." Further, simply caring and knowing about problems is not sufficient: "Developing oneself as a public leader means not only having public issue literacy but actually going public with it and being savvy about how to do so."[53]

Conclusion

Just six months after the storm, when I first brought a class to study the post-Katrina church, we spent most of one day in Baton Rouge talking with church leaders intimately involved in decision-making. We also visited with Robert Mann, communications director for Governor Kathleen Blanco at the time of the storm. A committed United Methodist layperson, he not only explained why some of the circumstances unfolded as they did but was also quite forthcoming about what he felt were his own and the administration's mistakes.

I had known Bob for years, so we visited after class. He asked, "Are you going to make this class a regular offering?" I shrugged and said, "I don't know, but I've been thinking about repeating it in the fall." Suddenly the fact that it was a perfectly legitimate question sank in. Would I indeed be bringing students to consider this situation for years to come? In that moment, I truly began to internalize what I had already said many times—that it would be ten to twelve years before Louisianians could even hope to say, "We have recovered." And for those who reside in New Orleans—as well as those who remain in diaspora—the memories and changes that Katrina wrought remain indelible parts of their psyches.

This quote from Bishop Harvey's address to the 2014 annual conference gathering may bring to mind the discussion of *jeong* in the previous chapter: "I want us to be a people who are not only woven together but act like they are woven together, love that they are woven together even with all of our quirkiness, our uniqueness and all that we hold in common and in tension."[54] The Katrina experience is something that still offers the church a chance to make of it what we will, and to make of ourselves a woven-together people if that is what we choose.

When Mike Tidwell was in New Orleans in 2014 to celebrate the ten-year anniversary of *Bayou Farewell*'s publication, I asked him about the

53. Henderson, *God's Troublemakers*, 231.
54. Harvey, "Message from Bishop Cynthia Fierro Harvey."

church's anemic response to climate change and coastal erosion. Tidwell responded that he does the work he does as director of the Chesapeake Climate Action Network for three reasons. The first is for his son's future on the planet. The second is that he lived abroad when he was in the Peace Corps and saw firsthand the effects of environmental problems on poorer nations. The third, he said, is that "I am a Christian."[55]

For most of us, it apparently takes either a personal financial loss or a personal health crisis to acknowledge and be moved to take action about a massive environmental problem. Robert Gifford of Canada's University of Victoria has studied humans' "inability to deal with climate change" and concluded there are several reasons why we have been so slow to act. Although Gifford "is reluctant to pick out one barrier as being more powerful or limiting than another," he said, "If I had to name one, I would nominate the lack of perceived behavioral control; 'I'm only one person, what can I do?' is certainly a big one."[56]

According to Renee Lertzman, when people are aware of the extent of the problem that climate change presents but make no changes in how they live as a result of that knowledge, "neither apathy nor denial really explains the dissonance between our actions and beliefs." She blames "environmental melancholia," her term for "the simple fact that we care an overwhelming amount about both the planet *and* our way of life, and we find that conflict too painful to bear. . . . When we don't process the pain of that, that's when we get stuck and can't move forward."[57] Lertzman points to South Africa's post-apartheid Truth and Reconciliation Commission as an example of how to deal effectively with this collective pain. "There's a lot to be said for providing a means for people to talk together about climate change, to make it socially acceptable to talk about it."[58]

The exact same reasons and the same kind of fears prevent us from talking productively about race and class and gender discrimination. But it is just as important for us to tackle these issues, too, in part because silence and feelings of helplessness breed anger. There is often a strong link between depression and unexpressed or displaced anger.

The post-Katrina situation was so complex that it was hard in 2005 and still remains difficult in 2015 to decide exactly who it is that deserves to be a recipient of that anger. There is so much fault, and so many to bear it, that it is hard to parcel it out. Tens of thousands of New Orleanians are still

---

55. Tidwell, Presentation at Octavia Books.
56. Paramaguru, "Battle over Global Warming."
57. Ibid.
58. Ibid.

trying to make sense of things, still need to recount their experiences aloud in order to learn what the flood did to them and their loved ones and their neighbors and their city, to understand how they reacted, and to discover what next steps they should take. They and the church still need to recover or create a feeling of hope.

When I speak of hope, I quote Charles Wood, who says that it is precisely the Christian hope that frees us from having to be optimists. We don't have to pretend that things are fine and getting better. We can accept that things are bad and might get worse, and yet believe that God is working in us and creation and that there is reason for hope. As Vaclav Havel wrote, "Hope is not about believing we can change things; hope is about believing that what we do matters." Every moment of deliberate relationship building, especially the building of bridging social capital, matters.

The Persistent Widow

A saying attributed to Rabbi Tarfon translates to this: "You are not responsible for completing the work, but neither are you free to abandon it." And Luke's Gospel offers the parable of the persistent widow. It is a story about a woman who comes to a judge demanding justice. He refuses, but she keeps raising her voice until he grows weary and gives her what she wants.

As the second decade after Katrina begins, the church can look back on having accomplished an enormous amount of much-needed recovery work and on having done it very well. It should look forward to a decade of raising its voice in the continuing struggle against injustice. Katrina has presented an unprecedented moment for this redemptive work. Speak wisely and, like the widow, persistently until God's reign is someday a reality in this Holy City of God.

Appendix

Explanation of Some United Methodist Terms

The United Methodist Church employs a number of terms that many nonmembers (and members) may not understand without some clarification. In addition, the church follows several policies in matters of finances, pastoral assignments, congregational discipline, and so forth that are unique to the denomination. This appendix provides some brief explanation of these matters, particularly relative to issues faced by the post-Katrina church, to help readers navigate the terminology employed and better understand why things happened in New Orleans as they did. Many United Methodists will need to consult this section only if they encounter a term that confuses them.

What is General Conference?

The UMC's General Conference, which convenes every four years, is the body that sets the governance and policies of the church; it is this body which decides on any changes that are made to our *Book of Discipline*, the "rulebook" for UMC governance and more. Delegates come from around the world, but most are from the annual conferences within the United States.[1]

---

1. Because the church was officially formed and flourished in what would become the United States, its polity reflects the idea that the church proper is the church in the USA and with the exception of British Methodists, Methodists elsewhere are in "tacked-on" kinds of organizations called Central Conferences. In some countries, there are autonomous Methodist Churches, and these do not have vote at General Conference. It is important to note that the structure described in the text does not really acknowledge the "global church" that the UMC claims to be and that there is much discussion ongoing about how to correct our structure, but it is far beyond the scope of this project to provide even a rudimentary explanation of the complex reality that exists.

What is an annual conference?

There are two quite different meanings to the term "annual conference" within the UMC, which can be quite confusing. One is, as the words "annual" and "conference" suggest, a meeting held every year.

The other and more common use of the term is less intuitive, as it describes a place rather than a gathering. The annual conference is considered the basic unit of United Methodist Church (UMC) structure; it is a geographic area, comparable to diocesan areas or regions in certain other churches. There are over fifty annual conferences within the United States of America. Some of these encompass more than one of the fifty states, while other states contain multiple annual conferences. However, the boundaries of the Louisiana Annual Conference happen to be identical to the boundaries of the state of Louisiana, and this makes both writing and reading about it easier.

To avoid confusion I have slightly altered the usage. In this book, I use the term "annual conference" to mean the yearly gathering; the term "Louisiana conference" refers to the geographic area. United Methodists also informally use the term "the conference" in the same way that employees of a corporation might refer to "the management." I have avoided that use in this volume for clarity's sake.

What is a jurisdiction?

Annual conferences in the United States are also grouped into five jurisdictions, with Louisiana being included in the South Central Jurisdiction. Today, jurisdictions exist primarily for the election and assignment of bishops. Because this layer of the hierarchy has no bearing on the post-Katrina part of this project, there is no reason to discuss it extensively here.

Jurisdictions did play a big part in the racial history of the church, as they were created in 1939 to facilitate segregation and used to maintain segregation until 1968. That history is addressed in the material on the racial/ethnic diversity of the church in Chapter 3.

What is a bishop?

Bishops are the elected chief officials of the UMC. Each annual conference has a bishop as its spiritual and administrative leader. The number of active UMC bishops is not the same as the number of annual conferences. Each bishop is appointed to an "episcopal area" which can contain more than one annual conference. However, the Louisiana conference and the Louisiana episcopal area happen to be identical in boundary.

All bishops belong to the Council of Bishops. Only in very recent years has the council made the decision to elect a president, and this means little more than presiding at meetings during a two-year term in the office. The president does not have authority over other bishops. The Roman Catholic language that depicts the pope as "first among equals" is not applicable; in the case of the pope, it is a misnomer because it is clear that no one else is really an equal; in the case of the president of the UMC bishops, the individual is not in any real sense "first." A bishop's rule of law can be referred to the Judicial Council for a decision as to whether it is in keeping with the *Book of Discipline*; this council is the third branch of UMC government, accompanying the legislative branch (General Conference) and the executive branch (the Council of Bishops). A bishop (like other elders) can be brought up on charges and face a church trial for violating the *Book of Discipline*. However, it is valid to say that almost always, within his or her own episcopal area, what a bishop says, goes.

How are pastors assigned?
What is the itineracy?

Pastors are assigned to their charges by the bishop and the appointive cabinet. The appointive cabinet includes each District Superintendent (DS) in an episcopal area. In 2005, the Louisiana conference had seven districts, so the bishop, the provost, and seven district superintendents made up the appointive cabinet that was responsible for all decisions about where pastors would be sent.

Today the appointment process is a bit more humane than it once was. In the early 1800s, Bishop Francis Asbury was in charge of assigning pastors.

> Once the appointments were made, Asbury had neither the time nor the inclination to listen to complaints from preachers unhappy with their assignments. He developed the practice of having [a colleague] bring his horse to a side door while he read the appointments on the last day of conference so that he could make a quick getaway as soon as he had finished.[2]

As late as the mid-twentieth century, in many conferences pastors did not know where or even whether they would be moving until a couple of days before they had to leave for a new parsonage.

2. Wigger, *American Saint*, 381.

Nowadays, appointments are made using a process of consultation. District superintendents are expected to visit with the Staff-Parish Relations Committee at a church that will have a change of ministers to see what they hope for in their new pastor. District superintendents are also to consult with pastors who will move to see what issues are most important to them about their settings. A pastor can refuse the first appointment offered, and a church can refuse the first pastor offered. This is not encouraged, however, and a second refusal will probably cause an "unappointable" label to be attached to a pastor, or a failure to send any pastor to a church.

What is a charge?
What is a two-point charge?

A pastor is appointed to a charge. It may take two or more congregations sharing the expenses in order to pay for one minister's salary and benefits. If a pastor is at First Example UMC, a congregation that can provide her full support, then she is appointed to the First Example congregation, which is also the First Example charge. If she is appointed to Less Affluent UMC and Financially Challenged UMC and preaches at both congregations and receives part of her compensation from each of them, then she serves the Less Affluent-Financially Challenged charge. There have always been and still are charges made up of more than two congregations.

What are apportionments?

When the budget for the overall United Methodist Church is adopted, then a certain amount of it is assigned to each annual conference, based on a formula that includes the number of members in that conference. The conference then apportions the payment to each of its churches, based on the amount of money the churches spent the prior year. A small church will therefore pay a much smaller amount than a larger church. Every church is provided with a breakdown of where their money goes.

Paying 100 percent of apportionments is a very good thing for a church to have achieved, and it tends to put the church in good standing with the annual conference. When a church cannot pay its apportionments, it is an indication of a lack of financial health. When a church could have paid its apportionments but chooses not to, it is an indication that they are unhappy with the direction of the larger church, and this does not sit well with the conference at all.

The term "a portion meant for others" is often used to explain apportionments, and much of the money does go to fund activities to help others that no one church or conference could have financed on their own. However, another part of the apportionments goes to what would be termed "overhead" in a corporation and thus to keeping the institution functioning.

Who owns UMC property?

One primary reason that United Methodism presents a compelling case study is its stance on property ownership. The man who wrote the definitive textbook about the UMC's governance is Thomas Frank, and this discussion draws heavily on the "Church Property" chapter of his polity textbook.[3] The UMC is one of a few connectional denominations that occupies a middle ground between the diocese's outright ownership of all property (as in Roman Catholicism) and outright ownership and control of a building by the congregation that meets there (as in nondenominational churches and in congregationally autonomous denominations). In United Methodism, congregations do own their property, and they alone are responsible for its upkeep; however, every deed states that the property is being held "in trust" for the larger church.

What does this "trust clause" mean?

What does it mean to say that the property is being held in trust? Secular courts have been called upon numerous times to answer this question. Almost all have ruled in favor of the larger church's right to control the property, but a very few, more recent decisions have let the local congregation which paid for a building keep ownership of it when they left the denomination.

The idea that ultimate control of property rests with a larger body originated with founder John Wesley's desire to exercise control over who preached in Methodist meeting houses. Here in the United States, the most practical results have been to prevent some schisms that might have occurred and to prevent individual congregations from leaving when they do not agree with a stance the denomination has taken. In the mid-twentieth century, such disagreements usually involved racial equality. In the late twentieth century and in the early decades of the twenty-first, they tend to concern homosexuality.

3. Frank, *Polity, Practice, and the Mission*, 299–309.

Controversies about whether gay and lesbian people should be ordained or even be eligible to serve in lay leadership positions have been ongoing for decades. More recently, debates about homosexuality have centered on the question of whether same-sex couples can be married in UMC buildings or by UMC pastors. Although the UMC is not officially open on this topic—gay and lesbian people cannot be ordained, same-sex "holy union" or wedding ceremonies cannot be conducted in UMC buildings, and it is a chargeable offense for a UMC pastor to preside at same-sex ceremonies anywhere—the denomination's relatively minor moves toward openness have prompted some congregations to wish to disaffiliate with the church. The courts have ruled in favor of at least one congregation who wished to leave because the Western Jurisdiction has publicly taken more open stances; in that instance, the local congregation was allowed to keep ownership of the property. However, almost every court ruling throughout the years has upheld the trust clause.

This book is not the right venue to discuss legal implications of various court cases. For the consideration of the post-Katrina situation, it is enough to state that the trust clause is understood by United Methodists to prohibit decision making about land and buildings done solely by a local congregation. The rule is that if a congregation wishes to remodel a building and the cost will amount to more than 25 percent of the value of the current property, they have to have a vote of the district-wide committee on church extension to do so.[4]

Frank also notes, "While the bishop does not hold title, local church property and assets revert to the annual conference (if the local church is abandoned or discontinued) and thus are reserved for the exclusive use of the United Methodist Church." Furthermore, he adds, "A local church's very acceptance of a pastor under appointment indicates its willingness to be subject to the trust clause (even if the trust clause is not specifically written into a particular property deed)."[5]

The import of all this for the post-Katrina church is that, from a disciplinary standpoint, no congregation should have begun its repair or rebuilding without approval from the local church. In fact, the conference office issued an instruction that no congregation should be engaged in rebuilding until the larger church had approved it, but not every congregation followed this instruction.

---

4. *Book of Discipline*, 2012, para. 2521, 736.
5. Frank, *Polity, Practice, and the Mission*, 300, 303.

What are the UMC's Social Principles?

The Social Principles are found in Part V of the *Book of Discipline*. The preface says that the statements "are a prayerful and thoughtful effort on the part of the General Conference to speak to the human issues in the contemporary world from a sound biblical and theological foundation. . . ." The principles are "a call to faithfulness and are intended to be instructive and persuasive in the best of the prophetic spirit." They are also "a call to all members of The United Methodist Church to a prayerful, studied dialogue of faith and practice." They are grouped into six sections: the Natural World; the Nurturing Community; the Social Community; the Economic Community; the Political Community; and the World Community. In each of these areas, the General Conference adopts policy statements and recommendations for actions that individuals and churches should take. The *Book of Resolutions* contains even more statements about specific situations adopted by General Conference; a version of it is also published every four years.[6]

---

6. *Book of Discipline*, 2012, 103–42; *Book of Resolutions*, 2012. The complete text of the Social Principles can also be found on the General Board of Church and Society website, umc-gbcs.org.

Bibliography

After the Storm. DVD. Directed by Hilla Medalia. Priddy Brothers, 2009.
Alexander-Bloch, Benjamin. "In Post-Katrina Housing Discrimination Case, St. Bernard Agrees to Final $1.8 Million Payment." *New Orleans Times-Picayune,* December 19, 2014. Online: http://www.nola.com/crime/index.ssf/2014/12/in_post-katrina_housing_discri.html.
———. "St. Bernard Multifamily Housing Battle Opens New Front." *New Orleans Times-Picayune,* January 29, 2011. Online: http://www.nola.com/politics/index.ssf/2011/01/st_bernard_multifamily-housing.html.
———. "Support for Wetland Restoration Dramatically Increased Over Past Decade, Survey Shows." *New Orleans Times-Picayune,* February 11, 2014. Online: http://impact.nola.com/environment/print.html?entry=/2014/02/support_for_wetland_restoratio.html.
Archdiocese of New Orleans. "Archbishop Gregory Michael Aymond." Online: https://www.arch-no.org/aymond.
Arend, Orissa. "Racism and the Church: Episcopalians Search their Souls, Seek Atonement." *The Lens,* January 24, 2014. Online: http://thelensnola.org/2014/01/24/racism-and-the-church-episcopalians-search-their-souls-seek-atonement/?utm_medium=email&utm_campaign=Weekly+Newsletter+12414&utm_content=Weekly+Newsletter+12414+CID_78999e871dc6f08cc486b6f993ef1fde&utm_source=Email%20Campaign&utm_term=OPINION%20Racism%20and%20the%20church%20Episcopalians%20search%20their%20souls%20seek%20atonement.
Associated Press. "Archbishop Tasked with Outreach to Poor." *Tulsa World,* November 29, 2013.
———. "Pope Ramps Up Charity Office to Be Near Poor, Sick." *Washington Post,* November 29, 2013.
Backstrom, Betty. "Church Ministries Awarded Peace with Justice Grants." *Louisiana Now!* February 6, 2013. Online: http://www.la-umc.org/news/detail/1011.
Baker, Christopher. *The Hybrid Church in the City: Third Space Thinking.* 2nd ed. London: SCM, 2009.
Barth, Karl. "The Need and Promise of Christian Preaching." In *The Word of God and the Word of Man,* translated by Douglas Horton, 97–135. London: Hodder & Stoughton, 1928.
Bauers, Sandy. "Study Finds Sea Levels Rising Fast; Concerns Grow about Shore." *Philadelphia Inquirer,* January 8, 2014. Online: http://articles.philly.com/2014-01-08/news/45958874_1_sea-level-rise-sea-level-research-laboratory-coastal-sciences.

Bayou, Aziza Victoria. "United for the City: Multiethnic First Grace United Methodist Church in Post-Hurricane Katrina New Orleans." MA thesis, Colorado State University, Summer 2011.

Bebelle, Carol, et al. *Swimming Upstream: A Testimony, a Prayer, a Hallelujah, an Incantation*. Produced by Carol Bebelle and Eve Ensler. Howlin' Wolf, New Orleans, Louisiana, November 18, 2008.

Bennett, James B. *Religion and the Rise of Jim Crow in New Orleans*. Princeton: Princeton University Press, 2005.

Bergal, Jenni, et al. *City Adrift: New Orleans before and after Katrina, A Center for Public Integrity Investigation*. Baton Rouge: Louisiana State University Press, 2007.

Bloch, Matthew, et al. "Mapping Poverty in America: Data from the Census Bureau Show Where the Poor Live." *New York Times*, January 4, 2014. Online: http://www.nytimes.com/newsgraphics/2014/01/05/poverty-map/?nl=todaysheadlines&emc=edit_th_20140106.

Blue, Ellen. *St. Mark's and the Social Gospel: Methodist Women and Civil Rights in New Orleans, 1895–1965*. Knoxville: University of Tennessee Press, 2011.

———. "Women of the United Methodist Church: Giving (Re)Birth to the UMC in New Orleans." Presented at Newcomb College Center for Research on Women Visiting Scholar Series, Tulane University, New Orleans, LA, October 30, 2008.

———. "'Yes, We Are Everywhere': Thirty Years with the Women for Progressive Action, Lower Ninth Ward." *Methodist History* 52.1 (2013) 4–18.

Book of Discipline of the United Methodist Church, 2008. Nashville: United Methodist, 2008.

Book of Discipline of the United Methodist Church, 2012. Nashville: United Methodist, 2012.

Book of Resolutions of the United Methodist Church, 2012. Nashville: United Methodist, 2012.

Boyle, Gregory. *Tattoos on the Heart: The Power of Boundless Compassion*. New York City: Free Press, 2011.

Branson, Ken. "New Jersey Shore Likely Faces Unprecedented Flooding by Mid-Century." *Rutgers Today*, December 4, 2013.

Brite Divinity School. "Soul Repair Center: Moral Injury Recovery." Online: http://brite.edu/programs.asp?lefnav=sr&BriteProgram=soulrepair.

Browne, Kate. "Soapbox: 'Culture Brokers' have Role to Play in Flood Disaster Recovery." *The Coloradoan*, October 4, 2013.

Carmelite NGO. "UN Issues Focused on by the Carmelite NGO." Online: http://carmelitengo.org/.

———. "We the Peoples: A Call to Action for the UN Millennium Declaration: Goals and Targets." Online: http://carmelitengo.org/annual%20conferences/57th%20conference%20-%202004/millennium%20goals.htm.

Chiseri-Strater, Elizabeth, and Bonnie Stone Sunstein. *FieldWorking: Reading and Writing Research*. Upper Saddle River, NJ: Prentice-Hall, 1997.

Clarke, Erika. "Teaching Nonviolence on New Orleans' Mean Streets." *CNN*, July 18, 2013. Online: http://www.cnn.com/2013/07/18/us/cnnheroes-fitzpatrick-new-orleans-youth/.

Cobb, John B., Jr. *Grace & Responsibility: A Wesleyan Theology for Today*. Nashville: Abingdon, 1995.

BIBLIOGRAPHY

Cooper, Anderson. *Dispatches from the Edge: A Memoir of War, Disasters, and Survival.* New York: HarperCollins, 2006.

Cowart, Courtney. *An American Awakening: From Ground Zero to Katrina the People We Are Free to Be.* New York: Seabury, 2008.

Daniell, Anne. "Incarnating Theology in an Estuary-Carnival Place: New Orleans in the Pontchartrain Basin." PhD diss., Drew University, October 2005.

Davis, Valerie Bridgeman. "Retribution as First Response: Did God Punish New Orleans?" In *The Sky Is Crying: Race, Class and Natural Disaster,* edited by Cheryl A. Kirk-Duggan, 3–12. Nashville: Abingdon, 2006.

DeBerry, Jarvis. "The Hurt from Hurricane Katrina Bridge Blockade Remains Incalculable." *New Orleans Times-Picayune,* October 4, 2011. Online: http://www.nola.com/opinions/index.ssf/2011/10/the_hurt_from_hurricane_katrin.html.

DeVore, Donald. "Water in Sacred Places: Rebuilding New Orleans Black Churches as Sites of Community Empowerment." *Journal of American History* 94.3 (2007) 762–69.

Driver, Tom F. *The Magic of Ritual: Our Need for Liberating Rites that Transform Our Lives and Our Communities.* San Francisco: Harper San Francisco, 1991.

Emerson, Michael O., and Rodney M. Woo. *People of the Dream: Multiracial Congregations in the United States.* Princeton: Princeton University Press, 2006.

Fink, Sheri. *Five Days at Memorial: Life and Death in a Storm-Ravaged Hospital.* New York: Crown, 2013.

Flaherty, Jordan. *Floodlines: Community and Resistance from Katrina to the Jena Six.* Chicago: Haymarket, 2010.

Frank, Thomas Edward. *Polity, Practice, and the Mission of The United Methodist Church.* Nashville: Abingdon, 2006.

Gillis, Justin. "The Flood Next Time." *New York Times* (13 January 2014). No pages. Online: http://www.nytimes.com/2014/01/14/science/earth/grappling-with-sea-level-rise-sooner-not-later.html?_r=0.

Gonzales, John Moreno. "Sign of Katrina Fatigue? Storm Memorial Delayed." *Washington Post,* July 13, 2008. Online: http://www.washingtonpost.com/wp-dyn/content/article/2008/07/13/AR2008071300375_pf.html.

Goodman, Amy. "Governor Gives Troops Shoot-to-Kill Orders." *Democracy Now!* September 2, 2005. Online: http://www.democracynow.org/2005/9/2/headlines#927.

Harbaugh, Gary. *Act of God, Active God: Recovering from Natural Disasters.* Minneapolis: Fortress, 2001.

Harper, Robert Henry. *Louisiana Methodism.* Washington, DC: Kaufmann, 1949.

Harris-Lacewell, Melissa Victoria. *Barbershops, Bibles, and BET: Everyday Talk and Black Political Thought.* Princeton: Princeton University Press, 2006.

Harvey, Cynthia Fierro. "A Message from Bishop Cynthia Fierro Harvey." *Louisiana Now* (2014) 3.

Heifetz, Ronald A. *Leadership without Easy Answers.* Cambridge: Belknap, 1994.

Heitzenrater, Richard P. "The Poor and the People Called Methodists." In *The Poor and the People Called Methodists,* edited by Richard Heitzenrater, 15–38. Nashville. Kingwood, 2002.

———. *Wesley and the People Called Methodists.* Nashville: Abingdon, 1995.

Helgesen, Sally, and Julie Johnson. *The Female Vision: Women's Real Power at Work.* San Francisco: Berrett-Koehler, 2010.

Henderson, Freddie C. "Gloria Listach Henderson." In *Journal of the Fortieth Session of the Louisiana Annual Conference, United Methodist Church*, 2010, edited by Carl Rhoads, 261–62. Baton Rouge: Louisiana Annual Conference, UMC, 2010.

Henderson, Katharine Rhodes. *God's Troublemakers: How Women of Faith Are Changing the World*. New York: Continuum, 2006.

Hiles, Sara Shipley. "The Environment." In *City Adrift: New Orleans before and after Katrina, A Center for Public Integrity Investigation*, edited by Jenni Bergal et al., 7–19. Baton Rouge: Louisiana State University Press, 2007.

Hirsch, Arnold R. "(Almost) a Walk Closer with Thee: Historical Reflections on New Orleans and Hurricane Katrina." *Journal of Urban History* 35.5 (2008) 614–26.

Hoerth, Pat. "Changing the Climate: Use of Language in Worship to Move Away from Anthropocentrism." Presentation at ReMind & ReNew conference, Phillips Theological Seminary, Tulsa, Oklahoma, January 22, 2014.

Horne, Jed. *Breach of Faith: Hurricane Katrina and the Near Death of a Great American City*. New York: Random, 2008.

Horowitz, Andy. "Hurricane Betsy and the Politics of Disaster in New Orleans's Lower Ninth Ward, 1965–1967." *Journal of Southern History* 70.4 (2014) 893–934.

Ishisaka, Naomi. "After the Storm: Hurricane Katrina and People of Color." *ColorsNW Magazine*, November 2005. Online: http://www.naomiishisaka.com/writing/cover-story-after-the-storm-hurricane-katrina-and-people-of-color.

Joh, Wonhee Anne. *Heart of the Cross: A Postcolonial Christology*. Louisville: Westminster John Knox, 2006.

"Juanita Arrieta Ramos." Missionary Profiles, UMC General Board of Global Ministries. Online: http://www.umcmission.org/Explore-Our-Work/Missionaries-in-Service/Missionary-Profiles/550001.

Kelman, Ari. "Boundary Issues: Clarifying New Orleans's Murky Edges." *Journal of American History* 94.3 (2007) 695–703.

Kemper, Thomas. "The Theology behind Disaster Relief and Recovery." *United Methodist Reporter*, June 11, 2013. Online: http://www.unitedmethodistreporter.com/2013/06/11/the-theology-behind-disaster-relief-and-recovery/?utm_source=twitterfeed&utm_medium=facebook.

Kirk-Duggan, Cheryl A. ed. *The Sky Is Crying: Race, Class, and Natural Disaster*. Nashville: Abingdon, 2006.

Kraemer, Craig, and Cynthia Fransen. *Swimming against the Holy See*. DVD. Produced and edited by Craig Kraemer. New Orleans: Craig Kraemer, 2009.

Kwok, Pui-Lan. *Postcolonial Imagination & Feminist Theology*. Louisville: Westminster John Knox, 2005.

Landphair, Juliette. "'The Forgotten People of New Orleans': Community, Vulnerability, and the Lower Ninth Ward." *Journal of American History* 94.3 (2007) 837–45.

Laska, Shirley. "'Mother of Rorschachs': New Orleans Recovery from Hurricane Katrina." *Sociological Inquiry* 78.4 (2008) 580–91.

Lawton, Dan, "New Orleans Church Protests Arrests of Immigrants." *Baton Rouge Advocate*, December 15, 2013. Online: http://theadvocate.com/news/7822957-123/new-orleans-church-protests-arrests.

Lawton, Kim. "Finding New Meaning in Holy Week." *Washington Post*, April 15, 2006.

———. "Lance Eden: Extended Interview." *Religion and Ethics Newsweekly*, April 6, 2007. Online: http://www.pbs.org/wnet/religionandethics/2007/04/06/april-6-2007-lance-eden-extended-interview/3590/.

LeDoux, Jerome G. *War of the Pews: A Personal Account of St. Augustine Church in New Orleans.* Donaldsonville, LA: Margaret Media, 2011.
Lee, Spike, and Sam Pollard. *When the Levees Broke: A Requiem in Four Acts.* Directed by Spike Lee. HBO Documentary Film and 40 Acres and a Goat Filmworks, 2006.
Living Cultures Project. "Sunday in Tremé: A Living Cultural Heritage Tour." Brochure compiled in conjunction with a collaborative policy research project of Tulane University, the University of New Orleans, and the Urban Institute, n.d.
Logsdon, Joseph, and Arnold R. Hirsch, eds. *Creole New Orleans: Race and Americanization.* Baton Rouge: Louisiana State University Press, 1992.
Long, Alecia P. *The Great Southern Babylon: Sex, Race, and Respectability in New Orleans, 1865–1920.* Baton Rouge: Louisiana State University Press, 2004.
"Louisiana Still Needs Assistance in Recovery from Isaac: Calling All Response Teams!" *Louisiana Now!* November 9, 2012.
MacKenzie, Tracy. "The 'R' Word." *(Alexandria) Town Talk,* August 17, 2013.
Maddox, Randy. *Responsible Grace: John Wesley's Practical Theology.* Nashville: Kingswood, 1994.
——— . "'Visit the Poor': John Wesley, the Poor, and the Sanctification of Believers." In *The Poor and the People Called Methodists, 1729–1999,* edited by Richard P. Heitzenrater, 59–81. Nashville: Kingswood, 2002.
Maestri, William F. *A Story of Hope in a Time of Destruction: The Archdiocese of New Orleans and Hurricane Katrina.* Strausbourg: Éditions du Signe, 2010.
Marshall, Bob. "Day After Boasting of Gulf's Health, BP Confirms 25,000-Pound Tar Mat." *The Lens,* March 18, 2015. Online: http://thelensnola.org/2015/03/18/bp-confirms-25000-pound-tar-mats-two-dead-dolphins-found-nearby/.
——— . "More Massive Tar Balls from BP Oil Spill Discovered on Louisiana Beaches." *The Lens,* December 18, 2013. Online: http://thelensnola.org/2013/12/18/more-massive-tar-mats-from-bp-oil-spill-discovered-on-louisiana-beaches/?utm_medium=email&utm_campaign=Weekly%20Newsletter%20122013&utm_content=Weekly%20Newsletter%20122013+CID_d1986424f27b80c3afa98b684a2535d2&utm_source=Email%20Campaign&utm_term=More%20massive%20tar%20mats%20from%20BP%20oil%20spill%20found%20on%20Louisiana%20beaches.
Marti, Gerardo. *Worship across the Racial Divide: Religious Music and the Multiracial Congregation.* New York: Oxford University Press, 2012.
Martin, Naomi. "New Orleans Murder Victim was 'Always Smiling,' Dillard Classmates Say." *New Orleans Times-Picayune,* October 3, 2012. Online: http://www.nola.com/crime/index.ssf/2012/10/new_orleans_murder_victim_was.html.
McCoy, Beth. "Second Line and the Art of Witness: Steve Prince's *Katrina Suite.*" *Image* 78 (2013) 63–74.
McFague, Sallie. *The Body of God: An Ecological Theology.* Minneapolis: Fortress, 1993.
McMullen, Michael D. ed. *Prayers and Meditations of Susanna Wesley.* London: Trustees for Methodist Church Purposes, 2000.
Meister, Susan J. "Cleaning Buckets a Tangible Expression of Care." Online: http://new.gbgm-umc.org/umcor/newsroom/releases/archives09/cleaning buckets/.
Michaelson, Jay. "Climate Change is a Sin—Here's How to Repent for It." *Religion Dispatches,* January 15, 2014. Online: http://www.religiondispatches.org/archive/culture/7505/climate_change_is_a_sin_here_s_how_to_repent_for_it/.

Miles, Margaret. *The Word Made Flesh: A History of Christian Thought*. Malden, MA: Blackwell, 2005.

Mitchell, Stephen, trans. *Tao Te Ching*. New York: Harper Perennial, 1988.

Mullen, Jethro. "Super Typhoon Haiyan, One of Strongest Storms Ever, Hits Central Philippines." *CNN*, November 8, 2013. Online: http://www.cnn.com/2013/11/07/world/asia/philippines-typhoon-haiyan/

Naples, Nancy A. *Feminism and Method: Ethnography, Discourse Analysis, and Activist Research*. New York: Routledge, 2003.

"New Reconciling Congregations—Parker Memorial United Methodist Church." Reconciling Ministries Network. November 15, 2012. Online: http://www.rmnetwork.org/rmnnews/new-reconciling-communities/page/8/.

"New Reconciling Congregations—Rayne Memorial United Methodist Church." Reconciling Ministries Network, October 16, 2012. Online: http://www.rmnetwork.org/rmnnews/new-reconciling-communities/page/8/.

Ng-A-Fook, Nicholas. *An Indigenous Curriculum of Place: The United Houma Nation's Contentious Relationship with Louisiana's Education Institutions*. New York: Peter Lang, 2007.

Nolan, Bruce. "After Years of Struggle, Prayer and Protest, St. Henry Church will Host Regular Masses." *New Orleans Times-Picayune*, June 10, 2012.

———. "Bishop Charles Jenkins Retires after 12 Years of Leading the State's Episcopalians." *New Orleans Times-Picayune,* January 6, 2010. Online: http://www.blog.nola.com/religion_impact/print.html?entry=/2010/01/bishop_charles_jenkins_retires_after_12_years_of_leading_the_states_episcopalians.html.

———. "Episcopal Bishop Charles Jenkins Charts a New Course after Being Traumatized by Hurricane Katrina." *New Orleans Times-Picayune*, January 17, 2009. Online: http://www.nola.com/news/index.ssf/2009/01/episcopal_bishop_charles_jenki.html.

Nolan, Bruce, and Susan Finch. "Police Clear out Church Holdouts: 2 Arrested as Archdiocese Regains Uptown Worship Sites." *New Orleans Times-Picayune*, January 7, 2009.

Oppenheimer, Mark. "Young Methodists Plant Churches with Environmental Gospel." *New York Times*, September 4, 2015.

"Oscar Ramos." Missionary Profiles, UMC General Board of Global Ministries. Online: http://www.umcmission.org/Explore-Our-Work/Missionaries-in-Service/Missionary-Profiles/Ramos-Gallardo-Oscar.

Paramaguru, Kharunya. "The Battle over Global Warming Is All in Your Head." *Time*, August 19, 2013. Online: http://science.time.com/2013/08/19/in-denial-about-the-climate-the-psychological-battle-over-global-warming/.

Parekh, Trushna. "Of Armed Guards and Kente Cloth: Afro-Creole Catholics and the Battle for St. Augustine Parish in Post-Katrina New Orleans." In *In the Wake of Hurricane Katrina: New Paradigms and Social Visions*, edited by Clyde Woods, 131–55. Baltimore: Johns Hopkins University Press, 2010.

Park, Andrew Sung. *The Wounded Heart of God: The Asian Concept of Han and the Christian Doctrine of Sin*. Nashville: Abingdon, 1993.

Penner, D'Ann R., and Keith C. Ferdinand. *Overcoming Katrina: African American Voices from the Crescent City and Beyond*. New York: Palgrave MacMillan, 2009.

Phillips, Brenda D. "Gendered Disaster Practice and Policy." In *The Women of Katrina: How Gender, Race, and Class Matter in an American Disaster*, edited by Emmanuel David and Elaine Enarson, 233–44. Nashville: Vanderbilt University Press, 2012.

Pope, John. "Exclusive Interview with Archbishop." *New Orleans Times-Picayune*. January 9, 2009. Online: http://videos.nola.com/times-picayune/2009/01/video_archbishop_alfred_hughes.html.

———. "Hughes 'At Peace' in Church Eviction." *New Orleans Times-Picayune*, January 10, 2009.

———. "Lt. Gen. Elvin 'Vald' Heiberg III, who Apologized after Katrina for New Orleans' Deficient Protection, Dies at 81." *New Orleans Times-Picayune*, October 7, 2013. Online: http://www.nola.com/military/index.ssf/2013/10/lt_gen_elvin_vald_heiberg_iii.html.

———. "Pat Evans, Feminist and Political Activist, Dies at 81." *New Orleans Times-Picayune*. March 20, 2013. Online: http://www.nola.com/politics/index.ssf/2013/05/post_515.html.

Putnam, Robert D. "Bowling Alone: America's Declining Social Capital." *Journal of Democracy* 6.1 (1995) 65–78.

———. *Bowling Alone: The Collapse and Revival of American Community*. New York, Simon & Schuster, 2000.

Putnam, Robert D., and Lewis M. Feldstein. *Better Together: Restoring the American Community*. New York: Simon and Schuster, 2003.

Reckdahl, Katy, et al. Presentation at the "Cultures of Rebuilding" conference, Louisiana State Museum, New Orleans, LA, November 8, 2008.

Rhoads, Carl, ed. *Journal of the Thirty-Fifth Session of the Louisiana Annual Conference, United Methodist Church, 2005*. Baton Rouge: Louisiana Annual Conference, UMC, 2005.

Rieger, Joerg. "Contemporary Issues and Models of Ministry with the Poor, the Underrepresented, and the Ignored: A Panel Discussion." In *The Poor and the People Called Methodists*, edited by Richard P. Heitzenrater, 195–208. Nashville: Abingdon, 1995.

Rioux, Paul. "Crescent City Connection Blockage Lawsuit in Federal Court Comes to an End." *New Orleans Times-Picayune*, December 28, 2010. Online: http://www.nola.com/katrina/index.ssf/2010/12/crescent_city_connection_block.html.

Robertson, Campbell. "Ex-Mayor of New Orleans Guilty on Corruption Charges." *New York Times*, February 12, 2014.

Rodriguez, Maya. "Talks Reopen about Future of Uptown Churches." WWL-TV, November 22, 2009. Online: http://www.wwltv.com/story/news/local/2014/08/25/14279650/

———. "Three Years after Closure, St. Henry Catholic Church to Reopen for Daily Mass." WWL-TV, June 10, 2012. Online: http://www.wwltv.com/story/news/local/2014/09/03/14512768/.

Rose, Chris. *1 Dead in Attic*. 2nd ed. New York: Simon & Schuster, 2007.

Russman, Gretchen B., and Sharon F. Rallis. *Learning in the Field: An Introduction to Qualitative Research*. Thousand Oaks, CA: Sage, 2003.

Russell, Gordon. "Mastermind Puts the Mayor in City Hall: Political Strategist's Win Record with Go Down in N.O. History." *New Orleans Times-Picayune*, June 11, 2006.

Sanders, Cheryl J. "Conducting Effective Research, among Other Things." Presentation at the Lilly Theological Research Grants 2009 Conference, Pittsburgh, Pennsylvania, February 29, 2009.

———. *Saints in Exile: The Holiness-Pentecostal Experience in African American Religion and Culture*. New York: Oxford University Press, 1996.

Snedeker, Rebecca. "Holding It Together, Falling Apart." In *Unfathomable City: A New Orleans Atlas*, edited by Rebecca Solnit and Rebecca Snedeker, 142–46. Berkeley: University of California Press, 2013.

Solnit, Rebecca. "Juju and Cuckoo." In *Unfathomable City: A New Orleans Atlas*, edited by Rebecca Solnit and Rebecca Snedeker, 142. Berkeley: University of California Press, 2013.

Starr, S. Frederick, ed. *Inventing New Orleans: Writings of Lafcadio Hearn*. Jackson: University of Mississippi Press, 2001.

Stewart, Marilyn. "Always Pursuing Excellence Youth Center in New Orleans Wins $50,000." *New Orleans Times-Picayune*, December 16, 2013. Online: http://blog.nola.com/new_orleans/2013/12/always_pursuing_excellence_you.html.

———. "Luke's House 'Suitcase Clinic' is Moving Free Medical Services to a Permanent Location." *New Orleans Times-Picayune*, March 18, 2012. Online: http://www.nola.com/health/index.ssf/2012/03/lukes_house_suitcase_clinic_mo.html.

———. "Prayers for Medical Help Answered: Luke's House Aids, Teaches Less Fortunate." *New Orleans Times-Picayune*, March 12, 2009.

Suchocki, Marjorie Hewitt. "What *Is* Process Theology?" Booklet produced by Process and Faith, 2003. Online: http://old.processandfaith.org/publications/RedBook/What%20Is%20Process%20Theology.pdf.

Thiele, William. *Monks in the World: Seeking God in a Frantic Culture*. Eugene, OR: Wipf & Stock, 2014.

Thomas, James. *Methodism's Racial Dilemma: The Story of the Central Jurisdiction*. Nashville: Abingdon, 1992.

Thomas, Oliver. "New Orleans Church Bridges Racial Divide." *USA Today*, August 1, 2013.

Tidwell, Mike. *Bayou Farewell: The Rich Life and Tragic Death of Louisiana's Cajun Coast*. New York: Vintage, 2004.

———. Presentation at Octavia Books, New Orleans, Louisiana, October 20, 2014.

———. *The Ravaging Tide: Strange Weather, Future Katrinas, and the Coming Death of America's Coastal Cities*. New York: Free Press, 2006.

Tierney, Kathleen. "Disaster Research, Social Inequality, Gender, and Hurricane Katrina." In *The Women of Katrina: How Gender, Race, and Class Matter in an American Disaster*, edited by Emmanuel David and Elaine Enarson, 245–58. Nashville: Vanderbilt University Press, 2012.

Tippett, Krista. *Speaking of Faith*. New York: Viking, 2007.

Trujillo-Pagan, Nicole. "Recovering Latinos' Place in New Orleans." *Louisiana History* 55.2 (2014) 177–97.

Tuggle, Lindsay. "Encrypting Katrina: Traumatic Inscription and the Architecture of Amnesia." *InVisible Culture* 16 (2011). Online: http://www.rochester.edu/in_visible_culture/Issue_16/articles/tuggle/tuggle.html.

Turner, Billy V. *God's Calling: Discerning His Claim on Our Life*. Bloomington, IN: CrossBooks, 2011.

United Methodist Committee on Relief (UMCOR). "About Us." Online: http://www.umcor.org/UMCOR/About-Us.

"United Methodists Rally to Help Survivors of Hurricane Sandy through Housing, Donations." *Louisiana Now!* November 9, 2012.

Vernon, Walter N. *Becoming One People: A History of Louisiana Methodism.* Bossier City: Commission on Archives and History, Louisiana Annual Conference of the United Methodist Church, 1987.

Warner, Coleman. "New Orleans Police Remove Parishioners Occupying Closed Uptown Churches." *New Orleans Times Picayune*, January 6, 2009. Online: http://www.nola.com/news/index.ssf/2009/01/new_orleans_police_swarm_uptow.html.

Washington, Erica. "Prioritizing Patient Safety." Post on the White House "Champions of Change" Online: http://www.whitehouse.gov/blog/2013/09/09/prioritizing-patient-safety.

Wesley, John. "The Use of Money." In *John Wesley's Sermons: An Anthology*, edited by Albert Outler and Richard Heitzenrater, 347–57. Nashville: Abingdon, 1991.

Wigger, John. *American Saint: Francis Asbury and the Methodists.* New York: Oxford University Press, 2009.

Wimberly, Edward P. *African American Pastoral Care.* Rev. ed. Nashville: Abingdon, 2008.

Wink, Walter. *Unmasking the Powers: The Invisible Forces That Determine Human Existence.* Philadelphia: Fortress, 1986.

Witt, Howard. "Katrina Aftermath Still Roils Gretna: Town Cut Off Escape Route Out of New Orleans." *Chicago Tribune*, September 4, 2008. Online: www.chicagotribune.com/news/nationworld/chi-gretna_wittsep04,0,7262286.story.

Wood, Charles M. *The Question of Providence.* Louisville: Westminster John Knox, 2008.

Wood, Charles M., and Ellen Blue. *Attentive to God: Thinking Theologically in Ministry.* Nashville: Abingdon, 2008.

Zander, Rosamund Stone, and Benjamin Zander. *The Art of Possibility: Transforming Professional and Personal Life.* Cambridge: Harvard Business School Press, 2000.

www.ingramcontent.com/pod-product-compliance
Lightning Source LLC
Chambersburg PA
CBHW031426150426
43191CB00006B/409